Bloomberg
BNA

SECURITIES PRACTICE SERIES

THE FEDERAL LAW OF ASSET-BACKED SECURITIES: THE OFFERING PROCESS AND PERIODIC REPORTING

By

Charles A. Sweet
Bingham McCutchen LLP

Charlie Sweet is the Managing Director of the Shared Legal Services Team and the Practice Development Leader for the Structured Transactions Group at Bingham McCutchen LLP. Charlie regularly advises clients on all aspects of the federal laws and regulations affecting asset-backed securities and other structured finance products. He has represented financial industry groups in their responses to many of the regulatory changes that have affected these products since the financial crisis, and his securitization experience encompasses many asset types and structures, including innovations such as the first automobile lease securitizations. Charlie received his B.A. from Yale University, and his J.D., with high honors, from the University of Texas School of Law, where he was a member of the Order of the Coif, a member of the Chancellors (the school's highest honorary organization), and an associate editor of the Texas Law Review.

The following cataloging data is provided by the Bloomberg BNA Library

Sweet, Charles A.
  The federal law of asset-backed securities.
    (Bloomberg BNA's securities practice series, ISSN 2331-5067; no. 206)

Bibliography: p.

  1. Asset-backed financing—Law and legislation—United States. I. Title. II. Series.
III. Bloomberg BNA. KF1432.S43 no. 206l
ISBN 978-1-61746-912-1

SECURITIES PRACTICE SERIES

PORTFOLIO DESCRIPTION SHEET

The Federal Law of Asset-Backed Securities: The Offering Process and Periodic Reporting

PORTFOLIO DESCRIPTION SHEET

Securities Practice Series Portfolio No. 206, *The Federal Law of Asset-Backed Securities: The Offering Process and Periodic Reporting*, provides an up-to-date summary of the complex web of federal laws and rules that governs the offer and sale of asset-backed securities and subsequent periodic reporting, including the myriad changes that have been proposed or adopted in response to the financial crisis.

The disclosure requirements for asset-backed securities offerings and subsequent periodic reporting are governed primarily by Regulation AB, which the Securities and Exchange Commission has proposed to revise dramatically in a comprehensive proposal known as "Regulation AB II." If adopted as proposed, Regulation AB II would for the first time require that investors be provided with detailed asset-level data, and would impose substantially the same disclosure obligations in connection with private offerings of structured finance products as are required in registered public offerings. The portfolio analyzes all of these issues, as well as the investor communications framework for offerings of asset-backed securities, including the ways that free writing prospectuses and "ABS informational and computational materials" may be used as marketing tools, and the many significant regulatory changes that have been proposed or adopted pursuant to the mandates of the Dodd-Frank Act and the JOBS Act. These changes include the requirement for an issuer review of the pool assets, repurchase demand reporting, the obligation of asset-backed issuers to continue periodic reporting for the life of the deal, and the ability to use "general solicitation" in private offerings of asset-backed securities.

This portfolio may be cited as Charles A. Sweet, *The Federal Law of Asset-Backed Securities: The Offering Process and Periodic Reporting*, 206 Securities Practice Series (BNA).

SECURITIES PRACTICE SERIES PORTFOLIOS

This portfolio is part of Bloomberg BNA's *Securities Practice Series,* a unique library of practice-oriented analysis and tools addressing the full range of securities issues and practice areas. Authored by experienced practitioners, each Portfolio provides concise legal analysis and clear practical guidance to facilitate a quick grasp of the issues, an understanding of the nuances and risks, and the development of an actionable solution. Areas of coverage include securities enforcement, capital formation, regulation of trading and markets, investment management regulation, derivatives and commodities, and more. The *Securities Practice Series* Portfolios, available both in print and online in 2014, will be updated regularly.

Other Bloomberg BNA and Bloomberg Law Products

Securities Law Daily™ and *Securities Regulation & Law Report*™ provide comprehensive and objective coverage of developments in the regulation of federal, state, and international securities and futures trading from a team of experienced reporters and a roster of leading securities experts. These publications help you know what's important when advising clients on compliance with complex securities laws, and Securities and Exchange Commission and Commodities Futures Trading Commission regulations.

World Securities Law Report^{TM} brings you a global perspective on legal and regulatory developments affecting securities around the world, providing both news and invaluable practical analysis from an unmatched roster of experts from around the globe, with a special focus on cross-border developments.

Bloomberg BNA's *Corporate Practice Series*^{TM} Portfolios provide concise legal analysis from experienced practitioners on a myriad of legal areas affecting business organizations, including corporate compliance, corporate governance, corporate transactions, corporate political activity, corporate and alternative entities, antitrust and trade regulation, and labor and employment—among others.

Bloomberg BNA's *Corporate Law Resource Center*^{SM} provides essential insights to help corporate law practitioners research, plan, and implement effective strategies to resolve the broad spectrum of legal, regulatory, and/or operational challenges their company or corporate clients may encounter. This all-in-one solution integrates together — in one easily searchable platform — actionable guidance from Bloomberg BNA's trusted, practitioner-written *Corporate Practice Series,* industry-leading news and commentary, relevant primary sources, and time-saving practice tools.

Bloomberg Law's Securities Practice Center makes it easy to search securities dockets and decisions, stay on top of the latest industry issues, and provide clients with proven solutions. Enjoy unlimited access to a specialized EDGAR Search functionality; sample transactional documents and clauses; deep regulatory materials (including an advanced SEC No-Action Letter Search); comprehensive primary sources including laws, regulations and case law; and trusted secondary sources, including Bloomberg BNA's *Securities Practice Series* and *Corporate Practice Series*^{TM} Portfolios, *Securities Law Daily*^{TM}, and *Securities Regulation and Law Report*^{TM} and an extensive selection of Practising Law Institute securities law treatises.

For further information on these or other Bloomberg BNA publications, call Customer Relations at: 1-800-372-1033, or visit our web site at: http://www.bna.com.

TABLE OF CONTENTS

I.
What Is an Asset-Backed Security?

A. Asset-Backed Securities in General

Generally, asset-backed securities (ABS) are securities whose payments are derived from the cash flows on a specified pool of underlying financial assets. Securitized assets may consist of common consumer receivables, such as mortgage loans, credit card receivables, automobile loans or leases, or student loans. These securities also may be backed by more esoteric assets, such as airplane leases, franchise fees, time-share receivables or life settlements.

Through securitization, it is possible to spread the risk of many individual financial assets in a pool among multiple investors, as well as to tailor the types of ABS issued by credit risk, interest rate, and other characteristics in accordance with those investors' needs. Issuing ABS may enable a company to raise funds from the capital markets at lower overall cost than accessing the corporate equity or debt markets. If all of the accounting requirements are met, it is even possible to move the securitized financial assets completely off the balance sheet of the securitizing entity.

B. Structure of a "Plain Vanilla" Securitization

There are a wide variety of securitization structures, which are often extremely complex. However, there are a number of characteristics that are common among many securitization structures. It is only by understanding the basic structure of a "plain vanilla" securitization that we can understand the still-developing federal regulatory scheme for the securitization process.

The entity that creates a securitization, which often is the entity that originated the securitized financial assets, is referred to as the "sponsor" of the securitization. The sponsor will transfer the assets that it desires to securitize to a "special purpose vehicle" formed solely for the purpose of facilitating securitizations. This special purpose vehicle, which ordinarily is a corporation or a limited liability company, is known as the "depositor."

The goal of most securitizations is for investors to evaluate the ABS solely on the basis of the expected performance of the pool assets and the structure of the securitization itself, unencumbered by the risks that would go along with holding corporate debt or equity issued directly by the sponsor. Therefore, the transfer of the securitized assets from the sponsor to the depositor, and the depositor itself, usually are structured to meet a variety of legal requirements intended to isolate the securitized financial assets from the risks of the sponsor's business. When the transfer of assets is structured to be a "true sale" (as opposed to a secured financing) under applicable state law, and to avoid substantive consolidation of the depositor with the estate of the sponsor in the event of the sponsor's bankruptcy or insolvency, the depositor is commonly referred to as a "bankruptcy remote" special purpose vehicle.

The depositor transfers the pool assets interest to an issuing entity, which usually is a trust formed under state law. The type of trust used will depend upon tax and other factors, but often it is either a common-law trust or a special type of trust known as a Delaware "statutory trust." The trust is the entity that actually issues the ABS.

ABS may be issued in the form of debt instruments issued under an indenture with an institutional trustee, or "pass-through certificates" of interest directly in the trust. Most types of ABS will have a stated amount (a principal amount for notes, or a notional amount for certificates) and will bear interest at either a fixed or floating rate. ABS are usually tranched, i.e., issued in multiple classes with differing risk profiles and interest rates. Cash flows on the pooled assets are applied in accordance with a "waterfall" set forth in the transaction documents, in which principal and interest on the more senior classes are paid before principal and interest on the more subordinated classes.

ABS usually are issued by the trust to the depositor. The depositor then conducts the offer and sale of the ABS to outside investors.

For purposes of the federal securities laws, the depositor in an ABS transaction, acting solely in its capacity as depositor to the issuing entity, is the "issuer" of the ABS in that transaction. When the depositor acts as a depositor in a separate ABS transaction (or issues its own securities), it is a different "issuer."[1]

A diagram of a "plain vanilla" note and certificate ABS structures is included as Practice Tool 1.[2]

C. Definition under Regulation AB

1. Use of the Regulation AB definition

Regulation AB provides an overlay to the federal regulatory scheme for registered public offerings of securities.[3] It is primarily a disclosure regulation, tailored specifically to the types of disclosures that are relevant to investors in ABS. Regulation AB applies only to "asset-backed securities" as specifically defined in Regulation AB Item 1101(c),[4] whether offered pursuant to the more streamlined "shelf" registration process on Form S-3, or in a stand-alone registration on Form S-1.

Most public offerings of ABS that qualify as "asset-backed securities" under Regulation AB use the shelf registration process on Form S-3, which provides several advantages over stand-alone registration on Form S-1. These include the ability to "take down" offerings off the shelf without the need to file a new registration statement, the ability to "incorporate by reference" from other documents filed with the Securities and Exchange Commission (SEC), and the ability to use special marketing materials called "free writing prospectuses" and "ABS informational and computational materials" in addition to the official prospectus.

For ABS, factors such as the nature of the security determine the availability of the shelf registration process; the status of the issuer as a reporting company and its public float are irrelevant. Because Regulation AB's definition of "asset-backed security" serves partially to delineate the types of ABS that are eligible for shelf registration, it is a somewhat restrictive definition. Not all securities characterized by the market as

---

[1] Securities Act Rule 191, 17 C.F.R. § 230.191.

[2] 206 SPS Practice Tool 1, *Diagram of a "Plain Vanilla" Securitization.*

[3] 17 C.F.R. §§ 229.1100–23.

[4] 17 C.F.R. § 229.1101(c).

ABS meet the definition of "asset-backed security" under Regulation AB. If a security does not meet this definition, it may not be offered off the shelf. It may be publicly offered only in a stand-alone registration on Form S-1, using the SEC's rules applicable to ordinary corporate offerings.

> **Comment:** Because these rules are not well-suited to ABS, such a stand-alone registration likely would entail lengthy (and costly) dialogue with the SEC's staff to properly tailor the disclosure. Because of the difficulty of such an undertaking, except in rare cases ABS that do not meet the Regulation AB definition of "asset-backed security" are offered in unregistered private placements.

2. Elements of the definition

Regulation AB Item 1101(c)[5] sets forth the definition of "asset-backed security." In general, an "asset-backed security" is:

> a security that is primarily serviced by the cash flows of a discrete pool of receivables or other financial assets, either fixed or revolving, that by their terms convert into cash within a finite time period, plus any rights or other assets designed to assure the servicing or timely distributions of proceeds to the security holders; provided that in the case of financial assets that are leases, those assets may convert to cash partially by the cash proceeds from the disposition of the physical property underlying such leases.

In addition to meeting this basic definition, a security must comply with several other conditions. Neither the depositor nor the "issuing entity" (i.e., the trust) may be (or become as a result of the securitization) an "investment company" subject to registration under the Investment Company Act The activities of the issuing entity must be limited to passively owning or holding the asset pool, issuing the ABS and other reasonably incidental activities. No non-performing assets[6] as described below may be included in the asset pool, and delinquent assets may not constitute 50 percent or more of the dollar volume of the asset pool. If leases are in the asset pool, their aggregate "residual value" may not exceed 65 percent of the dollar volume of the asset pool for automobile leases, or 50 percent for other types of leases.

3. Eligible financial assets

The concept of eligible financial assets—receivables or other financial assets, either fixed or revolving, that by their terms convert into cash within a finite time period—is key to understanding the definition of "asset-backed security." An eligible financial asset must represent a payment obligation that reduces to zero by its own terms over the life of the asset—in other words, it must be self-liquidating.

A loan of any type, whether a mortgage loan, an automobile loan, a student loan, a credit card loan, or otherwise, generally will have terms that ultimately require full payment within a fixed period of time. Therefore, loans generally are eligible financial assets. On the other hand, neither physical

property (such as a commodity) nor capital stock is an eligible financial asset, because it does not represent a payment obligation that reduces to zero by its own terms. The value of physical property or stock, or the fact that the market for such an asset may be well developed, does not matter, because the owner must take affirmative steps to sell the property in order to generate cash and the price to be realized is also usually not certain. As neither physical property nor stock is self-liquidating, it does not constitute an eligible financial asset.

The treatment of leases under Regulation AB is somewhat complicated. A lease by itself may well be a self-liquidating financial obligation. However, ABS backed by a pool of leases may also depend on cash flows from the "residual value" of the lease (the amount received upon disposition of the leased physical property on default or at the end of the least term). One common example of ABS backed by leases with residual value is a securitization of automobile leases. Unless the lessee is obligated to purchase the leased property at a fixed residual value, it is very difficult to conclude that the residual value of a lease is self-liquidating.

In order to address this difficulty, Regulation AB creates a special rule for residual values, requiring that they not exceed 65 percent of the dollar volume of the asset pool for automobile leases, or 50 percent for other types of leases. The residual value is determined as of the "measurement date." The measurement date generally is the designated cut-off date for the transaction (the date after which collections on the pool assets accrue for the benefit of the ABS holders), though for master trusts, the measurement date is the date as of which certain required financial information is presented in the prospectus.[7]

Delinquent and non-performing financial assets also pose interpretive issues under the general definition of "asset-backed security." Because it is much less likely that a receivable that is in default or is seriously delinquent ultimately will be paid, it is difficult to conclude that such financial assets are self-liquidating.

Regulation AB generally prohibits any non-performing assets from inclusion in the asset pool as of the measurement date.[8] Under Regulation AB, an asset is considered non-performing if it would be treated as wholly or partially charged off under:

- the securitization's transaction documents;

- the policies of the sponsor, the originator (if the originator is an affiliate of the sponsor) or the servicer; or

- the policies established by the primary safety and soundness regulator of the sponsor, the originator (if the originator is an affiliate of the sponsor), or the servicer, or by the regulator that oversees the asset's origination program.[9]

---

[5] *Id.*

[6] For more about non-performing assets, *see* 206 SPS § I-C3, *Eligible financial assets.*

[7] For more about master trusts, *see* 206 SPS § I-C4, *"Discrete pool" requirement.*

[8] Regulation AB Item 1101(c)(2)(iii), 17 C.F.R. § 229.1101(c)(2)(iii).

[9] Regulation AB Item 1101(g), 17 C.F.R. § 229.1101(g).

An asset is not non-performing just because it is in a grace period, forbearance or deferment.[10]

Regulation AB limits the inclusion of delinquent assets in the asset pool to less than 50 percent, by dollar amount, as of the measurement date.[11] An asset is delinquent for purposes of Regulation AB if it is 30 or 31 days (or a single payment cycle) past due under:

- the securitization's transaction documents;

- the policies of the sponsor, the originator (if it is an affiliate of the sponsor), or the servicer; or

- the policies established by the primary safety and soundness regulator of the sponsor, the originator (if the originator is an affiliate of the sponsor), or the servicer, or by the regulator that oversees the asset's origination program.[12]

4. "Discrete pool" requirement

Because the asset pool must be a "discrete pool," it cannot be actively managed in the manner of a mutual fund, or of a collateralized debt obligation. There are only three exceptions to this rule, which may be used alone or in combination.

First, Regulation AB permits the use of master trusts. A master trust, which is often used to securitize revolving financial assets (such as credit card debt and dealer floorplan loans) and short-term receivables, continuously acquires receivables in accordance with the transaction documents and periodically issues ABS backed by their proportionate share of the asset pool. The only requirement that Regulation AB imposes on the use of master trusts is that the "offering . . . contemplates adding additional assets to the pool that backs [the ABS] in connection with future issuances of [ABS] backed by such pool."[13]

Second, Regulation AB permits the use of revolving periods. During a revolving period, some of the cash flows on the pool assets are used to acquire additional pool assets. Revolving periods can lengthen the life of the ABS issued in securitization of short-term assets, permit the financing of short-term assets with structures developed for longer-term assets, and finance additional draws under securitized revolving assets. For these reasons, revolving periods are common in master trust structures. Regulation AB requires that the new pool assets acquired during the revolving period be of the "same general character" as the original pool assets. For ABS that are not backed by revolving assets, the revolving period cannot exceed three years from the issuance date of the ABS.[14]

Comment: The SEC did not elaborate on the meaning of "same general character," though general industry consensus is that the new assets must be of the same asset class and have the same material characteristics as the initial pool assets.

Third, Regulation AB permits the use of pre-funding periods. In a transaction with a pre-funding period, ABS are issued with a principal balance greater than would be supported by the aggregate principal balance of the asset pool at closing. The "excess" proceeds are held in a trust account and used to acquire additional qualifying pool assets in the future, during a designated pre-funding period. This structure allows a sponsor with access to a steady supply of quality receivables to finance some of those receivables before they are originated or acquired, which makes the securitization larger and therefore more efficient as a financing mechanism. Regulation AB does not permit a pre-funding period to exceed one year from the date of issuance of the ABS. In addition, the pre-funding account may not exceed 50 percent of the proceeds of the offering (or, for master trusts, 50 percent of the total pool balance as of the measurement date).[15]

Comment: The offering document generally describes the parameters that pre-funded assets must satisfy. Other legal considerations, such as ERISA and tax rules, may limit the use of pre-funding mechanisms.

"Synthetic" securitizations do not involve the issuance of "asset-backed securities" under Regulation AB, because they are not serviced by cash flows from a "discrete pool" of eligible financial assets. Instead, payments on the securities derive from a derivative that merely references an asset pool (or the value of a commodity or index).[16]

D. Definition under Securities Exchange Act

The Dodd-Frank Wall Street Reform and Consumer Protection Act (Dodd-Frank Act) added a new definition of "asset-backed security" as Exchange Act § 3(a)(79).[17] Under this definition, an "asset-backed security" is "a fixed-income or other security collateralized by any type of self-liquidating financial asset (including a loan, a lease, a mortgage, or a secured or unsecured receivable) that allows the holder of the security to receive payments that depend primarily on cash flow from the asset." This definition, which is sometimes referred to as "Exchange Act ABS" to distinguish it from the Regulation AB definition of "asset-backed security," encompasses a much broader range of instruments than Regulation AB definition, drawing many more types of securities into the new regulatory framework imposed by the Dodd-Frank Act.

For example, while collateralized debt obligations are not ABS for purposes of Regulation AB because the pool of underlying assets is not "discrete," collateralized debt obligations are specifically included within the ambit of Exchange Act ABS. The definition of Exchange Act ABS makes no distinction between securities that are offered publicly or privately, and includes securities that are exempt from registration under the Securities Act, such as ABS issued or guaranteed by a government sponsored entity such as Fannie Mae or Freddie Mac, and municipal ABS.

---

[10] Asset-Backed Securities, 70 Fed. Reg. 1506, 1518 n.92 (Jan. 7, 2005).

[11] 17 C.F.R. § 229.1101(c)(2)(iii).

[12] 17 C.F.R. § 229.1101(g).

[13] 17 C.F.R. § 229.1101(c)(3)(i).

[14] 17 C.F.R. § 229.1101(c)(3)(iii).

[15] *Id.*

[16] *See* 70 Fed. Reg. at 1514.

[17] 15 U.S.C. § 78c(a)(79).

The definition of Exchange Act ABS is used for a variety of federal securities law purposes other than determining the eligibility of securities for shelf registration. For example, Exchange Act Rule 15Ga-1,[18] which requires an issuer or sponsor to make disclosures related to fulfilled and unfulfilled asset repurchase requests for the pool assets underlying its securitizations, applies to Exchange Act ABS.[19]

---

[18] 17 C.F.R. § 240.15Ga-1.

[19] *See* 206 SPS § VI-I, *Repurchase Demand Reporting on Form ABS-15G.*

II.
Public Offerings of Asset-Backed Securities

A. The Registration Requirement of § 5

Section 5 of the Securities Act is not a model of clarity.[1] According to § 5:

(a) Unless a registration statement is in effect as to a security, it shall be unlawful for any person, directly or indirectly—

(1) to make use of any means or instruments of transportation or communication in interstate commerce or of the mails to sell such security through the use or medium of any prospectus or otherwise; or

(2) to carry or cause to be carried through the mails or in interstate commerce, by any means or instruments of transportation, any such security for the purpose of sale or for delivery after sale.

(b) It shall be unlawful for any person, directly or indirectly —

(1) to make use of any means or instruments of transportation or communication in interstate commerce or of the mails to carry or transmit any prospectus relating to any security with respect to which a registration statement has been filed under this title, unless such prospectus meets the requirements of section 10; or

(2) to carry or cause to be carried through the mails or in interstate commerce any such security for the purpose of sale or for delivery after sale, unless accompanied or preceded by a prospectus that meets the requirements of subsection (a) of section 10.

(c) It shall be unlawful for any person, directly or indirectly, to make use of any means or instruments of transportation or communication in interstate commerce or of the mails to offer to sell or offer to buy through the use or medium of any prospectus or otherwise any security, unless a registration statement has been filed as to such security, or while the registration statement is the subject of a refusal order or stop order or (prior to the effective date of the registration statement) any public proceeding or examination under section 8.

While there are nuances to a variety of other issues raised by this section, it clearly prohibits any sale of securities unless a registration statement is in effect for the offering, unless an exemption from registration is available, either for the type of security offered or for the transaction.[2] At the present time, asset-backed securities (ABS) offerings may be registered either pursuant to shelf registration on Form S-3 if the requirements for shelf registration and the use of Form S-3 are met, or on a stand-alone basis on Form S-1. A shelf registration permits an issuer to register securities that will be offered on an imme-

diate, delayed or continuous basis over a three-year period, with a streamlined "takedown" process at the time of the actual offering.

B. Eligibility for registration types

1. Shelf registration and Form S-3

Currently, in order to use Form S-3 for offerings of ABS,[3] those securities must be "asset-backed securities" within the Regulation AB definition of the term, including the prohibition on non-performing assets, the limitations on delinquent assets and residual values of leased property, and the limitations on the use of revolving periods and pre-funding accounts.[4] In addition, the offering must meet the following transaction-specific requirements imposed by Form S-3:[5]

- the ABS must be offered for cash;

- the ABS must be "investment grade securities," meaning that at the time of sale, at least one nationally recognized statistical rating organization has rated the securities in one of its generic rating categories signifying that they are investment grade (normally, one of the four highest rating categories, without regard to "+" or "−" modifiers);

- the dollar volume of delinquent assets as of the measurement date may not constitute 20 percent or more of the dollar volume of the total asset pool. This is a stricter limit on delinquent assets than the one contained within the definition of "asset-backed security;" and[6]

- for ABS backed by leases other than motor vehicle leases, the dollar volume of the portion of the asset pool consisting of residual values of the leased property may not constitute 20 percent or more of the dollar volume of the total asset pool. This is a stricter limit on residual values than the one contained within the definition of "asset-backed security."[7]

In addition, Form S-3 also imposes a special registrant requirement for offerings of ABS. If the depositor (or any issuing entity previously established, directly or indirectly, by the depositor or its affiliates) is or was at any time during the 12 calendar months (and any portion of a month) preceding the filing of the registration statement required to file periodic reports under § 12 or 15(d) of the Exchange Act with respect to

---

[1] 15 U.S.C. § 77e.

[2] The restrictions of § 5 on "offers" are described further in 206 SPS § III, *Investor Communications in Public Offerings of ABS*. For more about exempt securities and exempt offerings, *see* 206 SPS § V, *Exempt Securities and Transactions*.

[3] Securities Act Rule 415(a)(x) permits shelf registration (i.e., an offering made on a continuous or delayed basis) of securities that are registered (or qualified to be registered) on Form S-3, and which are offered for sale on an immediate, continuous or delayed basis by or on behalf of, among others, the registrant. 17 C.F.R. § 230.415(a)(x).

[4] *See* Sec. & Exch. Comm'n (SEC), Form S-3: Registration Statement Under the Securities Act of 1933, at 5 (General Instruction I(B)(5)(a): Offerings of Investment Grade Asset-Backed Securities). For more information about the requirement of the definition of "asset-backed security," *see* 206 SPS § I-C, *Definition Under Regulation AB*.

[5] SEC Form S-3, at 5 (General Instruction I(B)(5)(a)).

[6] For more information about delinquent assets and the measurement date, *see* 206 SPS § I-C3, *Eligible financial assets*.

[7] For more information about residual values, *see id.*

ABS backed by pool assets of the same asset class,[8] then all such required reports must have been filed. In addition, all such reports must have been filed timely,[9] other than any Form 8-K filed solely with respect to certain required items.[10] This requirement is tested as of the date of the initial filing of the Form S-3 registration statement.[11]

Therefore, even a single late Exchange Act filing by the depositor or any of its affiliates with respect to ABS backed by the same asset class can preclude the depositor from filing a new shelf registration statement for a full year. This issue is especially troublesome for ABS sponsors, given that much of the information required to be contained in regular periodic reports comes from third parties, such as trustees and servicers, over whom the sponsor may have no direct control. However, under current law, such a lapse in reporting would not preclude the depositor from continuing to make offerings off of the existing shelf until its expiration.[12]

> **Comment:** Issuers preparing to file a shelf registration statement should diligence their periodic Exchange Act filings before anything else.

2. *Form S-1*

Offerings of ABS that do not qualify for registration on Form S-3 may be registered on a one-off basis on Form S-1.[13] Unlike Form S-3, Form S-1 is not tailored specifically for use in offerings of ABS.

> **Comment:** While as a practical matter one might expect that the Securities and Exchange Commission (SEC) staff would require disclosures very similar to those that would be required by Form S-3 and Regulation AB in a registration of ABS under Form S-1, any such registration statement is very likely to be selected for SEC staff review, and additional or differing requirements could be imposed during the review process.

C. Shelf Registration Mechanics

1. *Base prospectus and prospectus supplements*

Currently, an ABS shelf registration statement will contain one or more "base" prospectuses that contemplate future offerings, or "takedowns," of different series of securities with a variety of different features. A separate form of base prospectus will be required for every contemplated securitization involving a different asset type, for each country of origin of the

securitized assets, and for each contemplated securitization involving a different combination of asset types or countries of origin (unless asset types or countries of origin differ for less than 10 percent of the asset pool by dollar volume).[14]

While not every feature of the securities to be offered must be described specifically, all of the types of securities must at least be contemplated by the base prospectus. Currently, the base prospectus must include all information other than "information that is unknown or not reasonably available to the issuer."[15] A post-effective amendment to the registration statement (which will be required to be declared effective by the SEC staff) will be needed to permit the use of the shelf for a type of security that is not contemplated by the base prospectus. Therefore, among differing features that should be described in the base prospectus are

- the types of assets that may be included in a securitized pool;

- the various structures of the securities that are contemplated (including interest rate;

- indices and methodologies, entitlements to interest and principal, and redeemability features);

- possible forms of credit support for the securities; and

- the plan of distribution.

> **Comment:** One limitation that has been imposed by the SEC staff is that derivatives other than interest rate caps or swaps, currency swaps or market value swaps, including credit default swaps, are not been permitted to be contemplated by a base prospectus, due to the SEC's position that synthetic securities do not constitute "asset-backed securities" within the meaning of Regulation AB.[16]

The registration statement also will contain one or more forms of prospectus supplement that "outline the format of deal-specific information"[17] that is unknown or not reasonably available to the issuer at the time of filing the registration statement, and so will be included in the prospectus supplement prepared and filed at the time of each takedown. Of necessity, then, the forms of prospectus supplement filed with the registration statement will contain numerous blanks and bracketed items.

The exhibits to be filed with a shelf registration statement will include forms of the proposed underwriting agreement and other transaction documents,[18] as well as legal opinions regarding the legality of the securities to be offered and relevant tax issues, subject to appropriate assumptions and qualifications

---

[8] For more information about Exchange Act periodic reporting requirements for ABS, *see* 206 SPS § VI, *Periodic and Other Reporting Requirements*.

[9] SEC Form S-3, at 5 (General Instruction I(A)(4): Rights Offerings, Dividend or Interest Reinvestment Plans, and Conversions or Warrants and Options).

[10] SEC, Form 8-K: Current Report Pursuant to Section 13 or 15(d) of the Securities Exchange Act of 1934 (Items 1.01–02, 2.03–06, 4.02(a), 6.01, 6.03, 6.05).

[11] *See* Securities Act Rule 401(a), 17 C.F.R. § 230.401(a); *see also* Asset-Backed Securities, 70 Fed. Reg. 1506, 1526 (Jan. 7, 2005).

[12] For more information about shelf expiration, *see* 206 SPS § II-C3, *Shelf expiration and adding capacity*.

[13] SEC, Form S-1: Registration Statement Under the Securities Act of 1933.

[14] *See* SEC, Form S-3: Registration Statement Under the Securities Act of 1933, at 10 (General Instruction V(A)(2): Disclosure).

[15] Securities Act Rule 430B(a), 17 C.F.R. § 230.430B(a).

[16] For more information about synthetic securitizations, *see* 206 SPS § I-C4, *"Discrete pool" requirement*.

[17] Asset-Backed Securities, 70 Fed. Reg. 1506, 1513 (Jan. 7, 2005).

[18] The underwriting agreement is required by Regulation S-K Item 601(b)(i). 17 C.F.R. § 229.601(b)(1). The other transaction documents are required by Regulation S-K Item 601(b)(10). 17 C.F.R. § 229.60.1(b)(10).

due to the fact that the securities in question have not yet been issued.[19]

2. Takedowns

When the issuer decides to issue securities off of an effective shelf registration statement (i.e., a takedown), several steps must be taken.

Any free writing prospectuses or asset-backed informational and computational materials that were used in the offering of the securities, must be filed within the required time.[20]

The issuer must file the final prospectus supplement. For ABS, there is a special rule permitting the prospectus supplement to be filed no later than the second business day following the date it is first used after effectiveness, which generally is the second business day after closing.[21]

Final versions of the underwriting agreement and other transaction documents must be filed under cover of Form 8-K. Traditionally, statements in the base prospectus have committed the issuer to make this filing no later than 15 days after the closing date, though the SEC staff more recently required the depositor either to commit to do this filing by the time of the takedown, or at least to disclose the material terms of the transaction documents in the prospectus supplement and to file the actual documents as promptly as practicable.

Final legality and tax opinions must be filed under cover of Form 8-K, without the assumptions and qualifications that were contained in the opinions filed with the registration statement.[22]

3. Shelf expiration and adding capacity

A shelf registration statement expires three years from the date when it was first declared effective by the SEC. However, if a new registration statement covering the same type of securities has been filed before the end of that three year period, securities may continue to be offered and sold off the old shelf registration statement until the earlier of the effective date of the new registration statement or 180 days after the expiration of the old registration statement.[23]

An ABS sponsor may use up all of the capacity under a shelf registration statement (i.e., the amount of securities that may be registered in takedowns, based on the filing fee paid) before it expires. The solution is the same as at expiration of the old shelf — file a new shelf registration statement covering the same type of securities.[24]

Any remaining capacity under an expiring or used-up shelf may be carried forward to a new shelf under Securities Act Rule 429 (which allows securities registered under both registration statements to continue to be offered and sold under a combined prospectus filed with the new registration statement),[25] Securities Act Rule 457(p) (which in certain circumstances allows the remaining unused registration fees paid under the old shelf to be applied to the new registration statement),[26] or Securities Act Rule 415(a)(6) (which allows a new registration statement covering the same type of securities and filed before the end of the three year effective period of the old registration statement to include any securities that remain unsold under the old registration statement).[27]

D. Other Issues

1. Updating the base prospectus

Often, items in the base prospectus will be required to be updated before a new shelf registration statement is filed. According to the undertaking required in the shelf registration statement, a post-effective amendment (which would be required to be declared effective by the SEC staff) is required to reflect new facts or events which, individually or in the aggregate, represent a "fundamental change" to the registration statement.[28] Disclosure of a change that is merely "material" but does not rise to the level of "fundamental" may be accomplished by other means, such as by filing a new base prospectus under Securities Act Rule 424(b).[29]

"Fundamental" has never been defined by the SEC, nor has the SEC or its staff given interpretive guidance as to its meaning in the context of an ABS offering. It is clear that adding a new type of security requires a post-effective amendment,[30] and that many smaller changes that individually are not fundamental can become fundamental when aggregated together.[31] The addition of a new asset class is so important that it appears the SEC will require the filing of an entirely new registration statement.[32]

2. Issuer review of pool assets

As mandated by § 945 of the Dodd-Frank Act, Securities Act Rule 193 requires the issuer in any registered offering of Exchange Act ABS to perform a review of the pool assets that is, at a minimum, "designed and effected to provide reasonable assurance that the disclosure regarding the pool assets in the . . .

---

[19] The legality opinion is required by Regulation S-K Item 601(b)(5)(i). 17 C.F.R. § 229.601(b)(5)(i). The tax opinion is required by Regulation S-K Item 601(b)(8). 17 C.F.R. § 229.601(b)(5)(ii). For more information regarding these opinion filing requirements and the limitations and qualifications that may be included, *see* SEC Staff Legal Bulletin No. 19, Legality and Tax Opinions in Registered Offerings (Oct. 11, 2011).

[20] For more information about free writing prospectuses and asset-backed informational and computational materials, *see* 206 SPS § III-D4, *ABS informational and computational materials*; 206 SPS § III-D5, *Free writing prospectuses*.

[21] *See* Securities Act Rule 424(b), 17 C.F.R. § 230.424(b) instruc.

[22] *See* 206 SPS § II-C1, *Base prospectus and prospectus supplements*.

[23] Securities Act Rules 415(a)(5)–(6), 17 C.F.R. §§ 230.415(a)(5)–(6).

[24] Securities Act Rule 413(a), 17 C.F.R. § 230.413(a).

[25] 17 C.F.R. § 230.429.

[26] 17 C.F.R. § 230.457(p).

[27] 17 C.F.R. § 230.415(a)(6).

[28] Regulation S-K Item 512(a)(1)(ii), 17 C.F.R. § 229.512(a(1)(ii).

[29] 17 C.F.R. § 230.424(b).

[30] Asset-Backed Securities, 70 Fed. Reg. 1506, 1524 (Jan. 7, 2005).

[31] Adoption of Integrated Disclosure System, 47 Fed. Reg. 11,380, 11,395 n.79 (Mar. 16, 1982).

[32] *See* 70 Fed. Reg. at 1524.

prospectus . . . is accurate in all material respects."[33] This review may be performed by the issuer itself, or by a third-party diligence provider engaged to perform the review. The SEC has acknowledged that—

> while "reasonableness" is an objective standard, there is a range of judgments that an issuer might make as to what will provide "reasonable assurance." Thus, the term "reasonable assurance" . . . does not imply a single methodology, but encompasses the full range of reviews an issuer may perform to ensure that its review [meets the required standard].[34]

Among the disclosures that are required to be made in the prospectus regarding this review[35] is whether a third-party diligence provider was engaged. Securities Rule 193 requires that, if the issuer attributes the findings and conclusions of the review to a third-party diligence provider, that provider must be identified in the registration statement and consent to being named as an "expert." Being named as an expert would subject the provider to potential liability under § 11 of the Securities Act.[36] The third-party diligence provider need not be named in the registration statement or consent to expert status if the issuer attributes the findings and conclusions of the review to itself.

3. Resecuritizations, repacks and registration of underlying or separate securities

A "resecuritization" is a securitization where the pool assets consist of one or more previously issued ABS. A "repack" is a securitization where the pool assets consist of one or more previously issued corporate notes or bonds. For convenience, in this section, both will be referred to as resecuritizations. In both cases, the purpose is usually to re-tranche the underlying securities into new instruments with different payment or credit characteristics. Most resecuritizations are accomplished by means of private placements, rather than registered public offerings, due in large part to the SEC's position on the need to register underlying securities, as set forth in Securities Act Rule 190.[37]

Unless the underlying securities are themselves exempt securities pursuant to § 3 of the Securities Act,[38] in addition to the resecuritization ABS, the issuer also is deemed to be offering the underlying securities. That underlying offering must be registered as a primary offering unless:

- neither the issuer of the underlying nor any of its affiliates has a direct or indirect agreement, arrangement or understanding relating to the underlying securities and the resecuritization;

- neither the issuer of the underlying nor any of its affiliates is an affiliate of the sponsor, depositor, issuing entity or underwriter of the resecuritization; and

- the depositor would be free to publicly resell the underlying without registration (e.g., if the underlying are restricted securities but qualify for resale without restriction under Securities Act Rule 144,[39] or if the underlying were publicly offered and the resecuritization does not constitute part of their initial distribution).

If the sponsor, depositor or underwriter in the resecuritization is affiliated with the underwriter of registered underlying securities, then the resecuritization will not constitute part of the initial distribution of the underlying securities only if they were purchased in an arms' length, secondary market sale at least three months after the sale by the affiliated underwriter of its entire allotment of the underlying securities.

Unless all of these requirements are met, the deemed separate offering of the underlying securities must be registered as a primary offering in accordance with a litany of very specific rules, including:

- if the resecuritization is registered on Form S-3, the offering of the underlying securities must be eligible to be registered under Form S-3 or F-3 as a primary offering;

- the plan of distribution in the base prospectus must contemplate the offering of the underlying securities;

- the prospectus for the underlying securities must be delivered simultaneously with the resecuritization prospectus, and the resecuritization prospectus must disclose that the prospectus for the underlying securities will be delivered contemporaneously;

- the resecuritization prospectus must identify the issuing entity, depositor, sponsor and each underwriter in the resecuritization as an underwriter for the offering of the underlying securities; and

- neither prospectus may disclaim any responsibility by the issuing entity, sponsor, depositor, trustee or any underwriter for information regarding the underlying securities.

Comment: As a practical matter, unless the depositor of the underlying securities and the resecuritization are affiliated (or there is some other means to force or entice the depositor of the underlying securities to cooperate), and the offering of the underlying securities was set up to comply with all Regulation AB disclosure requirements, it generally is impractical or even impossible for the resecuritization depositor to cause the registration of the underlying securities.

Other obstacles to public resecuritizations that are just as, if not more, significant include the difficulty of obtaining from the issuer of the underlying securities the information required to satisfy the issuer's periodic reporting requirements under the Exchange Act, and the difficulty of pro-

---

[33] 17 C.F.R. § 230.193.

[34] Issuer Review of Assets in Offerings of Asset-Backed Securities, 76 Fed. Reg. 4231, 4235 (Jan. 25, 2011).

[35] For more information about these disclosures, *see* 206 SPS § IV-A7, *Pool assets, including disclosure regarding the issuer's review of the pool assets.*

[36] 15 U.S.C. § 77k.

[37] 17 C.F.R. § 230.190.

[38] For more information on exempt securities, *see* 206 SPS § V-A, *Exempt Securities.*

[39] 17 C.F.R. § 230.144.

viding the requisite Sarbanes-Oxley Act certifications as to information regarding the underlying securities.

Some securitization structures, such as some credit card and automobile lease securitizations, bundle up the securitized assets into an intermediate instrument and then securitize that intermediate instrument as part of the securitized asset pool. While the distribution of the intermediate instrument must be registered, Securities Act Rule 190(c) provides an exemption from the remainder of its requirements regarding that registration, so long as the issuing entity for the ABS and the issuer of the intermediate instrument both were established under the direction of the same sponsor and depositor, the intermediate instrument was "created solely to satisfy legal requirements or otherwise facilitate the structuring of" the ABS issuance, and the intermediate instrument is not part of a scheme to avoid registration.[40]

Sometimes deal structures rely on the obligations of third parties to securityholders—for example, guarantees, insurance, commitments to purchase the offered ABS, and other forms of third-party credit enhancement. If these obligations rise to the level of a "separate security" under applicable case law,[41] then unless the separate security is an exempt security,[42] its offer and sale also must be registered. Ordinarily, this will be impractical, so structures that involve the offer and sale of a separate, non-exempt security usually are sold in exempt private placements.[43]

4.　Incorporation by reference

Form S-3 generally requires the registrant to specifically incorporate by reference into the registration statement its most recent annual report on Form 10-K, and all other Exchange Act reports filed since the end of the fiscal year covered by that 10-K. In addition, all subsequently filed Exchange Act reports must be incorporated by reference.[44]

> **Comment:** For an operating company, this requirement makes sense, as most of the applicable disclosure regard-

ing the registrant will be contained in its periodic reports, so the incorporation by reference of future periodic reports often can keep the disclosure in the prospectus complete and updated.

For ABS, the depositor on behalf of each trust constitutes a separate "issuer,"[45] and almost all of the material disclosure regarding the securities and the pool assets is contained only in the prospectus supplement. Therefore, the SEC permits an ABS issuer to modify this language and incorporate by reference only current reports on Form 8-K subsequently filed by that ABS issuer (i.e., the depositor for the benefit of the issuing entity in that transaction only) "prior to the termination of the offering."[46] The downside of limiting incorporation by reference is that if the ABS issuer needs to update its disclosure during the prospectus delivery period,[47] it will not be able to rely on information incorporated by reference from the excluded Forms 10-D or 10-K.[48]

5.　*Signing the registration statement*

An ABS registration statement must be signed by the depositor, the depositor's principal executive officer or officers, the principal financial officer, and the controller or principal accounting officer, as well as by at least a majority of the depositor's board of directors or persons performing similar functions.[49]

---

[40] 17 C.F.R. § 230.190(c).

[41] The voluminous law on this topic is well beyond the scope of this Portfolio.

[42] For more information on exempt securities, *see* 206 SPS § V-A, *Exempt Securities*.

[43] For more information about exempt offerings, *see* 206 SPS § V-B, *Private Placements*. Note that while Item 1114 of Regulation AB prescribes disclosure requirements for third-party credit enhancement, it does not address if or when those obligations must be registered as a separate security. 17 C.F.R. § 229.1114.

[44] SEC, Form S-3: Registration Statement Under the Securities Act of 1933, at 11–12 (Items 12(a)–(b): Incorporation of Certain Information by Reference).

[45] *See* 206 SPS § I-B, *Structure of a "Plain Vanilla" Securitization*.

[46] DIV. OF CORP. FIN., SEC, MANUAL OF PUBLICLY AVAILABLE TELEPHONE INTERPRETATIONS—REGULATION AB AND RELATED RULES § 15.02 (2007). There is little law on what constitutes the "termination" of an offering, though at least one case has analogized to the SEC's anti-manipulation rules (not Regulation M) as to when a "distribution" ends. *See, e.g.*, Kenilworth Partners LP v. Cendant Corp., 59 F. Supp. 2d 417, 426 (D. N. J. 1999). Under Rule 100 of Regulation M, "completion of participation in a distribution" occurs when the "distribution is completed," for an underwriter "when such person's participation has been distributed . . . and any stabilization arrangements and trading restrictions . . . have been terminated," and for any other participant "when such person's participation has been distributed." 17 C.F.R. § 242.100.

[47] *See* 206 SPS § III-E2, *The final prospectus and "access equals delivery."*

[48] In any event, the SEC has cast doubt on whether the information contained in Forms 10-D and 10-K subsequent to an ABS offering is sufficient to properly update the prospectus, given that ordinarily it will not update much of the required information regarding the asset pool. 70 Fed. Reg. at 1531 n.193.

[49] *See* SEC Form S-3, at 10 (General Instruction V(B): Signatures); SEC, Form S-1: Registration Statement Under the Securities Act of 1933, at 3 (General Instruction VI(C): Signatures).

III.
Investor Communications in Public Offerings of ABS

A. The Basic Investor Communications Framework of § 5

As described in 206 SPS § II-A, *The Registration Requirement of § 5*, § 5 of the Securities Act is far from a model of clarity.[1] However, the provisions that form the basis of the investor communications regime in registered public offerings are:

- Section 5(c), which prohibits any "offer" of a security for sale, through the use of a "prospectus" or otherwise, unless a registration statement has been filed;

- Section 5(b)(1), which prohibits the use of any "prospectus" relating to a security unless it meets the requirements of § 10 of the Securities Act; and

- Section 5(b)(2), which prohibits the delivery of a security after sale, unless accompanied or preceeded by a prospectus that meets the requirements of § 10 of the Securities Act.

The basic definition of "prospectus" in § 2(a)(10) is broad enough to include any written communication that "offers" a security for sale.[2] Section 2(a)(3) states that an "offer" includes "every attempt or offer to dispose of, or solicitation of an offer to buy, an interest in a security, for value."[3] In the view of the Securities and Exchange Commission (SEC), any publicity that "may in fact contribute to condition the public mind or arousing public interest in . . . [an] issuer or in . . . [its] securities . . . in a manner is an "offer" which raises a serious question whether the publicity is not in fact part of the selling effort."[4]

Putting these rules and guidance together, the basic requirements of § 5 are that:

- before a registration statement has been filed, it is unlawful to make any communication, written or oral, that could reasonably be expected to condition the market for the securities to be offered;

- after the registration statement has been filed, it is unlawful to use any written materials that could reasonably be expected to condition the market for the securities being offered, other than the statutory prospectus contained in the registration statement; and

- the final statutory prospectus must be delivered to a buyer before or at the same time as the securities themselves are delivered.

There are many exceptions and nuances to this scheme, which are explored further in this chapter.

B. Some Necessary Definitions

1. Issuer classifications

The securities offering reform rules adopted by the SEC in 2005 dramatically changed the regulatory framework surrounding the investor communications regime.[5] Under the offering reform rules, the types of communications that are permitted or prohibited at various times during the offering process differ depending upon how the issuer is classified. Therefore, in order to understand the investor communications regime, in addition to understanding the basic statutory framework of § 5, it is crucial to understand the issuer classification scheme of the offering reform rules.

- A "well-known seasoned issuer" (WKSI) generally is a company that is eligible to use the SEC's shelf registration forms, has a minimum public float of at least $700 million of common equity held by non-affiliates, or has issued at least $1 billion in registered non-convertible debt securities during the preceding three years, and is not an asset-backed securities (ABS) issuer, a registered investment company, a business development company, or an "ineligible issuer."[6]

- A "seasoned issuer" is a company that is eligible to use the SEC's shelf registration forms, but does not meet the minimum public float or minimum nonconvertible debt issuance tests required to be a WKSI. An issuer of ABS registered on Form S-3 is a seasoned issuer.

- An "unseasoned issuer" is a company that is required to file Exchange Act periodic reports, but is not eligible to use the SEC's shelf registration forms. An issuer of ABS registered on Form S-1 is an unseasoned issuer.[7]

- A "non-reporting issuer" is a company that is not required to file Exchange Act periodic reports, including a "voluntary filer" that files such reports anyway.[8]

The SEC's rules also define a category of "ineligible issuer" that is foreclosed from using much of the liberalized communications framework of the offering reform rules. A company is an "ineligible issuer" if, among other things:

- it is required to file Exchange Act periodic reports but has not filed all required such reports for the preceding 12 months, or any shorter period as it has been required to file (or, for an ABS issuer, if the depositor or any issuing entity directly or indirectly established by the depositor is required to file Exchange Act periodic reports with respect to the same asset class, but has not filed all required such reports for the preceding 12 months or any shorter period as it has been required to file), other than certain reports on Form 8-K;

---

[1] 15 U.S.C. § 77e.

[2] 15 U.S.C. § 77b(10).

[3] 15 U.S.C. § 77b(3).

[4] *See, e.g.*, Statement of the Commission Relating to Publication of Information Prior to or After the Effective Date of a Registration Statement, 22 Fed. Reg. 8359 (Oct. 24, 1957).

[5] Securities Offering Reform, 70 Fed. Reg. 44,722 (Aug. 3, 2005).

[6] Securities Act Rule 405, 17 C.F.R. § 230.405.

[7] SEC, Form S-1: Registration Statement Under the Securities Act of 1933.

[8] 70 Fed. Reg. at 44,730–31. The categories of seasoned issuer, unseasoned issuer and non-reporting issuer are used colloquially by the SEC, but are not defined in the SEC's rules.

- within the past three years, it has been the subject of certain bankruptcy or insolvency proceedings, has been convicted of certain crimes, or has been the subject of a judicial or administrative decree that prohibits conduct under the federal securities laws, requires it to "cease and desist" from violating the anti-fraud provisions of the federal securities laws, or determines that it violated the anti-fraud provisions of the federal securities laws; or

- it has filed a registration statement that is the subject of any pending proceeding or examination or has been the subject of a refusal or stop order under § 8 of the Securities Act.[9]

2. *Written and oral communications*

Much of the regulatory scheme surrounding investor communications depends on whether a particular communication is written or oral. For the SEC's purposes, a written communication includes anything written or printed, a radio or television broadcast (however transmitted), or a "graphic communication." A "graphic communication" includes all types of electronic media, including audio and video tapes, fax transmissions, CDs, email, Internet websites, and messages widely disseminated through voice mail systems and computer networks. On the other hand, a communication that originates live, in real time, to a live audience (and not as a recording or as some other form of graphic communication) is not itself a graphic communication, even if it is transmitted by graphic means.[10]

C. Pre-Filing Period

1. *General prohibition against gun-jumping*

As described above, before a registration statement has been filed, the general rule is that it is illegal to make any written or oral "offer" for the securities. Because of the SEC's broad definition of what constitutes an "offer," any communication, written or oral, that could reasonably be expected to condition the market for the securities to be offered, is prohibited. Such communications are known as "gun-jumping."

> **Comment:** Most ABS that are publicly offered are registered for the shelf on Form S-3, which may be filed far in advance of an actual offering. Therefore, when most ABS offerings are commenced, a registration statement already is on file and effective.

There can be serious adverse consequences to gun-jumping. Because most public offerings require opinions of counsel addressing compliance with the Securities Act in connection with the registration of the offering, counsel may require that the offering be delayed for a "cooling off" period or that other remedial steps be taken in order to mitigate the effect of an improper communication. The SEC may refuse to accelerate the effectiveness of the registration statement, and may issue a cease-and-desist order. Perhaps most importantly, under § 12 of

the Securities Act, an investor that purchases securities issued in violation of § 5 may have a "put" on those securities back to the underwriter and issuer for a full year after they were purchased.[11]

For these reasons, securitization sponsors should carefully monitor their communications to the public to ensure that they cannot be reasonably construed as a prohibited "offer" of securities.

There are several narrow exceptions to the general prohibition of gun-jumping during the pre-filing period.

2. *Rule 168*

Securities Act Rule 168 allows an ABS issuer, or a depositor, sponsor, servicer or affiliated depositor, whether or not that entity is the issuer (among other types of entities), to continue to regularly release or disseminate "factual business information" or "forward-looking information," which is deemed not to constitute an offer, subject to several conditions:

- the information must be released "by or on behalf of" the relevant entity;

- the relevant entity must have previously released or disseminated such information in the ordinary course of its business; and

- the timing, manner and form of the release must be consistent in material respects with previous such releases.[12]

As little as a single previous release of information may establish the required track record, unless it comes just before a registered offering.[13] "Factual business information" includes factual business information about the issuer, its business or financial developments, or other aspects of its business, as well as advertisements of and information about its products and services. For ABS, it includes information about prior transactions or asset pools.[14] "Forward-looking information" includes financial projections, statements about management's future plans and objectives, statements about future economic performance, and any assumptions underlying such statements.[15]

3. *Rule 135*

Securities Act Rule 135 permits an issuer, and any person acting on behalf of an issuer, to publish a notice of an upcoming registered offering, but the information notice must be very

---

[9] Securities Act Rule 405, 17 C.F.R. § 230.405 (definition of "ineligible issuer").

[10] *Id.* (definitions of "graphic communication" and "written communication").

---

[11] 15 U.S.C. § 77l. The one year statute of limitations for this remedy is contained in § 13. 15 U.S.C. § 77m.

[12] 17 C.F.R. § 230.168.

[13] Securities Offering Reform, 70 Fed. Reg. 44,722, 44,737 (Aug. 3, 2005).

[14] 70 Fed. Reg. at 44,735.

[15] Securities Act Rule 168 is a non-exclusive safe harbor. The SEC had given similar interpretive guidance long before the adoption of Rule 168, which encouraged companies to continue to market products and services and engage in usual business activities even during the pendency of a public offering. This guidance may still apply, even if a communication is not within the four corners of Rule 168. *See, e.g.,* Use of Electronic Media, 65 Fed. Reg. 25,843, 25,850 (May 4, 2000).

limited.[16] The permitted information of relevance to an ABS offering includes:

- the issuer's name;

- the title, amount and basic terms of the securities to be offered;

- the anticipated timing of the offering;

- a brief statement of the manner and purpose of the offering, but without naming the underwriters;

- whether the offering will be directed towards a particular class of buyers; and

- any statements or legends required by state or foreign laws or regulators.

The notice must also include a statement that it does not constitute an offer of any securities for sale.

Comment: For ABS, practitioners generally consider the title, amount and basic terms of the securities to be offered to include principal amount, interest rate, maturity date, yield, weighted average life, ratings, and pool asset type.

4. Rule 163A

Under Securities Act Rule 163A,[17] any communication made by or on behalf of the issuer more than 30 days before the registration statement is filed is deemed not to constitute an offer, so long as the communication does not reference a potential securities offering, and the issuer "takes reasonable steps within its control" to prevent further distribution or publication of the communication within the 30 days before filing.

Comment: It is not clear what constitute the required "reasonable steps," but a wise ABS sponsor will scrutinize its website to ensure that information for which no other exemption is available is deleted at least 30 days before filing a registration statement.[18]

Rule 163A does not apply to shelf registrations, where the registration statement is already on file. Nor does it specify when a "cooling off" period of a particular length will be sufficient to cure a gun-jump in any particular context, though the market and practitioners have viewed it as instructive, often concluding that a 30-day period between a gun-jump and the commencement of the offering (generally considered to be when the underwriter is identified) is sufficient. This is not surprising, given the SEC's statement that "the 30-day timeframe adequately assures that . . . communications will not condition the market for a securities offering by providing a sufficient time period to cool any interest in the offering that might arise from the communication."[19]

D. Waiting Period

1. The waiting period generally, and the shelf offering analogy

As described above, after the registration statement has been filed, it is illegal to use any written materials that could reasonably be expected to condition the market for the securities being offered, other than the statutory prospectus contained in the registration statement, unless an exemption is available.[20] The period beginning when the registration statement is filed, and ending when it is declared effective by the SEC, is known as the "waiting period."

There is no waiting period in most shelf offerings, as the registration statement is already filed and effective. Nevertheless, § 5(b)(1) still generally prohibits the use of any written materials (other than the statutory prospectus) to offer the ABS. The base prospectus alone will not contain sufficient information to constitute a statutory prospectus—for these purposes, the base prospectus combined with the prospectus supplement filed at the time of takedown will constitute the statutory prospectus.

2. Rule 134

The use of a Securities Act Rule 134 notice is permitted at any time after the registration statement (containing a preliminary prospectus or, for a shelf offering on Form S-3, the base prospectus) has been filed. The contents of a Rule 134 notice are limited to the matters specified by the rule, including factual information about the issuer, the names of the underwriters, a description of the offering schedule, the title and amount of the securities offered, and the expected ratings and Employee Retirement Income Security Act (ERISA) status of the securities.[21] A Rule 134 notice also must include a required legend if the registration statement has not been declared effective.

Comment: Note that many other basic terms of the securities, which may be included in a Rule 135 notice,[22] are not permitted in a Rule 134 notice. Originally, Rule 134 was used primarily for "tombstone" advertisements, but its use has been broadened to include, among other things, Bloomberg notices, Internet postings, emails, and press releases. Form S-3 ABS registrants may be able to treat such materials as a free writing prospectus. However, for Form S-1 registrants that intend to broadly disseminate such materials (making it impossible to ensure that their receipt is accompanied or preceded by the most recent statutory prospectus), it is strongly advisable to stay within the bounds of Rule 134, no matter how limiting they may be.

3. The preliminary prospectus

A "preliminary prospectus" (commonly referred to as a "red herring" or a "red," in reference to the color of the legend printed on the cover) is a statutory prospectus that omits only

---

[16] 17 C.F.R. § 230.135.

[17] 17 C.F.R. § 230.163A.

[18] For example, regularly released factual information under Securities Act Rule 168 or information clearly designated as "historical" under Securities Act Rule 433, is permissible. *See* 206 SPS § III-C2, *Rule 168*; 206 SPS § III-F, *The Internet and Statements on Websites.*

[19] 70 Fed. Reg. at 44,730.

[20] For more information on the distinction between written and oral communications, *see* 206 SPS § III-B2, *Written and oral communications.*

[21] Securities Act Rule 134, 17 C.F.R. § 230.134.

[22] *See* 206 SPS § III-C3, *Rule 135.*

pricing-related information such as the offering price, coupon, underwriting discounts or commissions, discounts or commissions to dealers, the amount of proceeds, and other matters that depend on the offering price. Because a preliminary prospectus is deemed to meet the requirements of § 10 of the Securities Act,[23] it is a statutory prospectus, and therefore may be used to offer securities during the waiting period.[24]

A preliminary prospectus must be delivered to any purchaser at least 48 hours before delivery of the confirmation of sale unless the issuer of the securities is already required to file periodic reports under the Exchange Act. ABS that qualify for shelf registration on Form S-3 currently are exempt from this requirement.[25] Because there usually is a separate "issuer" for most ABS offerings (i.e., the depositor for the benefit of the particular trust),[26] the preliminary prospectus delivery requirement will apply to most stand-alone ABS offerings registered on Form S-1. The "access equals delivery" rules applicable to the final prospectus do not apply to the preliminary prospectus,[27] so an electronic or paper copy of the final prospectus must be actually delivered to each prospective purchaser.

> **Comment:** In an offering that is being reviewed by the SEC staff (normally a Form S-1 filing; Form S-3 shelf filings ordinarily are reviewed only at the time of the initial filing, not at the time of a takedown for an offering), the preliminary prospectus should not be printed and finalized until the SEC examiner has signed off. By that time, all of the SEC's comments should have been incorporated into the registration statement by means of one or more pre-effective amendments.

Except for the delivery requirement in ABS offerings registered on Form S-1, there is no rule that requires the use of a preliminary prospectus to market the securities.

> **Comment:** Securities Act Rule 159 fixes the liability of the issuer and underwriter for material misstatements and omissions in the information conveyed to the purchaser at the time of sale.[28] Since its adoption, most ABS issuers (including in shelf takedowns off a Form S-3 registration statement) now circulate to prospective investors before the sale is consummated either a formal preliminary prospectus or a so-called "virtual red"—a free-writing prospectus in the form of a preliminary prospectus that contains almost all of the information that would be required in a preliminary prospectus.

4. ABS informational and computational materials

Securities Act Rule 167 permits the use of written "ABS informational and computational materials" (ABSICM) to market ABS offered off a shelf after effectiveness of the registration

statement.[29] Rule 167 and other relevant rules impose several conditions on the use of ABSICM:

- the securities must be offered pursuant to an effective Form S-3;
- ABSICM that are required to be filed must be filed on Form 8-K by the later of the date the final prospectus is required to be filed (for ABS shelf offerings, two business days after first use of the final prospectus), and two business days after first use of the ABSICM;[30]
- ABSICM are deemed incorporated by reference into the registration statement;[31] and
- the cover page of the ABSICM must include the depositor's and issuing entity's names, the file number of the registration statement, a statement that the materials are ABSICM being used in reliance on Rule 167, and a required legend urging investors to read the base prospectus and prospectus supplement and explaining how to access those documents on the SEC's website.

The SEC also takes the position that it is not permissible to use disclaimers in ABSICM that would be inappropriate in a prospectus, such as disclaimers regarding accuracy or completeness, statements requiring investors to read or acknowledge that they have read any disclaimers or legends or the registration statement, language indicating that the communication is neither a prospectus nor an offer to sell, or statements that the information is privileged or confidential.[32]

Item 1101(a) of Regulation AB specifies the contents that are permitted in ABSICM,[33] which include:

- factual information regarding the securities, including their terms and their tax and ERISA status;
- factual information regarding the underlying pool assets;
- identification and a brief description of the key parties to the offering;
- static pool data;[34]
- hypothetical yield, average life, expected maturity, interest rate sensitivity, cash flow characteristics, total rate of return, option adjusted spread, and other financial or statistical information relating to any class of the offered securities under assumed prepayment interest rate, loss or other scenarios (often referred to as "derived information");
- underwriter names and a description of how to submit indications of interest or conditional offers to purchase the securities; and

---

[23] Securities Act Rule 430(a), 17 C.F.R. § 230.430(a).

[24] See 206 SPS § III-D1, *The waiting period generally, and the shelf offering analogy.*

[25] Exchange Act Rule 15c2-8(b), 17 C.F.R. § 240.15c2-8(b).

[26] See 206 SPS § I-B, *Structure of a "Plain Vanilla" Securitization.*

[27] See 206 SPS § III-E2, *The final prospectus and "access equals delivery."*

[28] For more about Rule 159, see 206 SPS § III-D7, *Liability and "time of sale" considerations.*

[29] 17 C.F.R. § 230.167.

[30] Securities Act Rules 426(a)–(b), 16 C.F.R. §§ 426(a)–(b) (filing requirements for ABSICM); Securities Act Rule 424(b), 17 C.F.R. § 230.424(b) instruc. (filing deadline for ABS prospectuses).

[31] Securities Act Rule 462(a), 17 C.F.R. § 230.462(a).

[32] See Asset-Backed Securities, 70 Fed. Reg. 1506, 1557 (Jan. 7, 2005).

[33] 17 C.F.R. § 229.1101(a).

[34] For more information about static pool data, see 206 SPS § IV-A2, *Static pool information.*

- the projected offering schedule, including roadshow dates and times.

Under Rule 167, issuers and underwriters may provide information regarding the pool assets and cash flows in a securitization to third-party analytics services so that investors can perform their own cash flow analyses using those services, so long as the information is filed as ABSICM in "understandable form" (and not as executable computer code).[35] ABSICM must be filed with the SEC if:

- they relate to a particular class of ABS and the investor to whom they were delivered indicates that it proposes to purchase those ABS or

- they were distributed to any prospective investor after the final offering terms were established for all classes of offered ABS.

Materials related to abandoned structures and materials that do not contain new or different information from previously filed ABSICM need not be filed.[36]

An "immaterial or unintentional" failure to file (or delay in filing) ABSICM is not a violation of § 5 if:

- a "good faith and reasonable effort" was made to comply with the filing requirement, and

- the ABSICM were filed as soon as practicable after discovery of the failure.[37]

Because ABSICM are incorporated by reference into the registration statement, in addition to potential liability for material misstatements and omissions under § 12(a)(2) and Rule 10b-5, the underwriter and issuer may be liable for material misstatements or omissions under § 11 of the Securities Act.[38]

5. *Free writing prospectuses*

An alternative type of permitted written communication is the "free writing prospectus," (FWP). A free writing prospectus is any type of written communication[39] that constitutes an offer to sell securities,[40] other than a statutory prospectus, a notice issued under Securities Act Rules 134 or 135 (or any other communication that by reason of any other SEC position does not constitute an "offer"),[41] ABSICM, or traditional free writing.[42]

As described above,[43] an ABS issuer in a shelf offering registered on Form S-3 is a "seasoned issuer," which means that FWPs may be used at any time after the registration statement has been filed (which will almost always be true). An ABS issuer in a stand-alone offering registered on Form S-1 is a "non-reporting issuer," so an FWP may be disseminated only if it is accompanied or preceded by the most recent preliminary prospectus or, if available, final prospectus.[44]

An ineligible issuer is much more limited in its use of FWPs. An ineligible ABS issuer's FWPs generally may contain only ABSICM, but may not contain derived information.[45] The eligibility determination is made as of the filing date of the registration statement (for an ABS issuer in a stand-alone offering registered on Form S-1), or as of the time of the first bona fide offer of the registered securities (for an ABS issuer in a shelf offering registered on Form S-3).

Unless an exemption applies, each FWP must contain a mandated legend that informs the reader how to access a copy of the registration statement and prospectus for the offered securities.[46] Otherwise, there are virtually no limits on the information that can be included in an FWP. An FWP may contain information not included in the registration statement, so long as it does not conflict with any information included in the registration statement.[47]

As with ABSICM, the SEC also takes the position that it is not permissible to use disclaimers in an FWP that would be inappropriate in a prospectus, such as disclaimers regarding accuracy or completeness, statements requiring investors to read or acknowledge that they have read any disclaimers or legends or the registration statement, language indicating that the communication is neither a prospectus nor an offer to sell, or statements that the information is privileged or confidential.[48]

The filing requirements for FWPs are complicated. The following generally are required to be filed by the issuer no later than the date of first use:

- an "issuer free writing prospectus" (an FWP prepared "by or on behalf of" the issuer, depositor, sponsor or servicer);[49]

- "issuer information" (generally, material information about the issuer or the securities provided "by or on behalf" of the issuer, and contained in an another party's FWP);[50] and

- a description of the final terms of the offered securities or of the offering contained in any FWP of the issuer or any other party, after such terms have been established for all classes of securities.

In addition, an offering participant other than the issuer must file any FWP that it uses or refers to and distributes "in a

---

[35] 70 Fed. Reg. at 1556-57.

[36] Securities Act Rules 426(b)–(c), 17 C.F.R. §§ 426(b)–(c).

[37] Securities Act Rule 167(e), 17 C.F.R. § 230.167(e).

[38] For more about potential liability under ABSICM, *see* 206 SPS § III-D7, *Liability and "time of sale" considerations*; 206 SPS § III-D8, *Choosing between ABSICM and FWPs*.

[39] *See* 206 SPS § III-B2, *Written and oral communications*.

[40] For more information about what constitutes an "offer," *see* 206 SPS § III-A, *The Basic Investor Communications Framework of § 5*.

[41] *See* Securities Offering Reform, 70 Fed. Reg. 44,722, 44,745 n.207 (Aug. 3, 2005).

[42] Securities Act Rule 405, 17 C.F.R. § 230.405. For more information about traditional free writing, *see* 206 SPS § III-E, *Post-Effective Period and Traditional Free Writing*.

[43] *See* 206 SPS § III-B1, *Issuer classification*.

[44] Securities Act Rule 433(b), 17 C.F.R. § 230.433(b).

[45] Rule 164(e), 17 C.F.R. § 230.164(e). For more information about ineligible issuers, *see* 206 SPS § III-B1, *Issuer classification*.

[46] Securities Act Rule 433(c)(2), 17 C.F.R. § 433(c)(2).

[47] Securities Act Rule 433(c)(1), 17 C.F.R. § 433(c)(1).

[48] *See* 70 Fed. Reg. 44,749.

[49] Securities Act Rule 433(h), 17 C.F.R. § 230.433(h).

[50] *Id.*

manner reasonably designed to lead to its broad unrestricted dissemination."[51]

An FWP is prepared "by or on behalf of" the issuer (and thus is an issuer FWP), and information is provided "by or on behalf of" the issuer (and thus is issuer information), if the issuer (or its agent or representative) authorized or approved it before it was used.[52] "Authorized or approved" refers to control over substance, rather than use. An FWP or information is not prepared or provided "by or on behalf of" the issuer just because the underwriting agreement requires the issuer to consent to its use. The issuer's actions must "amount to adoption of or entanglement with" an FWP (or information therein) for it to be deemed "authorized or approved" by the issuer, and therefore prepared or provided "by or on behalf of" the issuer.[53]

According to the SEC, virtually all of the information that would constitute ABSICM also would be deemed to constitute issuer information under the FWP rules, including:

- factual information regarding the securities;

- factual information regarding the underlying pool assets;

- identification and a brief description of the key parties to the offering;

- static pool data; and

- derived information, but only to the extent provided by the issuer, depositor, affiliated depositor, or sponsor—derived information is not issuer information when prepared by an underwriter or dealer, even if it was derived from issuer information).[54]

For these purposes, "derived information" clearly includes the kinds of information regarding hypothetical yield, average life, expected maturity, interest rate sensitivity, cash flow characteristics, total rate of return, option adjusted spread, and other financial or statistical information under assumed prepayment interest rate, loss or other scenarios as would be permitted to be included in ABSICM.[55]

Comment: It is common for an underwriter to provide derived information to investors without filing it as an FWP, in reliance on the foregoing exception. Whether "custom loan stats" (i.e., customized statistical information prepared according to specific criteria requested by a particular investor) must be filed is a more controversial issue. Many practitioners advise that such materials be filed, or that the full "loan tape" (with personal information redacted in an effort to avoid privacy concerns) should be filed in order to then rely upon the exemption from

filing an FWP that does not contain a substantive change from or addition to a previously filed FWP.[56]

While the general rule is that an FWP or required issuer information must be filed no later than the date of first use, an FWP or portion thereof that contains only ABSICM need not be filed until the time that the ABSICM would be required to be filed—the later of the date the final prospectus is required to be filed (for ABS shelf offerings, two business days after first use of the final prospectus), and two business days after first use.[57]

In addition to special rules for media reports and roadshows,[58] there are a variety of more general exemptions from the filing requirements for FWPs:

- an FWP need not be filed if there is no substantive change from or addition to a previously filed FWP;[59]

- issuer information included in an FWP of an offering participant other than the issuer need not be filed if the information is included in an FWP or prospectus previously filed with respect to the same offering;[60] and

- an FWP or a portion thereof containing a description of the "terms of the issuer's securities in the offering or the offering" need not be filed if it does not reflect the final terms (i.e., it is a preliminary term sheet).[61]

The SEC has equated the "terms of the issuer's securities in the offering or the offering" for purposes of an ABS to ABSICM, with the exception of derived information.[62]

Comment: It is common practice to file the last version of a preliminary term sheet if no final term sheet is prepared and circulated, because much of the information in a preliminary term sheet (especially the last version) is likely to be final and therefore would not qualify for the filing exemption. It also is common practice to prepare and file a final term sheet consisting solely of ABSICM by the time that the final prospectus is filed, so any pricing or other final terms information that was disseminated in writing by the underwriter or other offering participants arguably need not be filed because it does not differ from a previously filed FWP.

An issuer or other offering participant must retain its FWPs that were not filed for three years after the initial bona fide offer of the securities in the offering.[63]

An "immaterial and unintentional" failure to include the required legend on an FWP is not a violation of § 5 if:

- a "good faith and reasonable effort" was made to comply with the legend requirement,

- the FWP is amended to include the legend as soon as practicable after discovery of the omission, and

---

[51] Securities Act Rule 433(d)(1), 17 C.F.R. 230.433(d)(1).

[52] Securities Act Rule 433(h)(3), 17 C.F.R. 230.433(h)(3).

[53] Div. of Corp. Fin., *Securities Offering Reform Questions and Answers*, SEC.GOV (Nov. 30, 2005) (answering Question 9).

[54] 70 Fed. Reg. at 44,751 n.271.

[55] *Id.. See also* 206 SPS § III-D4, *ABS Informational and computational materials* (discussing ABSICM).

[56] *See* Securities Act Rule 433(d)(3), 17 C.F.R. § 230.433(d)(3).

[57] *See* 306 SPS § II-C2, *Takedowns*.

[58] *See* 206 SPS § III-D6, *Media reports, road shows and other special FWP rules*.

[59] Securities Act Rule 433(d)(3), 17 C.F.R. § 230.433(d)(3).

[60] 17 C.F.R. § 230.433(d)(4).

[61] 17 C.F.R. § 230.433(d)(8).

[62] *See* Securities Act Rule 164, 17 C.F.R. § 230.164.

[63] Securities Act Rule 433(g), 17 C.F.R. § 230.433(g).

- the FWP with the legend is re-transmitted by substantially the same means and to substantially the same prospective purchasers.[64]

Similarly, an "immaterial or unintentional" failure to file (or delay in filing) an FWP is not a violation of § 5 if:

- a "good faith and reasonable effort" was made to comply with the filing requirement, and

- the FWP is filed as soon as practicable after discovery of the failure.[65]

Finally, an "immaterial or unintentional" failure to comply with the recordkeeping requirement is not a violation of § 5 if a "good faith and reasonable effort" was made to comply with the recordkeeping requirement.[66]

6. Media reports, roadshows and other special FWP rules

There are special FWP rules for media reports. If an offering participant prepares or pays for a publication or broadcast, it is treated just like any other FWP. For a non-reporting issuer, the prospectus delivery requirement will make such publications and broadcasts practically impossible. However, if the publication or broadcast is not paid for or prepared by an offering participant and is published by an unaffiliated media outlet, no FWP legend is required, filing is not required until four business days after the offering participant becomes aware of the media report, and (for non-reporting issuers, i.e., issuers of ABS registered on Form S-1) no prospectus is required to be delivered. No filing is required if the substance of the media report has previously been filed.[67]

There also are special FWP rules for roadshows and for visual aids and other materials disseminated at roadshows. In general, a roadshow is a marketing presentation for the securities being offered, usually made by management of the issuer with the assistance of the underwriter, to one or more institutional investors. Because oral offers clearly are permitted once the registration statement has been filed,[68] roadshows that qualify as oral communications clearly are permitted as well. However, the FWP rules substantially clarified the legal treatment of slides and other demonstration materials used in roadshows, and liberalized the use of electronic roadshows.

For the SEC's purposes, a "roadshow" means an offer (other than a statutory prospectus) that contains a presentation regarding an offering by (for ABS issuers) one or more members of management involved in the securitization or servicing function of the depositor, sponsor or servicer, that includes a discussion about the issuer, such management and the offered securities.

Comment: To take advantage of the SEC's special rules regarding roadshows, it is important to include one or more appropriate management members in the presentation. A presentation solely by the underwriter will not qualify.

With respect to visual aids, a communication that is "provided or transmitted simultaneously" with a roadshow "in a manner designed to make the communication available only as part of the roadshow and not separately" is treated as part of the roadshow.[69] Therefore, if a roadshow is an oral communication, so too are any visual aids that meet this test, which means that they need not be filed as an FWP or otherwise.

Comment: The classic example of a visual aid that qualifies for this special rule is a PowerPoint presentation shown on a screen during a live roadshow presentation. Handouts also may fall within the scope of this special rule, if they are carefully collected at the end of the presentation under procedures designed to make it impossible for them to be kept by participants. Otherwise, a handout is a written communication that should be filed as an FWP.

A live, in-person roadshow clearly is an oral presentation. Under the SEC's rules, if a roadshow is transmitted electronically (or by other "graphic" means) but originates live, in real time, to a live audience, it is still an oral communication. On the other hand, a recorded electronic roadshow is a graphic communication, and therefore a written communication as well as a free writing prospectus. However, so long as it qualifies as a "roadshow" under the SEC's rules, it need not be filed.[70] Because of the SEC's special rule on visual aids, a visual aid in an electronic roadshow need not be filed if it is "provided or transmitted simultaneously" with the roadshow "in a manner designed to make the communication available only as part of the roadshow and not separately."[71] If the visual aid is "contained in a separate file from the roadshow, or otherwise transmitted separately," it remains subject to the filing requirement.

Comment: As a matter of practice, visual aids in an electronic roadshow generally should not be capable of being printed, downloaded or otherwise saved separately from the roadshow, unless they are filed as FWPs.

Included as Practice Tool 2 is a table detailing many types of FWPs commonly used in public offerings of ABS and their associated filing requirements.

7. Liability and "time of sale" considerations

Sources of potential liability for marketing materials under the federal securities laws include:

- Section 11 of the Securities Act,[72] which imposes potential civil liability on the issuer, its directors and principal officers, the underwriter, and certain named experts, if any part of the registration statement contains an untrue statement of a material fact or omits a material fact that is required or necessary to make the statements it does contain not misleading;

---

[64] Securities Act Rule 164(c), 17 C.F.R. § 230.164(c).

[65] Securities Act Rule 164(b), 17 C.F.R. § 230.164(b).

[66] Securities Act Rule 164(d), 17 C.F.R. § 230.164(d).

[67] Securities Act Rule 433(f), 17 C.F.R. § 230.433(f).

[68] See 206 SPS § III-D1, *The waiting period generally, and the shelf offering analogy.*

[69] Securities Act Rule 433(d)(8), 17 C.F.R. § 230.433(d)(8) note.

[70] 17 C.F.R. § 230.433(d)(8).

[71] 17 C.F.R. § 230.433(d)(8) note.

[72] 15 U.S.C. § 77k.

- Section 12(a)(2) of the Securities Act,[73] which imposes potential civil liability on any person who offers or sells a security in a public offering[74] by means of a prospectus (i.e., a written communication that "offers" the security) or oral communication that contains an untrue statement of a material fact or omits a material fact that is necessary in order to make the statements it does make contain, in light of the circumstances in which they were made, not misleading;

- Rule 10b-5 under the Exchange Act,[75] which makes it unlawful for any person to make any untrue statement of a material fact or to omit to state a material fact necessary in order to make the statements made, in light of the circumstances under which they were made, not misleading; and

- Section 17(a) of the Securities Act,[76] which makes it unlawful for any person in the offer or sale of a security to obtain money or property by means of any untrue statement of a material fact or any omission to state a material fact necessary in order to make the statements made, in light of the circumstances under which they were made, not misleading.

Under Securities Act Rule 159,[77] potential liability under §§ 12(a)(2) and 17(a)(2) of the Securities Act for statements to investors that contain material misstatements and omissions is determined on the basis of information that has been conveyed to the investor at the time of sale, which is the time the investor commits to purchase the securities in question. Because the final prospectus generally is not finalized until after contracts of sale have been entered into with investors, liability will rest on the materials that have been delivered to investors at the time they are "hard circled," which generally will include either a statutory preliminary prospectus or a virtual red, as well as any other FWPs and ABSICM.

If, after the time of sale and before closing, these documents are determined to contain a material misstatement or omission, whether through error or a change in circumstance, the SEC's view is that the only way to eliminate potential liability consistently with the federal securities laws is to terminate the existing contract of sale, convey the additional or changed information to the investor, and then enter into a new contract of sale.[78] According to the SEC, "any such procedure must be the substantive equivalent of the termination by mutual agreement of the prior contract of sale and the entering into a new contract of sale,"[79] and must include providing the investor with:

- adequate disclosure of the contractual arrangement,
- adequate disclosure of the investor's rights under the existing contract,
- adequate disclosure of the new information, and
- a meaningful ability to decide whether to terminate the prior contract and enter into the new contract.

Whether the procedure used complies with these requirements depends on the particular facts and circumstances, including:

- the manner and prominence of the disclosure of the contractual arrangements and the investor's rights under the old contract,
- the process by which the new or changed material information will be conveyed to the purchaser, and
- the method by which the purchaser is required to make or communicate its decisions.

While an affirmative communication is not necessarily required, the method chosen must give the purchaser a meaningful ability to make its decisions in light of the new information.[80]

Comment: Most broker-dealers have policies specifying the exact procedures to be used in order to terminate the existing contract of sale and enter into a new contract of sale.

If the investor decides not to terminate its old contract of sale and enter into a new one, the issuer and underwriter of course would not proceed on the basis of materially misleading disclosure. The investor then would have the theoretical right to sue for damages for breach of the initial contract of sale, although as a practical matter the more likely result would be a negotiated settlement.

8. Choosing between ABSICM and FWPs

FWPs have essentially eclipsed ABSICM in the marketplace for several reasons. ABSICM are limited to prescribed categories of information, while almost anything can be included in an FWP, so long as it does not conflict with the registration statement. All ABSICM must be filed, while many FWPs need not be filed. While the general filing requirement for FWPs is stricter than for ABSICM, FWPs consisting solely of ABSICM may be filed within the more relaxed time period for filing ABSICM. ABSICM may be used only in shelf offerings, while FWPs may be used in stand-alone offerings registered on Form S-1, subject to certain limitations. Finally, and perhaps most importantly, ABSICM are incorporated by reference into the registration statement,[81] which means that the issuer, its directors and officers, and the underwriter face potential liability under § 11 of the Securities Act for ABSICM. FWPs are not filed as part of the registration statement nor

---

[73] 15 U.S.C. § 77l.

[74] See Gustafson v. Alloyd Co, Inc., 513 U.S. 561, 569, 585 (1995).

[75] 17 C.F.R. § 240.10b-5. The courts have implied a private right of action for violations of Rule 10b-5. See, e.g., Ernst & Ernst v. Hochfelder, 425 U.S. 185, 196–97 (1976).

[76] 15 U.S.C. § 77q. While § 17(a) is a criminal provision, some courts have implied a private right of action. See, e.g., Kenilworth Partners L.P. v. Cendant Corp., 59 F. Supp. 2d 417, 426 (D. N. J. 1999).

[77] 17 C.F.R. § 230.159.

[78] 70 Fed. Reg. at 44,767.

[79] 70 Fed. Reg. at 44,768.

[80] Id.

[81] Securities Act Rule 462(a), 17 C.F.R. § 230.462(a).

incorporated by reference into the registration statement,[82] so they cannot give rise to § 11 liability.

> **Comment:** One of the only reasons for using ABSICM rather than an FWP is if the issuer is an ineligible issuer, due to the limitations on the content and use of FWPs by ineligible issuers.

E. Post-Effective Period and Traditional Free Writing

1. Generally

After the registration statement has been declared effective by the SEC, § 5 of the Securities Act no longer prohibits sales of the securities.[83] Oral offers continue to be permitted, as does the use of FWPs, ABSICM and the preliminary and final prospectuses.

Section 2(a)(10) of the Securities Act[84] provides that additional written materials (known as "traditional free writing") are not a "prospectus" subject to the prohibitions of § 5 if a statutory final prospectus was sent or given to the recipient concurrently or prior to the delivery of the additional free writing. The "access equals delivery" rules[85] do not apply here, so an electronic or paper copy of the final prospectus must actually have been delivered to the recipient prior to its receipt of the free writing materials.

> **Comment:** Once all of the offered securities have been sold by the underwriter, it is unlikely that any subsequent written communication could be deemed to condition the market for the securities offered. However, just because the closing has occurred does not mean that the underwriter will have sold all of the securities it has purchased from the issuer—it is common for an underwriter to retain an unsold allotment, sometimes for an extended period of time. Therefore, a careful issuer will exercise caution in the dissemination of post-closing materials referring to the offering, especially post-closing press releases. If the underwriter retains an unsold allotment, any post-closing press release or other widely disseminated materials should be limited to the contents permitted in a pre-closing press release under Securities Act Rule 134 or (for Form S-3 registrants) and should be treated as a free writing prospectus.

2. The final prospectus and "access equals delivery"

Securities Act § 5(b)(2) prohibits causing a security to be carried through the mails or in interstate commerce for purposes of delivery after sale, unless it is accompanied or preceded by a statutory prospectus.[86] In addition, Exchange Act Rule 10b-10(a) requires a broker-dealer to deliver to the purchaser of a security, at or before completion of the transaction,

a written confirmation containing certain required information regarding the transaction.[87] Because this written confirmation would be a "prospectus," in order for it to be permitted as traditional free writing it must be preceded or accompanied by a copy of the final statutory prospectus.

Alternatively, Securities Act Rule 172 enables "access equals delivery" to comply with all of these obligations—the final prospectus need not be actually delivered to the purchaser so long as the issuer has filed the statutory prospectus with the SEC (or if not yet filed, the issuer "will make a good faith and reasonable effort to file the prospectus within the time required under Securities Act Rule 424"[88] and files the prospectus as soon as practicable thereafter).[89]

The prospectus delivery requirement of § 5(b)(2) continues to apply to the underwriters until they completely sell out of their initial allotments of the offered securities.[90] Therefore, the prospectus should be updated to keep abreast of any material changes for so long as there are any unsold allotments. Material changes may be accomplished by preparing a supplement, or "sticker," and filing it pursuant to Securities Act Rule 424(b)(3)[91] by the fifth business day after first use.

Where access equals delivery does not apply and a prospectus must actually be delivered, delivery may be accomplished electronically, by email or posting on a website. In order for electronic delivery to be effective:

- the investor must receive notice that the prospectus is available electronically;

- the prospectus must be accessible, without restrictions so burdensome that the intended recipients cannot effectively access the information (e.g., having to navigate a complex set of onscreen menus); and

- there must be evidence of the delivery, such as the investor's consent to receive the prospectus electronically in the format provided.

Electronic delivery by email and website is presumptively permissible if there was adequate notice and investor consent to electronic delivery.[92]

---

[82] Securities Act Rule 433(d)(1), 17 C.F.R. § 230.433(d)(1).

[83] See 206 SPS § III-A, The Basic Investor Communications Framework of § 5.

[84] 15 U.S.C. § 77b(a)(10). This is the definition of "prospectus," which is used in the prohibitions of § 5.

[85] See 206 SPS § II-E2, The final prospectus and "access equals delivery."

[86] 15 U.S.C. § 77e(b)(2).

[87] 17 C.F.R. § 240.10b-10(a).

[88] For prospectuses and prospectus supplements in shelf offerings of ABS, the filing must be no later than the second business day following the date it is first used after effectiveness, which generally is the second business day after closing; for stand-alone ABS offerings, the filing must be no later than the second business day following the earlier of the date of determination of the offering price or the date it is first used after effectiveness, which generally is the second business day after pricing. 17 C.F.R. § 230.424(b)(1), instruc.

[89] 17 C.F.R. § 230.172.

[90] Cf. Securities Act § 4(a)(3), 15 U.S.C. § 77d(a)(3) (excepting dealers from the prospectus delivery requirement after a designated period of time, "including an underwriter no longer acting as an underwriter"—meaning that an underwriter with an unsold allotment must continue to comply).

[91] 17 C.F.R. § 230.424(b)(3).

[92] See Use of Electronic Media for Delivery Purposes, 60 Fed. Reg. 53,548, 53,460–61 (Oct. 13, 1995).

F. The Internet and Statements on Websites

Electronic delivery embodies the "envelope" theory—documents hyperlinked together are considered to be delivered together as if they were in the same paper envelope.[93] So, for example, when an email to an investor contains a hyperlink to a prospectus as well as a copy of the confirmation of sale, and the investor has consented to electronic delivery, the email with the hyperlink and the confirmation is analogous to an envelope containing both the prospectus and the confirmation, which will be considered to have been delivered together.

When a statutory prospectus is posted on the issuer's website, not everything on that website becomes part of the prospectus. Information only becomes part of the prospectus if the issuer takes action to make it so. For example, under the envelope theory, a hyperlink within the prospectus means that the hyperlinked information is part of the prospectus.[94]

Issuers are responsible for statements posted on their websites and can be held liable for material misstatements and omissions in those statements under the antifraud provisions of the federal securities laws. The SEC has provided guidance on when an issuer also may become responsible for information that is contained on other websites but hyperlinked from the issuer's website. In general, whether third-party information is attributable to an issuer depends upon whether the issuer has involved itself in the preparation of the information (known as the "entanglement" theory), or explicitly or implicitly endorsed or approved the information (known as the "adoption" theory).[95] According to the SEC, the key question in determining whether an issuer has adopted hyperlinked information is whether the context creates a reasonable inference that the issuer has approved or endorsed the hyperlinked information. Factors to be evaluated in making this determination include what is implied by the context of the hyperlink (e.g., whether the issuer specifically endorses the hyperlinked information or uses it to support its own statements, or merely states that it might be of interest), as well as the nature and context of the hyperlinked information (e.g., whether it is specific to the issuer or more general in nature). "Exit notices" (which state that the user is leaving the issuer's website) and disclaimers of responsibility for the hyperlinked information may be helpful, but neither conclusively absolves the issuer from responsibility for hyperlinked information.[96]

Under the SEC's rules, a website is a graphic communication as well as a written communication. Therefore, any statement on an issuer's website (or hyperlinked from an issuer's website) for which the issuer is responsible and that could be deemed to condition the market for the securities being offered (i.e., that constitutes an "offer") is a "prospectus."[97] Absent some other exemption, the information should (at least in a shelf offering) be filed as an FWP.[98] However, during a registered securities offering, Securities Act Rule 433 provides a safe harbor rule for most historical information contained on an issuer's website, which protects such information from being considered an "offer" of the securities. Historical information that is identified and located in a separate section of the website, that has not been incorporated by reference into or otherwise referred to in the prospectus, or otherwise been used or referred to in the offering, is not a current offer of the securities. Therefore, such information need not be filed as an FWP.[99]

---

[93] *See, e.g.*, Use of Electronic Media, 65 Fed. Reg. 25,843, 25,846 (May 4, 2000).

[94] 65 Fed. Reg. at 25,847.

[95] 65 Fed. Reg. at 25,848–49 (also discussing factors to be considered in determining whether issuer is entangled with or has adopted third-party statements).

[96] Commission Guidance on the Use of Company Websites, 73 Fed. Reg. 45,862, 45,871 (Aug. 7, 2008).

[97] *See* 206 SPS § III-A, *The Basic Investor Communications Framework of § 5*; 206 SPS § III-B2, *Written and oral communications*; *cf.* 65 Fed. Reg. at 25,848 (issuers are responsible for their statements on Internet websites).

[98] Securities Act Rule 433(e)(1), 17 C.F.R. § 230.433(e)(1).

[99] 17 C.F.R. § 230.433(e)(3).

IV.
Disclosure Requirements in Public Offerings of ABS

A. Regulation AB

Regulation AB provides an overlay to the Securities and Exchange Commission's (SEC) ordinary disclosure requirements for registered public offerings of asset-backed securities (ABS).[1] Most of the items of Regulation AB are required to be included in a registration statement for ABS.[2] The following summarizes some of the more important issues raised by the disclosure items of Regulation AB, as they are currently in effect,[3] and required to be addressed in the prospectus for an ABS offering.

1. Sponsor

Under Item 1101(*l*) of Regulation AB,[4] the "sponsor" is "the person who organizes and initiates the [ABS] transaction by selling or transferring assets, either directly or indirectly, including through an affiliate, to the issuing entity."

Item 1104 of Regulation AB[5] requires a variety of disclosures regarding the sponsor of the transaction, including:

- its name and form of organization;

- the general character of its business;

- a description of its securitization program; and

- its material roles and responsibilities in the securitization program.

Ordinarily, the sponsor of an ABS transaction will be an affiliate of the depositor. However, this is not always the case, and is not required by the definition.[6]

> **Comment:** In a so-called "rent-a-shelf" transaction, an entity without its own effective shelf registration statement securitizes assets by transferring them to an unaffiliated depositor that has an effective shelf registration statement. In this circumstance, the SEC believes that the unaffiliated transferor of the assets to the depositor is the sponsor.[7] A rent-a-shelf depositor usually is controlled by a broker-dealer.

If the transaction documents for the securitization contain a covenant to repurchase or replace an underlying asset for breach of a representation or warranty, then the sponsor must provide the information required by Exchange Act Rule 15Ga-1 for the past three years regarding assets securitized by the sponsor that were the subject of a demand for repurchase or replacement due to breach of a representation or warranty.[8]

2. Static pool information

"Static pool information" indicates how the performance of a "static pool" of financial assets has performed over time, providing comparisons between originations at similar points in the assets' lives.[9]

Under Item 1105 of Regulation AB, static pool information for ABS with an amortizing asset pool generally must be provided with respect to delinquencies, cumulative losses, and prepayments of prior securitized pools of the sponsor of the same asset type. This information must be provided for five years, or for so long as the sponsor has been securitizing assets of the same type, if less than five years. If the sponsor has less than three years of experience securitizing assets of the relevant type, it should "consider" instead providing static pool information by vintage origination years regarding originations or purchases by the sponsor for that asset type. Again, this information must be provided for five years, or for so long as the sponsor has been originating or purchasing assets of the same type, if less than five years.

In either case, the required delinquency, cumulative loss and prepayment data must be presented in periodic increments (e.g., monthly or quarterly) over the life of the relevant asset pool or vintage origination year, with the most recent increment being no later than 135 days before the date of first use of the prospectus. Summary information for the material origination characteristics of the reported securitized pools or vintage origination years also must be provided.

> **Comment:** Although not specified by the rule, it is common practice to include static pool data only for asset pools securitized in the preceding five years, rather than for all securitizations of the sponsor that existed at some point during the preceding five years.

For revolving asset master trusts, static pool information generally must be provided regarding delinquencies, cumulative losses, prepayments, payment rate, yield, and standardized credit scores (or other relevant measures of credit quality), in separate increments based on the date of origination of the pool assets. The rule does not specify the required reporting increments, but registrants should "consider presenting such data at a minimum in 12-month increments through the first five years of the account's life."[10]

Static pool information need not be provided if "the registrant determines that such information is not material."[11] However, the SEC has called static pool information an "increasingly valuable tool in analyzing performance . . . [that] allow[s] the detection of patterns that may not be evident from overall portfolio numbers and thus may reveal a more informa-

---

[1] 17 C.F.R. §§ 229.1100–23.

[2] SEC, Form S-3: Registration Statement Under the Securities Act of 1933, at 10 (General Instruction V: Offerings of Asset-Backed Securities).

[3] The SEC has proposed a wide variety of revisions to Regulation AB, in a proposal commonly known as "Regulation AB II." Asset-Backed Securities, 75 Fed. Reg. 23,328 (May 3, 2010). For more details about proposed Regulation AB II, *see* 206 SPS § VII-A, *Regulation AB II*.

[4] 17 C.F.R. § 229.1101(*l*).

[5] 17 C.F.R. § 229.1104.

[6] *Cf.* Asset-Backed Securities, 70 Fed. Reg. 1506, 1534 (Jan. 7, 2005) ("We do recognize that the facts and circumstances . . . may result in a sponsor that is unaffiliated with the depositor, or that there may even be more than one unaffiliated sponsor.").

[7] *See* 70 Fed. Reg. at 1534, 1541 n.267.

[8] *See generally* 17 C.F.R. § 240.15Ga-1; 206 SPS § VI-I, *Repurchase Demand Reporting on Form ABS-15G*.

[9] 70 Fed. Reg. at 1548.

[10] 17 C.F.R. § 229.1105(b).

[11] 17 C.F.R. §§ 229.1105(a)–(b).

tive picture of material elements of portfolio performance and risk."[12] The SEC also noted that it received "universal and sustained comment" from investors that static pool information is material, and that materiality determinations are made from the standpoint of a reasonable investor.[13]

> **Comment:** As a practical matter, static pool data should not be omitted unless there is a truly compelling argument for doing so.

If the static pool information that otherwise would be required is not material, but alternative static pool information would provide material disclosure, the alternative information must be provided instead. Static pool information regarding a party other than the sponsor may be provided in lieu of or in addition to static pool information of the sponsor, "if appropriate to provide material disclosure."[14] For example, if the sponsor's experience has been sporadic, there is a significant gap in its experience, or its origination or acquisition program has changed materially, information about the sponsor's vintage portfolio may be appropriate in addition to or instead of information about its prior securitized pools. For a new revolving asset master trust, information about prior master trusts or the sponsor's vintage portfolio may be appropriate in addition to or in lieu of information about the new asset pool.[15]

> **Comment:** In the absence of SEC guidance, industry practices vary widely as to when static pool information of third parties would be material (such as when a significant portion of the securitized assets was originated by a third party rather than by the sponsor) and should be provided.

Item 1105(f) provides that if any otherwise required static pool information is "unknown and not available to the registrant without unreasonable effort or expense," it may be omitted if the registrant provides the information that it possesses (or can acquire without unreasonable effort or expense) and includes a statement "showing that unreasonable effort or expense would be involved in obtaining the omitted information."[16] This standard is almost identical to that of Securities Act Rule 409,[17] which more generally provides that any information required in a registration statement may be omitted if it is "unknown and not available to the registrant without unreasonable effort or expense," either because it would involve unreasonable effort or expense to obtain or "because it rests peculiarly within the knowledge of another person not affiliated with the registrant." Rule 409 also requires the registrant to provide the information that it possesses (or can acquire without unreasonable effort or expense) and to include a statement "either showing that unreasonable effort or expense would be involved or indicating the absence of any affiliation with the person within whose knowledge the information rest and stating the result of a request made to such persons for the infor-

mation." The "unreasonable effort or expense" standard in Rule 409 traditionally has been viewed by the SEC staff as setting a high threshold.

> **Comment:** Because of the SEC staff's narrow interpretation, issuers generally should be cautious about omitting otherwise required static pool information based on the "unreasonable effort or expense" standard, though it may be easier to reach the conclusion that unreasonable effort or expense would be required to obtain static pool information that is controlled solely by an uncooperative third party.

While the SEC used to permit static pool information to be provided on a separate website and incorporated into the prospectus, this was a temporary accommodation that expired on June 30, 2012.[18] At the present time, static pool information must be physically included within the prospectus (often as an appendix), or filed on Form 8-K and incorporated by reference into the registration statement (for Form S-3 shelf registrations), or included on a CD-ROM or other electronic media delivered with the prospectus.[19]

3. Depositor

Under Item 1101(e) of Regulation AB,[20] the "depositor" generally is "the depositor who receives or purchases and transfers or sells the pool assets to the issuing entity." As described above,[21] the depositor usually is a bankruptcy-remote special purpose corporation or limited liability company. Item 1105 of Regulation AB[22] requires a variety of disclosures regarding the depositor, including:

- its name and form of organization;

- the general character of its business;

- a description of its securitization program and its material roles and responsibilities in that securitization program (to the extent materially different from the information disclosed with respect to the sponsor);

- its ownership structure;

- the general character (and time period) of its activities other than securitizations; and

- any continuing duties regarding the offered ABS or underlying pool assets.

4. Issuing entity

Under Item 1101(f) of Regulation AB,[23] the "issuing entity" is "the trust or other entity created at the direction of the sponsor or depositor that owns or holds the pool assets and in whose name the [ABS] supported or serviced by the pool assets

---

[12] 70 Fed. Reg. at 1538.

[13] *Id.*

[14] 17 C.F.R. § 229.1105(c).

[15] 70 Fed. Reg. at 1541.

[16] 17 C.F.R. § 229.1105(f).

[17] Securities Act Rule 409 applies more generally to any information required to be contained in a registration statement. 17 C.F.R. § 230.409.

[18] Regulation S-T Item 312(a), 17 C.F.R. § 232.312(a).

[19] 70 Fed. Reg. at 1541-42.

[20] 17 C.F.R. § 229.1101(3).

[21] *See* 206 SPS § I-B, *Structure of a "Plain Vanilla" Securitization.*

[22] 17 C.F.R. § 229.1105.

[23] 17 C.F.R. § 229.1101(f).

are issued." As described above,[24] the issuing entity usually is either a common-law trust or a Delaware statutory trust.[25]

Among the disclosures required by Item 1107 about the issuing entity are:

- its name and form of organization;

- the activities that are permissible and restricted under its organizational documents and any discretionary activities regarding the pool assets or ABS;

- its assets other than the pool assets and liabilities other than the ABS;

- the terms of any management or administration agreement;

- the sale and transfer of the pool assets to the issuing entity and any security interest in the pool assets in favor of the issuing entity, the trustee, or the ABS holders, including the material terms of any sale or security agreement;

- the market price of any pool assets that are securities; and

- any bankruptcy-remoteness characteristics of the issuing entity.

The issuing entity's organizational documents (which usually are a pooling and servicing agreement when certificates are issued and a trust agreement and indenture when notes are issued), any management or administration agreement with regard to the issuing entity, and any sale or security agreement with regard to the pool assets must be filed as an exhibit to the registration statement.

5. Servicers

Under Item 1101(j) of Regulation AB,[26] a "servicer" is "any person responsible for the management or collection of the pool assets or making allocations or distributions to holders of the [ABS]."

The concept of "making allocations or distributions of pool assets" is very broad—and intentionally so.[27] Therefore, whether an entity is a "servicer" can be a difficult factual determination. The definition specifically states that a trustee that makes allocations or distributions to holders of the ABS is not a servicer if it receives funds for allocation or distribution from a servicer and does not otherwise perform servicing functions, but where the trustee calculates and makes allocations and distributions and there is no other servicer (in, for example, a resecuritization), the trustee may also be a servicer. Transaction documents often provide for the trustee to take over as back-up servicer in certain circumstances, and if it does so it will be a servicer under Regulation AB. Subservicers and other

transaction parties whose responsibilities are limited to particular portions of the servicing function are still captured within the definition of "servicer." On the other hand, a credit risk manager that monitors and makes recommendations regarding the asset pool generally would not be a servicer, because it is not responsible for making or implementing decisions regarding the pool assets. Nor would a party holding the servicing rights—and therefore entitled to retain servicing fees in excess of those paid to the servicer and to appoint a successor servicer—be "responsible for the management or collection of the pool assets."

> **Comment:** An interim servicer that continues to service the pool assets only for a very limited time from the cut-off date (i.e., the date after which collections on the pool assets are for the benefit of the ABS holders) until around the closing date is still a "servicer." However, most practitioners would conclude that only the name of the servicer and a description of the servicing transfer (including its risks) need be included because most servicer disclosure items are required only "as applicable depending on the servicer's role."[28]

There may be multiple "servicers" in a transaction, including one or more master servicers (i.e., a servicer that oversees other servicers), primary servicers that are in privity with the issuing entity, and special servicers whose responsibilities are limited to specific servicing functions.[29] In that case, while a general description of their respective roles must be provided, not every disclosure required by Item 1108 must necessarily be made. Full disclosure is required for every master servicer, every affiliated servicer, every unaffiliated servicer that services 20 percent or more of the pool assets, and "[a]ny other material servicer responsible for calculating or making distributions to holders of the [ABS], performing work-outs or foreclosures, or another aspect of the servicing of the pool assets or the [ABS] upon which the performance of the pool assets or the [ABS] is materially dependent."[30] An unaffiliated servicer that services 10 percent or more of the pool assets (but less than 20 percent) must be identified, but the other disclosures are not required. The 10-percent and 20-percent calculations generally are made as of the cut-off date in amortizing transactions.[31]

> **Comment:** In a master trust, most practitioners would advise that the 10-percent and 20-percent determinations be made as of the issuance date. Many practitioners also would include within the 10-percent and 20-percent buckets any servicers identified after considering the expected servicing of assets intended to be acquired during the pre-funding or revolving period.

Where full disclosure is required regarding a servicer, the mandated items include, as applicable depending on its role:

- its name and form of organization;

---

[24] *See* 206 SPS § I-B, *Structure of a "Plain Vanilla" Securitization.*

[25] The "issuing entity" should not be confused with the "issuer," which is the depositor, acting solely in its capacity as depositor to the issuing entity. Securities Act Rule 191, 17 C.F.R. § 230.191; *see also* 206 SPS § I-B, *Structure of a "Plain Vanilla" Securitization.*

[26] 17 C.F.R. § 229.1101(j).

[27] 70 Fed. Reg. at 1535.

---

[28] Regulation AB Item 1108(a)(3), 17 C.F.R. § 229.1108(a)(3).

[29] 17 C.F.R. § 229.1108(a).

[30] 17 C.F.R. §§ 229.1108(a)(2)–(3).

[31] Div. of Corp. Fin., SEC, Manual of Publicly Available Telephone Interpretations—Regulation AB and Related Rules § 7.01 (2007).

- how long it has been servicing assets, including a general discussion of servicing experience for any asset type and details regarding servicing experience for the securitized asset type, including "to the extent material information regarding the size, composition and growth of the servicer's portfolio of serviced assets of the type included in the current transaction";[32]

- any material change to its policies or procedures for the same function and asset type during the past three years; and

- information regarding its financial condition, but only to the extent that there is a material risk that it "could have a material impact on pool performance or performance of the ABS."[33]

Comment: Whether financial information regarding the servicer is required will depend on a facts-and-circumstances analysis of whether its financial condition has or may reasonably be expected to be significantly impaired, including factors such as a recent material adverse financial occurrence or reduction in its credit rating or outlook.

Comment: Prior to the adoption of Regulation AB, prospectuses commonly provided statistical information in tabular form regarding the servicer's entire portfolio, including net loss and delinquency information. Because Regulation AB does not require this information, it is no longer commonly provided.

In addition, Item 1108 also requires a variety of disclosures regarding the terms of the servicing arrangements, including, to the extent material:

- the terms of the servicing agreement;

- the manner in which collections on the pool assets will be maintained;

- whether the servicer is required or permitted to advance collections, cash flows, or distributions, including any associated fees and how such advances are to be recovered;

- the servicer's process for handling delinquencies, losses, bankruptcies, and recoveries;

- arrangements regarding the safekeeping and preservation of pool assets for which the servicer has custody; and

- terms regarding replacement of the servicer and back-up servicing.

6. Originators

Regulation AB does not define "originator." However, the term could refer either to the entity from which the sponsor acquired the pool assets or to another other originating entity from which the selling entity acquired those assets.

    Comment: Many practitioners would advise that in a "correspondent lending" relationship, where one entity has a contractual agreement to acquire assets from a "correspondent lender" that meet certain preset criteria, the acquiror (and not the correspondent lender) is the originator. Without such a relationship, the party that actually originated the assets generally will be considered to be the originator.

It may be difficult to obtain the required information regarding an originator that is not affiliated with the sponsor or with which the sponsor does not have a contractual relationship. If so, then it may be impossible to structure a registered public securitization of those assets, unless the originator's concentration does not meet the 20 percent disclosure threshold discussed below or is otherwise immaterial.

    Comment: Many sponsors would conclude that originator disclosure is immaterial if the pool assets have been fully re-underwritten in accordance with the sponsor's own underwriting guidelines.

Full disclosure is required for every originator (other than the sponsor or its affiliates) that originated, or is expected to originate, 20 percent or more of the pool assets.[34] An originator (other than the sponsor or its affiliates) that originated, or is expected to originate, 10 percent or more of the pool assets (but less than 20 percent) must be identified, but the other disclosures are not required.[35]

    Comment: Most practitioners would advise that the 10-percent and 20-percent calculations be made as of the cut-off date in amortizing transactions, or as of the issuance date in a master trust.

Where full disclosure is required regarding an originator, the mandated items include:

- its name and form of organization;

- to the extent material, a description of its origination program and how long it has been originating assets, including its experience in the securitized asset type; and

- to the extent material, the size and composition of its origination portfolio and other information material to an analysis of the pool assets' performance, such as its underwriting criteria.

7. Pool assets, including disclosures regarding the issuer's review of the pool assets

Item 1111 of Regulation AB requires a long list of information regarding the pool assets, including:

- their type, terms, underwriting and selection criteria;

- the material characteristics of the assets on a pool-wide basis;

- delinquency and loss information;

- representations and warranties made regarding the pool assets;

- information about any revolving periods or prefunding accounts; and

---

[32] 17 C.F.R. § 229.1108(b)(2).
[33] 17 C.F.R. § 229.1108(b)(4).

[34] Regulation AB Item 1110(b), 17 C.F.R. § 229.1110(b).
[35] Regulation AB Item 1110(a), 17 C.F.R. § 229.1110(a).

- a description of any variation of any pool assets from the disclosed underwriting criteria, including data on the amount and characteristics of assets that did not meet the underwriting criteria.[36]

Currently, asset-level disclosure is not required.

Statistical information should be presented in tabular or graphical format and in appropriate distributional groups or incremental ranges in addition to overall pool totals, averages, and weighted averages "if such presentation will aid in the understanding of the data."[37] In addition to presenting the number, amount and percentage by distributional group or range, the data also should be presented by variables such as average balance, weighted average coupon, average age, remaining term, average loan-to-value, weighed average credit score, or other appropriate variables, to the extent material.[38]

Historical data is to be provided as appropriate to allow material evaluation of the pool data—the example given in the rule is for the lesser of three years or the time the assets have been in existence.[39] Wherever required in Regulation AB, historical delinquency and loss information is to be presented in 30 or 31-day increments beginning with assets that are 30 or 31 days delinquent (as applicable),[40] through the point when they are written off or charged off as uncollectible.[41]

> **Comment:** In most cases assets would not be included in the asset pool if they were charged off as of the cut-off date, so the main import of this requirement for a prospectus is to include delinquency and loss information for an extended period of time. SEC staffers have indicated that it may be acceptable to end the 30 or 31 day increments after a period of time such as six months, and thereafter include larger increments.

According to the SEC, although the requirement is not specified, Item 1111 requires an ABS prospectus to contain statistical information regarding an originator's "risk-layering" practices with respect to "multiple non-traditional features of a loan" that are bundled together.[42]

Item 1111 of Regulation AB requires each issuer to disclose in the prospectus the nature of the review performed by the issuer or sponsor pursuant to Securities Act Rule 193, as well as the findings and conclusions of the review. Section 945 of the Dodd-Frank Act, as codified at § 7(d) of the Securities Act,[43] mandated the adoption of the rule,[44] which requires ABS issuers to perform a review of the pool assets underlying the ABS. Section 7(d) refers explicitly to Exchange Act ABS, and it only requires the SEC to issue rules "relating to the registration statement." Accordingly, as adopted, Securities Act Rule 193 applies only to issuers of Exchange Act ABS that are offered in registered offerings.

Rule 193 requires that the review must, at a minimum, be designed and effected to provide "reasonable assurance" that the disclosure in the prospectus regarding the assets is "accurate in all material respects." Rule 193 does not mandate any particular type of review; according to the SEC, the scope of the review may vary depending on the circumstances, such as the nature of the securitized assets, and there is a range of judgments that an issuer might make as to what constitutes "reasonable assurance." Sampling may be appropriate depending on the circumstances, such as the type of ABS being offered, the number of pool assets, the size of the sample and whether further review was conducted if the initial review indicated that it was warranted. If sampling is used, the sample size and the criteria used to select the sampled assets should be disclosed.

Under Rule 193, the pool asset review is required to be performed by the "issuer" of the registered Exchange Act ABS. The required review may be performed by either the depositor or the sponsor, and Rule 193 permits an issuer to engage another third party to perform any part of the required review. However, a review of the assets by an unaffiliated originator would not suffice for purposes of Rule 193. In the view of the SEC, an unaffiliated originator may have different interests in the securitization and different review standards than the issuer or sponsor, particularly where it has contributed only a small portion of the pool assets.[45]

Item 1111 of Regulation AB requires the issuer to disclose whether it hired a third party to undertake any of the review required by Rule 193. The rule permits the issuer to choose whether to attribute the findings and conclusions of a third-party diligence provider to that third party or to itself. If the issuer attributes the findings and conclusions to the third party, then the diligence provider must be specifically named, and it must consent to being named as an "expert" pursuant to § 7(a)(1) of the Securities Act,[46] and Rule 436 thereunder,[47] and therefore be subject to liability under § 11 of the Securities Act.[48] If the issuer attributes the findings and conclusions of the third party to itself, then the diligence provider need not be specifically named and need not consent to expert status.

> **Comment:** Few, if any, third-party diligence providers have agreed to be named as experts.

Finally, Item 1111 mandates disclosure as to whether any pool assets deviate from the disclosed underwriting criteria or any other criteria or benchmark used to evaluate the assets, or any assets in the sample or assets otherwise known to deviate if only a sample was reviewed. Also to be disclosed are which entity or entities (e.g., the depositor, the sponsor, or the underwriter) made the decision to include the nonconforming assets in the pool and the factors used to make that decision. If the underwriting criteria provide that the originator may approve assets at multiple levels, but assets that failed to meet the first level of underwriting criteria are included in the pool, the determination to include these loans in the pool will trigger the required disclosures.

---

[36] 17 C.F.R. § 229.1111.

[37] 17 C.F.R. § 229.1111 intro.

[38] *Id.*

[39] *Id.*

[40] Historical delinquency data is always required. *See* DIV. OF CORP. FIN., REGULATION AB TELEPHONE INTERPRETATIONS, at § 9.01.

[41] Regulation AB Item 1100(b), 17 C.F.R. § 229.1100(b).

[42] 75 Fed. Reg. 23,328, 23377.

[43] 15 U.S.C. § 77g(d).

[44] 17 C.F.R. § 230.193.

---

[45] Issuer Review of Assets in Offerings of Asset-Backed Securities, 76 Fed. Reg. 4231, 4233 (Jan. 25, 2011).

[46] 15 U.S.C. § 77g(a)(1).

[47] 17 C.F.R. § 230.436.

[48] 15 U.S.C. § 77k.

Comment: This disclosure requirement has caused many issuers to revise their standard asset underwriting disclosure, in an effort to ensure that it clearly describes the loans that comply with their underwriting criteria. Issuers have taken different approaches in describing "exception loans" (i.e., loans that deviate from the disclosed underwriting criteria). For example, one public issuer includes a table with information on each exception loan, including why it failed to meet the disclosed underwriting criteria and any "offsetting" characteristics.

8. *Significant obligors*

"Significant obligor" is defined by Item 1101(k) of Regulation AB as:

- an obligor (or group of affiliated obligors) on any pool asset (or group thereof) if the pool asset (or group) represents 10 percent or more of the asset pool;

- a property (or group of related properties) securing a pool asset (or group thereof) if the pool asset (or group) represents 10 percent or more of the asset pool; or

- a lessee (or group of affiliated lessees) if the related lease (or group thereof) represents 10 percent or more of the asset pool.[49]

Cross-defaulted or cross-collateralized pool assets (or underlying properties) are aggregated for these purposes. The determination of significant obligors is made as of the cut-off date, except for master trusts for which there is no cut-off date, in which case it is made as of the issuance date. Where cash flow from leases supports the ABS, the calculation is based on those leases even if the asset pool consists of mortgages on the leased properties or other related assets, rather than the leases themselves. If a pool asset is a nonrecourse lease or mortgage of real property, and the obligor does not manage the property and has no other operations, then the obligor is not itself a significant obligor, even if the property is. While the disclosure requirements for significant obligors begin at the 10-percent level, enhanced disclosure is required with regard to significant obligors that present 20-percent or more of the asset pool.

Comment: Many practitioners also would include within the 10-percent and 20-percent buckets any additional servicers identified after considering the expected servicing of assets intended to be acquired during a pre-funding or revolving period.

Item 1112 of Regulation AB requires disclosure of the following for significant obligors:

- its name and form of organization;

- the general character of its business;

- the nature of the concentration of its pool assets;

- the material terms of the related pool assets and any agreements with the obligor involving the pool assets;

- for a significant obligor with 10 percent or more, but less than 20 percent, of the asset pool, selected financial data pursuant to Item 301 of Regulation S-K[50] generally is required (but only net operating income for the most recent fiscal year and any subsequent interim period if the obligor is a property or group of properties); and

- for a significant obligor with 20 percent or more of the asset pool, full audited financial statements meeting the requirements of Regulation S-X.[51]

No financial information is required with respect to the significant obligor if its obligations are backed by the full faith and credit of the U.S. or (in some circumstances) a foreign government. If the significant obligor is an asset-backed issuer (i.e., in a resecuritization), then the information required by Items 1104–15, 1117 and 1119 of Regulation AB also must be provided.

In lieu of providing required third-party information, including significant obligor information, in the prospectus (either directly or via incorporation by reference from a Form 8-K), it may be incorporated by reference from Exchange Act reports of the third party (or an entity that consolidates the third party) under certain conditions:

- the third party (or consolidating entity) must be required to file Exchange Act periodic reports (i.e., it may not be a voluntary filer);

- the third party (or consolidating entity) must have filed all reports and other materials required during the last 12 months (or any shorter time it was required to do so);

- the filed reports must include or properly incorporate by reference the third party's financial statements (or, if the significant obligor is an asset-backed issuer, the information required by Items 1104–15, 1117, and 1119 of Regulation AB); and

- the prospectus must state that all documents subsequently filed by the third party (or consolidating entity) before the termination of the offering are incorporated by reference.[52]

All other SEC rules regarding incorporation by reference must be followed,[53] meaning that for audited financial statements, the written consent of the third party's auditors may be required, which may be impracticable to obtain.

Because of the difficulty of obtaining the required consents from an unaffiliated third party, if there is no direct or indirect agreement or understanding relating to the transaction, and neither the third party nor any of its affiliates is an affiliate of the sponsor, depositor, issuing entity, or underwriter, then if one of the following conditions is satisfied to the knowledge of the registrant, the information regarding the third party may be merely referenced rather than formally incorporated by reference:

- the third party is eligible to use shelf registration on Form S-3 or F-3 for certain offerings of its own securities;

---

[49] 17 C.F.R. § 229.1101(k).

[50] 17 C.F.R. § 229.301.
[51] 17 C.F.R. § 229.1112. *See* 17 C.F.R. pt. 201 (Regulation S-K).
[52] Regulation AB Item 1100(c)(1), 17 C.F.R. § 229.1100(c)(1).
[53] 17 C.F.R. § 229.1100(c)(1) instrucs. 1–2.

- the related pool assets are themselves ABS, the third party is filing Exchange Act reports and the third party has filed all reports and other materials required during the last 12 months (or any shorter time it was required to do so); or

- the third party is a U.S. government-sponsored enterprise such as Fannie Mae and Freddie Mac, subject to certain conditions.

Comment: Significant obligor information would be required in a public resecuritization in which a single ABS issuer represents more than 10 percent of the entire pool of underlying securities. The difficulty of obtaining this information is one of the reasons that public resecuritizations are so rare.[54]

9. Transaction structure

Item 1113 of Regulation AB requires the description of a variety of specific matters relating to the structure of the ABS transaction and the securities to be issued.[55] These include:

- the securities and the transaction structure, including the types of securities to be offered, the flow of funds for the transaction, any liquidation, amortization, performance, or similar triggers (and the results of those triggers) and any overcollateralization percentage;

- the distribution dates and the related collection periods, as well as how cash is maintained pending its distribution;

- the fees and expenses payable out of cash flows from the pool assets, set forth in a table;

- how excess cash flows are to be used and the holders of any residual or retained interests that are affiliated with the sponsor, the depositor, the issuing entity, or certain other transaction parties, "if such person has rights that may alter the transaction structure beyond receipt of residual or excess cash flows";[56]

- any optional or mandatory redemption features, including a requirement that a class be titled "callable" if an optional redemption feature may be exercised when 25 percent or more of the original principal balance of the series in which the class was issued is still outstanding; and

- various prepayment, maturity, and yield considerations, including prepayment and interest rate sensitivity analyses to the extent material.

What constitutes "rights that may alter the transaction structure" beyond the right to receive excess cash flows from the pool assets is unclear. For example, the right to amend the transaction documents without the consent of securityholders would clearly qualify, but there are other common transaction features where the result is not so clear, such as the right to

repurchase the pool assets and cause the redemption of the outstanding ABS when the pool balance reaches a predetermined trigger.

> **Comment:** Many practitioners would advise that "original principal balance" for purposes of determining whether the "callable" designation is required should include amounts on deposit in any pre-funding account. Market practices differ as to whether to include the "callable" designation when the optional purchase is on behalf of a third party, rather than the issuer.

10. Credit support

Regulation AB Item 1114 requires a description of the material terms of any credit enhancement mechanism that is "designed to affect or ensure timely payment" of the ABS.[57] The related agreements must be filed as an exhibit to the registration statement. These include:

- external enhancement supporting ultimate payment of the ABS, such as a guarantee, insurance policy, or letter of credit;

- external credit enhancement supporting timely payment of the ABS, such as a liquidity facility or a minimum principal payment agreement;

- derivatives whose primary purpose is to provide credit enhancement related to the pool assets or the ABS;[58] and

- internal credit enhancement mechanisms, such as reserve accounts, subordination provisions, overcollateralization, and cash collateral or spread accounts.

When any entity (or group of affiliates) is liable or contingently liable for payments representing 10 percent (but less than 20 percent) of the cash flows from the asset pool, then the prospectus must include the selected financial data described in Item 301 of Regulation S-K with regard to the entity or group.[59] If the entity (or group of affiliates) is liable or contingently liable for payments representing 20 percent or more of the cash flows from the asset pool, then full audited financial statements of the entity or group meeting the requirements of Regulation S-X must be included.[60] This includes obtaining the required auditors' consent to include audited financial statements in a registration statement.

The 10-percent and 20-percent calculations are made based on the worst case scenario—i.e., without taking into account the probability that the enhancement will be called upon. It does not matter whether the enhancement functions at the pool asset level or is embedded in the structure of the securities. However, loan-level credit protection on individual pool assets, such as private mortgage insurance on individual

---

[54] *See also* 206 SPS § II-D3, *Resecuritizations, repacks and registration of underlying or separate securities.*

[55] 17 C.F.R. § 229.1113.

[56] 17 C.F.R. § 229.1113(d)(1).

---

[57] 17 C.F.R. § 229.1114.

[58] Disclosure regarding derivatives used for purposes other than credit enhancement is governed by Item 1115. 17 C.F.R. § 229.1114 instruc. 1; *see* 206 SPS § IV-A11, *Derivatives not primarily for credit support.*

[59] 17 C.F.R. § 229.301.

[60] 17 C.F.R. pt. 210.

mortgage loans, is not considered to be the type of credit enhancement that triggers disclosure under this item.[61]

If the obligations of the enhancement provider are guaranteed by the full faith and credit of the United States, or a foreign government with an investment grade credit rating, no financial information need be provided.[62] If the enhancement provider is a foreign business, its disclosure obligations are governed by Items 3.A. and 17 of Form 20-F rather than Regulation S-K Item 301 or Regulation S-X, respectively.[63]

In lieu of providing the required financial information in the prospectus (either directly or via incorporation by reference from a Form 8-K), the information may be incorporated by reference from Exchange Act reports of the third party (or an entity that consolidates the third party) under certain conditions.[64]

11. Derivatives not primarily for credit support

Item 1115 of Regulation AB[65] governs the required disclosures for derivatives "such as interest rate and currency swap agreements, that are used to alter the payment characteristics of the cashflows from the issuing entity and whose primary purpose is not to provide credit enhancement related to the pool assets or the [ABS]."[66] Whether the disclosures required by this item are required for such a derivative depends on its "significance percentage."

In order to calculate the significant percentage of a derivative, one first needs to determine its "significance estimate," which is a reasonable good faith estimate of the maximum probable exposure, made in substantially the same manner as the sponsor uses in its own internal risk management process for similar derivatives. The "significance percentage" is the percentage that the significance estimate represents out of the aggregate pool balance. The significance percentage of a derivative that relates only to certain classes of ABS is calculated by reference to the aggregate principal balance of those classes rather than the pool balance.

Comment: While the transaction parties are required to use the internal risk management policies of the sponsor to determine the significance percentage, the sponsor itself is not required to make the calculation, and others (such as the underwriter) often do so, especially when the sponsor has little experience with derivatives. Market perspectives differ as to whether the significance percentage of a derivative should be reduced by taking into account whether it is collateralized.

Regulation AB Item 1115 requires a description of certain descriptive information regarding any covered derivative, including:

- the name and organizational form of the counterparty and its general character of business;

- the material terms of the derivative instrument, including limits to and timing of payments; and

- whether the significance percentage is less than 10 percent, at least 10 percent but less than 20 percent, or 20 percent or more.

When the significance percentage of any entity (or group of affiliates) providing covered derivatives is 10 percent or more, but less than 20 percent, then the prospectus must include the selected financial data described in Item 301 of Regulation S-K with regard to that entity or group.[67] If the significance percentage of any entity (or group of affiliates) providing covered derivatives is 20 percent or more, then full audited financial statements of the entity or group meeting the requirements of Regulation S-X must be included. This includes obtaining the required auditors' consent to include audited financial statements in a registration statement.

If the obligations of the enhancement provider are guaranteed by the full faith and credit of the U.S., or a foreign government with an investment grade credit rating, no financial information need be provided.[68] If the enhancement provider is a foreign business, its disclosure obligations are governed by Items 3.A and 17 of Form 20-F,[69] rather than Regulation S-K Item 301 or Regulation S-X, respectively.[70]

Comment: If a derivative provider does not prepare separate financial statements, because it is a bank subsidiary of a holding company that prepares only consolidated financial statements or otherwise, it may not be able to provide the information required by Regulation AB. As a practical solution, if the significance percentage at the closing of the transaction does not exceed 10 percent or 20 percent, as applicable, such an entity may contract that if the significance percentage subsequently hits a trigger (typically set two percentage points below the 10-percent or 20-percent threshold), the entity will either demonstrate that it can provide the required financial information or substitute another counterparty that can do so.

In lieu of providing the required financial information in the prospectus (either directly or via incorporation by reference from a Form 8-K), the information may be incorporated by reference from Exchange Act reports of the third party (or an entity that consolidates the third party) under certain conditions.[71]

12. Credit ratings

Items 1103(a)(9) and 1120 of Regulation AB purport to require disclosure as to whether any class of the offered ABS is conditioned on the assignment of a credit rating from one or more nationally recognized statistical ratings organizations (NRSROs). If so, the agency, its minimum rating, and any ratings monitoring arrangements also must be disclosed.

---

[61] Div. of Corp. Fin., Regulation AB Telephone Interpretations, at § 10.01.

[62] Regulation AB Item 1114, 17 C.F.R. § 229.1114 instrucs. 2–3.

[63] 17 C.F.R. § 229.1114 instruc. 5.

[64] See 206 SPS § IV-A8, Significant obligors.

[65] 17 C.F.R. § 229.1115.

[66] Id.

[67] 17 C.F.R. § 229.301.

[68] 17 C.F.R. §§ 229.1115 instruc. 1, 229.1114 instrucs. 2–3.

[69] SEC, Form 20-F: Registration Statement Pursuant to Section 12(b) or (g) of the Securities Exchange Act of 1934.

[70] 17 C.F.R. §§ 229.1115 instruc. 1, 229.1114 instruc. 5.

[71] See 206 SPS § IV-A8, Significant obligors, above.

Rule 436 under the Securities Act[72] requires that if any portion of a registration statement has been reviewed by and is based on the authority of a third party, the consent of that "expert" must be filed as an exhibit. Subsection (g) of Securities Act Rule 436 formerly exempted NRSROs from this requirement, but § 939G of the Dodd-Frank Act effectively eliminated this exemption by providing that it would have no further force or effect, meaning that disclosure of a credit rating in a registration statement requires the consent of the issuing rating agency.

NRSROs generally have refused to provide such consents, meaning that the credit rating disclosures required by Regulation AB generally can no longer be included. Therefore, the staff of the SEC's Division of Corporation Finance issued no-action relief confirming that it would not recommend enforcement action if the otherwise required ratings information is omitted from a registration statement for ABS.[73]

> **Comment:** Ratings information now is commonly provided in a free writing prospectus instead of the registration statement. Because a free writing prospectus is not incorporated into the registration statement, the consent requirement of Rule 436 does not apply.

13. Other requirements

Other requirements of Regulation AB that apply to registration statements include:

- information about each trustee (Item 1109);[74]

- the federal tax treatment and material federal tax consequences of owning or trading the registered ABS, including the substance of tax counsel's opinion (Item 1116);[75]

- material pending legal proceedings involving the transaction parties (Item 1117);[76]

- the reports required to be provided to security holders by the transaction documents (Item 1118);[77] and

- affiliation and other relationships between the transaction parties (Item 1119).[78]

B. The FDIC Safe Harbor Rule and Its Effect on Disclosures

If the Federal Deposit Insurance Corporation (FDIC) is appointed as a receiver or conservator of a bank or other insured depository institution, it will succeed to the assets of that institution. In addition, the FDIC generally has the power, as receiver or conservator, to repudiate contracts made by failed banks. If a bank-sponsored securitization qualifies as a legal true sale of the securitized assets, the FDIC has no legal power to reclaim those assets.

However, if a bank-sponsored securitization represents the grant of a perfected security interest in the pool assets to secure debt ABS, the FDIC could repudiate the ABS and recover the assets by paying the damages specified in the Federal Deposit Insurance Act. If the FDIC does not repudiate debt ABS and they default, then the pool assets could be liquidated beginning 90 days after the FDIC is appointed as receiver (or 45 days after the FDIC is appointed as conservator) of the sponsoring bank. The FDIC originally adopted its "securitization safe harbor"[79] to address concerns that its repudiation powers could promote uncertainty as to the rights of investors in bank-sponsored securitizations and as to the accounting treatment of the transfers of pool assets by banks that do not qualify as a legal true sale.

Currently, Financial Accounting Standards (FAS) 166 and 167 focus on control of (i.e., servicing) and a continuing economic interest in special-purpose entities, rather than on permissible activities.[80] Many standard securitization structures that would have achieved sale accounting treatment under prior accounting rules are now consolidated for financial statement reporting purposes (on-balance sheet) under FAS 166 and 167. The FDIC revised the securitization safe harbor in 2010 in response to these changes. As currently in effect, the FDIC's rules provide two different safe harbors: one for securitizations that achieve off-balance sheet accounting treatment under generally accepted accounting principles (other than the "legal isolation," i.e., true sale, criterion), and one for securitizations that do not.

For securitizations that achieve off-balance sheet treatment under FAS 166 and 167 without a legal true sale, the safe harbor provides that the FDIC will not interfere with the transfers of securitized assets through its power to repudiate contracts of failed banks, so long as the securitization complies with a variety of additional conditions, including significant disclosure conditions.

> **Comment:** Because a legal true sale is a prerequisite for off-balance sheet treatment, this safe harbor is not very useful. Securitizations that achieve off-balance sheet treatment with a legal true sale have no need of the safe harbor.

For securitizations that fail to achieve off-balance sheet accounting treatment and which satisfy the FDIC's additional conditions, the safe harbor provides relief from two provisions of the Federal Deposit Insurance Act (as interpreted by the FDIC). The first is the requirement that no creditor actions to liquidate collateral can be taken without the FDIC's consent for the first 90 days after the FDIC is appointed as receiver (or the first 45 days after the FDIC is appointed as conservator).

Under the safe harbor, if the FDIC fails to "pay or apply collections from the financial assets received by it in accor-

---

[72] 17 C.F.R. § 230.436.

[73] Ford Motor Credit Co. LLC, SEC No-Action Letter (Nov. 23, 2010); Ford Motor Credit Co. LLC, SEC No-Action Letter (July 22, 2010).

[74] 17 C.F.R. § 229.1109.

[75] 17 C.F.R. § 229.1116.

[76] 17 C.F.R. § 229.1117.

[77] 17 C.F.R. § 229.1118.

[78] 17 C.F.R. § 229.1119.

---

[79] The current version of the securitization safe harbor is codified at 12 C.F.R. § 360.6.

[80] Fin. Accounting Standards Bd. (FASB), Statement of Fin. Accounting Standards No. 166, Accounting for Transfers of Financial Assets (2009) (amending FASB, Statement of Fin. Accounting Standards No. 140); FASB, Statement of Fin. Accounting Standards No. 167, Amendments to FASB Interpretation No. 46(R) (2009).

dance with the securitization documents" on behalf of a failed bank for 10 business days after receipt of a written notice, then the FDIC consents to the exercise of contractual rights under the securitization agreements, including self-help remedies to foreclose on the securitized assets, provided that no involvement of the FDIC is required (other than consents, waivers, or execution of transfer documents as may be reasonably requested in the ordinary course of business).

The second provision from which the safe harbor provides relief for securitizations that do not achieve off-balance sheet treatment is the requirement to calculate damages for repudiation as of the date of the FDIC's appointment, which precludes the further accrual of interest on the debt. Under the safe harbor, if the FDIC repudiates a securitization agreement, it must pay damages equal to the par value of the obligations of the securitization outstanding at the date of its appointment as conservator or receiver (less any payments of principal paid to investors to the date of repudiation), plus any unpaid accrued interest actually received through the date of repudiation, within 10 business days, or else it consents to the same exercise of contractual rights.

According to the rule, the FDIC will not seek to reclaim any interest payments made to investors in accordance with transaction documents and will consent to (or perform itself) any servicing activity required in furtherance of the securitization, including the making of payments to investors to the extent actually received through payments on the securitized assets.

> **Comment:** It is not uncommon for a securitization to constitute a legal true sale of the securitized assets, but not achieve off-balance sheet treatment for accounting purposes. While the FDIC has no legal authority to recover assets sold in a legal true sale, it generally takes the position that it will determine the assets owned by an institution on the basis of the institution's balance sheet. Therefore, while banks and other depositary institutions that engage in securitizations that achieve a legal true sale but remain on balance sheet may not legally need to comply with the requirements of the safe harbor, they generally do so anyway, in an effort to avoid conflict with the FDIC.

The rule requires compliance with a variety of other conditions as a condition to either safe harbor. Some of the additional conditions apply to all securitizations, while others apply only to residential mortgage-backed securities (RMBS) transactions. There are five categories of additional conditions: capital structure and financial assets, documentation and recordkeeping, compensation, origination and retention, and (most importantly for our purposes here) disclosures, as well as several additional miscellaneous conditions that do not fit into any of these categories.

The capital structure and financial assets conditions of the safe harbors require:

- Regulation AB-level disclosures for any underlying securities in a resecuritization or collateralized debt obligation;
- limitations on the use of derivatives, in that principal and interest distributions generally must be primarily based on the performance of underlying assets and not be contingent on independent events;

- for RMBS, no more than six credit tranches and, in general, no subtranches; and
- for RMBS, no external credit support at the pool level, though loan-level support (such as mortgage insurance) is permitted, as is credit support from Fannie Mae, Freddie Mac, Ginnie Mae and other government-sponsored entities.

The documentation and recordkeeping provisions of the safe harbors require:

- the transaction documents to define the contractual rights and responsibilities of the transaction parties and grant them sufficient authority;
- the use, as appropriate, of any available standard documentation for each asset class;
- for RMBS, that servicing agreements provide servicers with authority to maximize the net present value of mortgage loans underlying RMBS securitizations by executing certain loss mitigation strategies; and
- for RMBS, that servicing advances are limited by the transaction documents to payments of principal and interest for no more than three payment periods, unless alternative "financing or reimbursement facilities" are available.

The compensation conditions of the safe harbors are all applicable to RMBS only:

- any fees payable to credit rating agencies or "similar third-party evaluation companies" must be payable over a five-year period; and
- the transaction documents must include provisions to incentivize the servicer to maximize the net present value of the serviced assets.

The origination and retention conditions of the safe harbors consist primarily of credit risk retention requirements. Prior to the effective date of the credit risk retention regulations required by the Dodd-Frank Act, the transaction documents must require the sponsor to retain at least 5 percent of the credit risk of the securitized assets, either by retaining at least 5 percent of each tranche sold to investors or by retaining a "representative sample" of the securitized assets. Sales, pledges, or hedges of this retained credit risk are not permitted, except for the hedging of interest rate or currency risk.

Upon the effectiveness of the Dodd-Frank credit risk retention regulations, those rules will govern in lieu of the FDIC's requirements. In addition, for RMBS only:

- the transaction documents must require the sponsor to establish a reserve fund equal to 5 percent of the proceeds in order to cover any repurchases of mortgage loans due to material breaches of representations and warranties, to remain in place for one year; and
- the transaction documents must require securitized mortgage loans to have been originated in all material respects in compliance with all statutory, regulatory, and originator underwriting standards in effect at the time of

origination and include a representation that securitized loans were underwritten based upon the borrower's ability to repay the loan in accordance with its terms.

The disclosure conditions of the safe harbors mandate that the transaction documents require a wide variety of disclosures. At a minimum, the transaction documents must require that the disclosures made to investors comply with Regulation AB—including any future changes that may be made by the SEC, such as the long-awaited Regulation AB II. Therefore, all private offerings must have Regulation AB-compliant disclosure to qualify for the FDIC's safe harbor rules, even though this is not currently required by the SEC's rules.[81]

In addition, the transaction documents must require:

- that the capital structure, priority of payments, subordination features, and representations and warranties (along with associated remedies) be disclosed to investors, along with similar disclosures regarding any liquidity facilities or credit enhancements, waterfall triggers, and servicing policies governing servicing of delinquent assets;

- that investors be provided with credit performance information regarding the underlying assets, including delinquency and modification data, any additions or removals of assets, servicing advances, and losses to particular tranches;

- that investors be provided at issuance with disclosure detailing compensation paid to originators, sponsors, rating agencies, mortgage brokers, and servicers, that any credit risk retained by any of these parties be disclosed, and that any changes to compensation or retained interests be disclosed to investors as long as their interests are outstanding;

- for RMBS, that loan level data be disclosed, including information concerning loan type, loan structure, maturity, interest rate, and location of property;

- for RMBS, that the sponsor affirm compliance in all material respects with all applicable statutory and regulatory standards and supervisory guidance for origination of mortgage loans, including that loans are underwritten at a fully indexed rate and rely on documented income;

- for RMBS, that the sponsor disclose a third-party diligence report on compliance with the foregoing standards, which also describes compliance with representations and warranties with respect to the securitized loans; and

- for RMBS, that servicers disclose any ownership interest they (or their affiliates) own in whole loans secured by the same real property securing loans in the RMBS pool (e.g., second liens).

Finally, there are a variety of miscellaneous conditions to the use of the safe harbors, which include:

- transactions must be negotiated at arm's length and transaction documents must require that obligations issued in a securitization may not be predominantly sold to affiliates or insiders of the sponsor, other than its wholly owned, consolidated subsidiaries;

- the transaction documents must be in writing, must be approved by the sponsor's board of directors or loan committee, and must have been continuously in the official record of the sponsor; and

- securitizations must be entered into in the ordinary course of business and not in contemplation of a bankruptcy or with any intent to hinder, delay, or defraud creditors;

- transfers of securitized assets must be made for adequate consideration; and

- the transfer of assets or security interest must be properly perfected under the Uniform Commercial Code or other applicable state law.

---

[81] As proposed, Regulation AB II would require Regulation AB-compliant disclosure in all securitization transactions that rely on the exemptions from registration contained in Rule 506 and Rule 144A under the Securities Act. *See* 206 SPS § VII-A, *Regulation AB II*.

V.
Exempt Securities and Transactions

A. Exempt Securities

Section 3 of the Securities Act of 1933 contains a variety of exemptions from registration for specific types of securities, some of which are useful for certain types (or features) of asset-backed securities (ABS).[1]

Among other things, § 3(a)(2) exempts securities issued or guaranteed by:

- the U.S. or any of its territories;

- any state (or the District of Columbia);

- any political subdivision or public instrumentality of a state or territory; or

- any person controlled or supervised by and acting as an instrumentality of the U.S. pursuant to authority granted by Congress.

The list of entities that qualify for this exemption is quite long. It includes government-sponsored enterprises such as the Federal National Mortgage Association (Fannie Mae), the Federal Home Loan Mortgage Corporation (Freddie Mac) and the Federal Home Loan Banks, as well as the Government National Mortgage Association (Ginnie Mae).

What qualifies as a "guarantee" for these purposes is a somewhat more complicated question. According to the Securities and Exchange Commission (SEC), the guarantee "must completely protect the purchaser [of the exempt securities] in all circumstances,"[2] meaning that it must cover full payment of both principal and interest.

Comment: This means that the guarantee must apply to the securities themselves, not just the pool assets, as otherwise the investor would be exposed to loss resulting from errors or defaults of the trustee or securities administrator.

The guarantee generally must be enforceable directly by the securityholders.[3]

Also exempt under Securities Act § 3(a)(2) are securities issued or guaranteed by a national bank or by a bank chartered by a state, territory, or the District of Columbia. According to the SEC, this exemption also includes securities issued or guaranteed by a U.S. branch of a foreign bank, so long as it is subject to regulatory oversight that is substantially equivalent to that of a national bank or a state-chartered bank.[4] The depositor generally is the "issuer" of ABS for purposes of the federal securities laws.[5] However, because "any applicable exemptions from registration that [a] person may have with respect to its own securities are not applicable to [ABS],"[6] a bank cannot avoid the requirement to register (or find an applicable exemption for) its ABS by directly serving as the ABS depositor.[7]

Securities Act § 3(a)(8) provides a registration exemption for an "insurance or endowment policy or annuity contract or optional annuity contract, issued by a corporation subject to the supervision of the insurance commissioner, bank commissioner, or any agency or officer performing like functions, of any State or Territory of the United States or the District of Columbia."[8] To qualify for this exemption, it is not sufficient that the product in question be issued by an insurance company—the exemption is limited to the enumerated types of products.

Comment: In the context of ABS, the insurance exemption is most useful for credit enhancement products that take the form of insurance policies. Note, however, that while covered insurance products are exempt from registration as separate securities, any applicable disclosure required by Item 1114 of Regulation AB must still be provided.

Securities Act § 3(a)(3), the commercial paper exemption, exempts from registration—

any note, draft, bill of exchange, or banker's acceptance which arises out of a current transaction or the proceeds of which have been or are to be used for current transactions, and which has a maturity at the time of issuance of not exceeding nine months, exclusive of days of grace, or any renewal thereof the maturity of which is likewise limited.[9]

In addition to the statutory requirements, the commercial paper must also be "prime quality" and "of a type not ordinarily purchased by the general public,"[10] which generally is interpreted to require the offering to be made only to institutional and substantial individual investors and in minimum denominations of $100,000 or more. Both this exemption and the statutory private offering exemption of Securities Act § 4(a)(2) are commonly used for offerings of asset-backed commercial paper.[11]

Interest rate caps and swaps and currency swaps are often used in ABS structures, with the related disclosure generally governed by Item 1115 of Regulation AB.[12] As a result of the enactment of the Dodd-Frank Wall Street Reform and Consumer Protection Act (Dodd-Frank Act), "security-based

---

[1] 15 U.S.C. § 77c.

[2] SBA Guaranteed Loans, SEC No-Action Letter (Nov. 8, 1974).

[3] See, e.g., Fed. Deposit Ins. Corp., SEC No-Action Letter (July 12, 2010); Nat'l Credit Union Admin., SEC No-Action Letter (Sept. 24, 2010) (no-action advice granted where securityholders could opt out of the designation of the trustee or securities administer as their representative and directly enforce the guarantee).

[4] See Securities Issued or Guaranteed by United States Branches or Agencies of Foreign Banks, 51 Fed. Reg. 34,460, 34,461 (Sept. 29, 1986).

[5] See 206 SPS § I-B, *Structure of a "Plain Vanilla" Securitization*.

[6] Asset-Backed Securities, 70 Fed. Reg. 1506, 1536 (Jan. 7, 2005).

[7] 70 Fed. Reg. at 1526 n.156; see Bank of Am. Nat'l Trust & Savings Ass'n, SEC No-Action Letter (May 19, 1977).

[8] 15 U.S.C. § 77c(a)(8).

[9] 15 U.S.C. § 77c(a)(3).

[10] Interpretation of Section 3(a)(3), 26 Fed. Reg. 9158, 9159 (Sept. 29, 1961).

[11] 15 U.S.C. § 77d(a)(2). See 206 SPS § V-B1, *Section 4(a)(2)* (discussing the statutory private offering exemption).

[12] See 206 SPS § IV-A11, *Derivatives not primarily for credit support*.

swaps" are the only swaps that are "securities" for purposes of the Securities Act,[13] and are potentially subject to the registration requirements of the Securities Act.[14] A "security-based swap" generally is a swap that is based on a single security or loan, a "narrow-based security index" (generally, an index of fewer than nine securities, in which one security constitutes more than 30 percent of the index's weighting),[15] or the occurrence (or nonoccurrence) of an event relating to the issuer of a single security or the issuers of securities in a narrow-based index.[16] Because an interest-rate cap or swap or a currency swap is not a security-based swap, an issuer need not be concerned that it must be registered as a separate security, although Regulation AB Item 1115 disclosures must still be provided and applicable commodities laws must still be complied with.

B. Private Placements

1. Section 4(a)(2)

Section 4(a)(2) of the Securities Act (formerly § 4(2)) exempts from registration "transactions by an issuer not involving any public offering."[17] Early on, the SEC identified four main factors in determining whether an offering is public or private:

- the number of offerees and their relationship to each other and the issuer (the smaller the number and the more closely related to the issuer, the more likely the offering is to be a private placement);

- the number of units offered (the fewer offered, the more likely the offering is to be a private placement);

- the size of the offering (the smaller the offering, the more likely it is to be a private placement); and

- the manner of the offering (a directly negotiated transaction may be a private placement, but use of general solicitation or advertising or other mechanisms of public distribution are likely to preclude private placement status under § 4(a)(2)).[18]

The scope of the § 4(a)(2) private placement exemption was further circumscribed by the Supreme Court in *SEC v. Ralston Purina Co.*[19] The Court indicated that the exemption should be interpreted in light of its purpose, so that its applicability depends on whether the persons affected need the protection of the Securities Act. While an offering to a large number of offerees is more likely to be public, an offering may be public if it is made to even a small number of potential investors.

The main determinants of the availability of the § 4(a)(2) exemption are whether the offerees are able to "fend for themselves," and whether they have access to the same type of information that registration would provide.[20] ABS generally are marketed only to the most sophisticated institutional investors, so in most cases they will clearly be able to fend for themselves. The "access to information" factor does not necessarily mean that investors must have every item of information that would be included in a prospectus for a registered offering, but it is common practice in private ABS offerings to prepare and provide a private placement memorandum that contains substantially all of the disclosures that would be required in a prospectus. In sum, the more sophisticated the offerees are, and the more information concerning the issuer and the offering to which they have access, the more likely the transaction is to be considered private.

In determining whether any offering meets the requirements for exemption, it is not enough to look at each offer and sale individually. Instead, each particular transaction must be analyzed to determine whether it should be "integrated" into a broader offering. The factors to be considered in any determination of integration are:

- whether the transactions are part of a single plan of financing;

- whether the transactions involve the same class of securities;

- whether the transactions occur at or about the same time;

- whether the same type of consideration is received; and

- whether the transactions have the same general purpose.[21]

In determining whether an offering is exempt under § 4(a)(2), the securities must "come to rest" in the hands of the initial purchasers. If those purchasers are merely conduits for a wider distribution, then they are "underwriters" under § 2(a)(11), and their resales will be lumped together with the initial sales in determining whether the entire transaction meets the requirements for the exemption. In that case, the issuer will have violated the registration provisions of the Securities Act.[22] For this reason, strict transfer restrictions usually are imposed on privately placed securities, which therefore are often referred to as "restricted" securities. In order to be able to monitor compliance with these restrictions, privately-placed ABS usually are issued in definitive (i.e., certificated, as opposed to book-

---

[13] Securities Act § 2(a)(1), 15 U.S.C. § 77b(a)(1).

[14] Securities Act § 5(e), 15 U.S.C. § 77e(e); *see also* Securities Act Rule 240, 17 C.F.R. § 230.240 (exemption for certain security-based swaps).

[15] Or in which the lowest weighted component securities comprising an aggregate of 25 percent of the index's weighting have an average daily trading volume of less than $50 million (or for an index with 15 or more component securities, $30 million). Exchange Act § 3(a)(55)(B), 15 U.S.C. § 78c(a)(55)(B).

[16] Securities Act § 2(a)(17), 15 U.S.C. § 77b(a)(17) (referring to definition of "security-based swap" in the Commodities Exchange Act); Commodities Exchange Act § 1a, 7 U.S.C. § 1a (referring to definition of "security-based swap" in the Exchange Act); Exchange Act § 3(a)(68), 15 U.S.C. § 78c(a)(68) (defining "security-based swap").

[17] 15 U.S.C. § 77d(a)(2).

[18] Factors Involved in Determining Whether Transaction is "Public Offering," 11 Fed. Reg. 10,952 (Sept. 27, 1946), SEC Release No. 33-285 (Jan. 24, 1935).

[19] SEC v. Ralston Purina Co., 346 U.S. 119 (1953).

[20] 346 U.S. at 124–27.

[21] Non-Public Offering Exemption, 27 Fed. Reg. 11,316 (Nov. 16, 1962).

[22] *Id.*

entry) form, with detailed legends describing those restrictions. Generally, the transaction documents will require the trustee to receive certifications as to a variety of matters before registering the transfer of restricted ABS, including:

- that the security was not acquired by means of a general solicitation;

- that the security was acquired for investment and not with a view to a public distribution; and

- that the transferee is aware that the security has not been registered under the Securities Act and may be resold only pursuant to registration or an exemption from registration.

2. *Regulation D*

Because § 4(a)(2) can be so difficult to apply in practice, the SEC promulgated Regulation D, which offers three different "safe harbors" from the registration requirements of the Securities Act.[23]

Comment: Because of the stringent limitations on offering amount in Rule 504 ($1 million) and Rule 505 ($5 million), Rule 506 is the only one of the Regulation D exemptions that potentially could be useful for offerings of ABS. However, Rule 506 is not often used in ABS offerings.

Rule 506, which provides an exemption for a limited offering of an unlimited dollar amount of securities, is a regulatory safe harbor adopted under § 4(a)(2) of the Securities Act. The number of purchasers (not offerees) is limited to 35.[24] However, this number is a bit illusory, as Rule 501(e)[25] permits a number of exceptions when calculating the number of purchasers, including (most importantly) any "accredited investor." An "accredited investor" under Rule 501(a) currently includes persons and entities that fall within one of a number of specified categories (or which the issuer reasonably believes come within one of those categories). Of most relevance to ABS issuers are the following, which are known colloquially as "institutional accredited investors":

- a bank, savings and loan, or other regulated financial institution;

- a registered broker dealer;

- a licensed insurance company;

- a registered investment company;

- a licensed small business investment company;

- certain employee benefit plans, including a self-directed plan whose investment decisions are made solely by accredited investors;

- a private business development company under the Investment Advisers Act of 1940;

- a § 501(c)(3) organization, corporation, business trust, or partnership not formed specifically for the purpose of

investing in the offering, with total assets of more than $5 million; and

- a trust not formed specifically for the purpose of investing in the offering, with total assets of more than $5 million, if the person directing the purchase is "sophisticated" (as described below).[26]

Comment: The investor will usually represent as to accredited investor status in a separate representation letter or in the securities purchase agreement. The better practice is to require the investor to specifically indicate why it falls within this definition rather than merely reciting that it does so.

Each nonaccredited investor must, either alone or with its "purchaser representative," have such knowledge and experience in financial and business matters that it is capable of evaluating the merits and risks of the investment (or at least the issuer must reasonably believe that it meets this sophistication requirement).

A "purchaser representative" is someone who, among other requirements, has such knowledge and experience in financial and business matters that it is capable of evaluating the merits and risks of the investment, either alone, with the purchaser or with any other purchaser representatives (or whom the issuer reasonably believes meets those requirements).

Because ABS offerings are likely to be limited to institutional accredited investors, purchaser sophistication and purchaser representative issues are unlikely to arise.

Rule 506 incorporates the disclosure requirements of Rule 502(b).[27] There are no specific disclosure requirements if the offering is made solely to accredited investors, the most likely scenario for an offering of ABS.[28]

Comment: In any event, as noted above, it is common for private offerings of ABS to include a private placement memorandum containing substantially the same disclosures that would be required in the prospectus for a public offering.

Rule 506 also incorporates the integration requirements of Rule 502(a).[29] Under Rule 502(a), other sales within six months before or after the offering in question may be integrated with that offering. If they are integrated, then all of those offers and sales, taken as a whole, must meet the requirements of Rule 506.[30]

---

[23] 17 C.F.R. §§ 230.501–08.

[24] 17 C.F.R. § 230.506(b)(2)(ii).

[25] 17 C.F.R. § 230.501(e).

[26] 17 C.F.R. § 230.501(a).

[27] *See* Securities Act Rule 502(b), 17 C.F.R. § 230.502(b); Securities Act Rule 506(b)(1), 17 C.F.R. § 230.506(b)(1).

[28] 17 C.F.R. § 230.502(b)(2)(i)(B)(3).

[29] 17 C.F.R. § 230.502(a); *see* Securities Act Rule 506(b)(1), 17 C.F.R. § 230.506(b)(1).

[30] The factors to be considered in determining whether particular offers and sales should be integrated with a Rule 506 offering are the same integration factors used in a § 4(a)(2) private placement. *See* 206 SPS § V-B1, *Section 4(a)(2)*.

Further, Rule 506 incorporates the restrictions on resale imposed by Rule 502(d).[31] Under Rule 502(d), issued securities are "restricted"— in other words, they cannot be resold without a separate registration or exemption from registration. The issuer must take reasonable care that the purchasers do not resell in a manner that makes them into statutory underwriters. Reasonable care may be demonstrated by three actions:

- the issuer must make reasonable inquiry to determine if the purchaser is acquiring the securities for himself rather than for resale;

- the issuer must disclose before sale that the securities have not been registered and therefore cannot be resold without registration or an exemption from registration; and

- the certificate representing the security must contain a legend stating that the securities have not been registered and setting forth the restrictions on transfer and sale.

Comment: The reasonable inquiry requirement is usually met by means of a representation contained either within the securities purchase agreement or in a separate representation letter. Disclosure as to the restricted nature of the shares is usually contained within the securities purchase agreement and the private placement memorandum.

Rule 503(a) requires that the issuer file with the SEC a signed notice on Form D within 15 days after first sale in any Rule 506 offering.[32]

An offering made pursuant to Rule 506(b) incorporates the limitation on manner of offering imposed by Rule 502(c).[33] This rule prohibits any offer by means of any form of general solicitation or public advertising, including published and broadcast ads, and seminars or meetings to which the public is invited. The SEC staff views the most important factor as to whether a solicitation is "general" as whether the proposed offerees have a pre-existing relationship with the issuer (or its broker-dealer), which allows the issuer to know whether they have the knowledge and experience in financial matters to be able to analyze the risks of the investment.[34] In determining whether any particular type of publicity could be deemed an "offer" for purposes of this rule, the SEC staff has analogized to the authority on whether publicity constitutes "gun-jumping" under § 5 of the Securities Act.[35]

As required by the Jumpstart Our Business Startups Act of 2012 (JOBS Act), the SEC recently added new Rule 506(c) to permit the use of general solicitation in Rule 506 offerings that comply with various new conditions. Most importantly, all purchasers of securities in the offering must be accredited investors (including the "reasonable belief" standard embedded in the definition), and the issuer must take reasonable steps

to verify that all purchasers of the securities are accredited investors.[36]

The verification condition is a principles-based condition that requires the issuer to make an "objective determination . . . in the context of the particular facts and circumstances of each purchaser and transaction" that the steps taken to verify a purchaser's accredited investor status are reasonable.[37] According to the SEC, issuers should consider a number of factors to determine the reasonableness of the steps to verify that a purchaser is an accredited investor, including the nature of the purchaser and the type of accredited investor it claims to be, the amount and type of information that the issuer has about the purchaser and the nature of the offering.

For example, an issuer that solicits new investors through a website accessible to the general public or through a widely disseminated e-mail or social media solicitation would likely be obligated to take greater measures to verify accredited investor status than an issuer that solicits new investors from a database of pre-screened accredited investors created and maintained by a reasonably reliable third party, such as a registered broker-dealer. Also, a minimum investment requirement may be sufficiently high such that only accredited investors could reasonably be expected to meet it.

These factors are interconnected, and the information gained by looking at these factors would help an issuer assess the reasonable likelihood that a potential investor is an accredited investor. In addition, the SEC observed that "[i]f an issuer has actual knowledge that the purchaser is an accredited investor, then the issuer will not have to take any steps at all."[38]

Comment: Regardless of the particular steps taken, it is important for issuers to retain adequate records that document those steps.

In addition to the principles-based approach, Rule 506(c) provides four non-exclusive verification methods that are deemed to satisfy the required "reasonable steps" standard for natural persons (so long as the issuer or a person acting on its behalf does not have knowledge that a potential investor is not an accredited investor):

- Verification on the basis of net income, by reviewing copies of any Internal Revenue Service form that reports the potential investor's income for the two most recent years, along with a written representation from the potential investor that there is a reasonable expectation of reaching the required income level during the current year;

- Verification on the basis of net worth, by reviewing certain specified types of documentation, dated within the prior three months, and by obtaining a written representation from the potential investor that all liabilities necessary to make a determination of net worth have been disclosed;

- Third-party verification, by obtaining a written confirmation from a registered broker-dealer, an investment

---

[31] *See* 17 C.F.R. §§ 230.502(d), 230.506(b)(1).

[32] 17 C.F.R. § 230.503(a).

[33] *See* 17 C.F.R. §§ 230.506(b), 230.502(c).

[34] *See, e.g.*, Woodtrails-Seattle, Ltd., SEC No-Action Letter (July 8, 1982).

[35] *See, e.g.*, REMCO Sec. Co., SEC No-Action Letter (July 22, 1985); *see also* 209 SPS § III-A, *The Basic Investor Communications Framework of § 5* (discussing the meaning of "offer").

---

[36] Eliminating the Prohibition Against General Solicitation and General Advertising in Rule 506 and Rule 144A Offerings, 78 Fed. Reg. 44,771 (July 24, 2013).

[37] 78 Fed. Reg. at 44,778.

[38] 78 Fed. Reg. at 44,779 n.111.

adviser, an attorney, a certified public accountant or a similar reliable party that he or she has taken reasonable steps within the prior three months to verify that the potential investor is accredited and has so determined (and an issuer may be entitled to rely on a similar verification by some other type of person or entity so long as the issuer has a reasonable basis to rely on the verification); and

- Verification by means of existing relationship, by obtaining the certification of a natural person who invested in an issuer's Rule 506(b) offering as an accredited investor before September 23, 2013.

Comment: Market practices as to what constitutes "reasonable steps" are still developing. In the author's view, practices with regard to large institutional investors are likely to change very little.

Also added by the JOBS Act were new "bad actor" rules, which prohibit an issuer of securities from relying on Rule 506 if the issuer or certain affiliated persons (referred to colloquially by the SEC as covered persons) have had certain types of disqualifying legal problems (referred to colloquially by the SEC as disqualifying events).[39]

Among the covered persons subject to the bad actor rules are:

- the issuer, any predecessor and any affiliated issuer;

- the issuer's general partners, managing members, directors, and executive officers, as well as any other officer participating in the offering in more than transitory or incidental manner;

- holders of at least 20 percent of the issuer's aggregate voting securities, including any securities where the holders have or share the ability to significantly influence the management and policies of the issuer through a voting right;

- investment managers of investment funds;

- promoters;[40] and

- placement agents, institutional initial purchasers and others who are paid for soliciting purchasers in connection with the offering, together with any of their directors, officers, general partners and managing members.

Comment: If even a single junior officer of a placement agent or initial purchaser has had a disqualifying event, the issuer will be foreclosed from relying on Rule 506. An issuer would be advised to diligence this issue thoroughly, though market practices are still developing as to the scope of the assurances that financial institutions are willing to provide.

The laundry list of disqualifying events that trigger the bad actor prohibition includes:

- a criminal conviction within 10 years before the offering (or five years for the issuer and its predecessors and

affiliated issuers) for any felony or misdemeanor in connection with the purchase or sale of a security, involving a false SEC filing, or arising out of the conduct of business of an underwriter, broker, dealer or investment advisor;

- a court order, judgment or decree entered within five years before the offering that currently restrains or enjoins a covered person from engaging in any conduct in connection with the purchase or sale of a security, involving a false SEC filing, or arising out of the conduct of business of an underwriter, broker, dealer or investment adviser;

- a final order within 10 years before the offering from certain state securities, banking and insurance regulators, certain federal banking agencies or the Commodity Futures Trading Commission, that bars the covered person from associating with a regulated entity or engaging in a securities, insurance or banking business, or is based on a violation of law that prohibits fraudulent, manipulative or deceptive conduct;

- an SEC disciplinary order that suspends or revokes a covered person's registration as a broker, dealer or investment adviser, limits a covered person's activities, or bars a covered person from being associated with any entity or from participating in a penny stock offering;

- an SEC cease and desist order entered within five years before the offering as to certain anti-fraud provisions of the federal securities laws, or the registration requirements of § 5 of the Securities Act;

- suspension or expulsion of a covered person from a securities "self-regulatory organization" or from association with a member of a self-regulatory organization, such as a national securities exchange or national securities association, for any act or omission constituting conduct inconsistent with just and equitable principles of trade;

- an SEC refusal or stop order issued within five years before the offering with respect to a registration statement filed by a covered person or as to which it was an underwriter, or a pending investigation or proceeding to determine whether a covered person should be subjected to any such order; and

- a U.S. Postal Service false representation order entered within five years before the offering or a pending temporary restraining order or preliminary injunction concerning any scheme for obtaining money or property through the mail by false representations.

There is an exemption from the bad actor disqualification if the issuer establishes that it did not know and, in the exercise of reasonable care, could not have known that a disqualifying event existed because of the presence or participation of another covered person.

Comment: Because the SEC did not define "reasonable care" for purposes of this exemption, leaving its determination to facts and circumstances, reliance on the exemption significantly undermines the safety of the Rule 506 safe harbor.

---

[39] Securities Act Rule 506(d), 17 C.F.R. § 230.506(d).

[40] As defined in Securities Act Rule 405. 17 C.F.R. § 230.405.

The failure to meet any particular Regulation D requirement will not necessarily result in the loss of the exemption if the issuer made a good faith and reasonable attempt to comply, so long as the failure did not pertain to a requirement intended to protect the particular offeree or purchaser and was insignificant with respect to the offering as a whole. However, a failure to comply with the limitation on manner of offering where required by Rule 502(c), or any applicable maximum aggregate offering price and/or maximum number of purchasers requirement, is deemed to be significant. Also, the SEC still has enforcement power over any such failure.[41]

Reliance on Rule 506 confers one significant benefit. The Securities Act preempts state blue sky requirements for "covered securities," which include those issued in Rule 506 offerings. State securities regulators may require only a notice filing that is "substantially similar" to Form D as in effect.[42]

3. *Rule 144A*

Rule 144A provides a safe harbor exemption from registration under the Securities Act for resales of certain restricted securities if they are sold solely to "qualified institutional buyers" (QIBs) or purchasers that the seller reasonably believes are QIBs.[43] Although technically Rule 144A is a resale exemption, it is most often used for institutional private placements, particularly of debt securities and asset-backed securities, made through a financial intermediary acting as "initial purchaser" to which the initial sale is made pursuant to § 4(a)(2) or some other exemption from registration.

A QIB is one of a lengthy list of types of institutional investors that owns and invests on a discretionary basis at least $100 million in securities of unaffiliated issuers, including:

- insurance companies;
- registered investment companies;
- small business investment companies;
- retirement plans and trust funds whose participants are retirement plans;
- tax-exempt charitable organizations, corporations (other than banks and savings and loan associations), partnerships, and business trusts;
- registered investment advisers; and
- banks and savings and loan associations that also meet a $25 million net worth test.

In addition:

- securities dealers need have only a $10 million securities portfolio, or may use Rule 144A when acting in a riskless principal transaction on behalf of a QIB;
- a family of investment companies may in certain circumstances aggregate their investment portfolios to determine whether they add up to $100 million; and

- an entity wholly owned by QIBs also may be a QIB.[44]

There are detailed rules for determining the aggregate amount of securities owned and invested on a discretionary basis by an entity. Various interests are excluded, such as bank deposits, loan participations, repurchase agreements (and securities subject to repurchase agreements), and currency, interest rate, and commodities swaps. Value is determined based on cost, unless the entity reports them on its financial statements at market value and no current cost information has been published. Securities owned by subsidiaries that are consolidated in the entity's financial statements generally may be included.[45]

In determining whether a potential purchaser is a QIB, Rule 144A deems several verification methods to be acceptable, including:

- the prospective purchaser's most recent publicly available financial statements or other publicly available information filed with the SEC or another governmental agency (if no more than 16 months old for a U.S. purchaser or 18 months for a foreign purchaser); or
- a certification by the prospective purchaser's chief executive officer or chief financial officer.[46]

The seller must take reasonable steps to ensure that the purchaser is aware that the seller may be relying on Rule 144A. Further, the securities sold cannot be of the same class as (or fungible with) any exchange-listed securities.[47]

Comment: Registered classes of ABS are virtually never listed on a securities exchange.

Rule 144A does not currently require the preparation of an offering document, though as discussed above it is customary in ABS markets to provide a private placement memorandum containing substantially all the information that would be required in the prospectus for a registered offering. For issuers that are not required to file Exchange Act reports (as will be the case with most newly-issued ABS), the holder or any prospective purchaser of the securities must have the right to obtain certain specified financial and other information.[48] For ABS, the information required currently includes "basic, material information concerning the structure of the securities and distributions thereon, the nature, performance, and servicing of the assets supporting the securities, and any credit enhancement mechanism associated with the securities."[49]

Comment: In order to satisfy this requirement, ABS transaction documents usually require provision of the private placement memorandum, the transaction documents, the most recent servicer certifications and reports, distribution reports for the preceding year, and other information (if requested), to the extent reasonably available, that is di-

---

[41] Securities Act Rule 508, 17 C.F.R. § 230.508.

[42] Securities Act §§ 18(a), 18(b)(4)(D), 15 U.S.C. §§ 77r(a), 77r(b)(4)(D).

[43] 17 C.F.R. § 230.144A.

[44] 17 C.F.R. § 230.144A(a)(1).

[45] 17 C.F.R. §§ 230.144A(a)(2)–(4).

[46] 17 C.F.R. § 230.144A(d)(1).

[47] 17 C.F.R. §§ 230.144A(d)(2)–(3).

[48] 17 C.F.R. § 230.144A(d)(4).

[49] Resale of Restricted Securities; Changes to Method of Determining Holding Period of Restricted Securities Under Rules 144 and 145, 55 Fed. Reg. 17,933, 17,939 (Apr. 30, 1990).

rectly related to the performance of the pool assets and the ABS.

The SEC used to take the position that general solicitation was prohibited in Rule 144A offerings, because the rule required that the securities be offered (as well as sold) only to QIBs. As required by the JOBS Act, the SEC recently amended Rule 144A to remove the restriction on offers, thereby removing the ban on general solicitation.[50]

4.   Private Resales and "§ 4(1½)"

Section 4(a)(1) of the Securities Act[51] provides an exemption from registration for transactions by any person other than an "issuer, underwriter or dealer." However, because of a rather oblique phrase in the definition of "underwriter" under § 2(a)(11),[52] the exemption for resales in § 4(a)(1) does not cover resales by persons controlling, controlled by, or under common control with the issuer, commonly known as "affiliates." An affiliate of an issuer must always register any transfer of securities or find an independent exemption, even if the securities originally were acquired by the affiliate in a registered public offering.

Also, as described above, most issuer exemptions from registration require, either expressly or implicitly, that the securities issued be "restricted"—in other words, that resales be prohibited unless the resale itself is registered or a separate exemption is available. Therefore, the § 4(a)(1) exemption for resales generally applies only to unrestricted securities held by non-affiliates of the issuer. The resale of restricted securities (by an affiliate or otherwise) requires an independent exemption, as does the resale of any securities by an affiliate of the issuer (whether restricted or unrestricted).

In general, an "underwriter," whose sales are not exempt under § 4(a)(1), is anyone who purchases from an issuer with a view to, or offers or sells for an issuer in connection with, a "distribution."[53] The word "distribution" commonly is understood to be synonymous with "public offering." Purchasers of restricted securities who purchase with the appropriate investment intent, and whose securities "come to rest" in their hands before they determine to sell them, are not underwriters on behalf of the issuers, and their resale clearly is exempt in a straightforward application of § 4(a)(1).

Comment: The longer the holding period prior to resale, the more likely it is that the securities will be deemed to have "come to rest." But how long should such a holding period be? Practitioners have debated that question ad nauseam, with rules of thumb ranging from two years up to five years or more.

Contrast the situation where restricted securities acquired in a private placement have not yet come to rest, but the purchaser wishes to resell them in a private transaction. In this circumstance, the early resale does not mean that the securities

were purchased from the issuer with a view to, or offered or sold for the issuer in connection with, a distribution. Due to the private nature of the resale, the issuer's placement retains its nonpublic character. The initial purchaser is not an underwriter, and the resale therefore is exempt under § 4(a)(1). While in truth this is nothing but a specialized application of § 4(a)(1), because of the required private nature of the resale (which may implicate requirements analogous of those of § 4(a)(2)), this transaction commonly is known as a "§ 4(1½)" transaction. There is no statutory or regulatory codification of § 4(1½), although practitioners, courts, and the SEC's staff readily accept its existence.

Little authority exists on § 4(1½), and what does is remarkably inconsistent in describing its requirements. Conceptually, those requirements may well vary depending upon the use that is made of the exemption.

Assume that a security holder initially purchased restricted securities with the intent to hold them for investment. However, they have not yet come to rest in the security holder's hands. Shareholders are only protected under § 4(a)(1) if they are able to prove that they are not underwriters in a transaction by the issuer. Therefore, the security holder must establish the issuer's continued right to a private placement exemption. In such a case, it would be better to insist that the resales take on most of the character of a private placement by an issuer, so that the shareholder cannot be said to be continuing a public distribution of shares by the issuer.

But which of the § 4(a)(2) criteria should be applied? Practices vary. For example, some practitioners would insist that the transaction be analyzed just as if it were a § 4(a)(2) private placement by an issuer. Others would not require the purchaser to have full access to information regarding the issuer on the theory that the purchaser does not have the control over the issuer to ensure that it is providing access to complete information. On this theory, the selling shareholder could simply pass along the most complete information regarding the issuer to which there is access.

On the other hand, assume that an affiliate of an issuer wishes to resell unrestricted securities he originally acquired on the public market. The requirements for a private resale here do not derive from an effort to ensure that the issuer's initial private placement retains its exempt character. Rather, for securities registration purposes, the affiliate stands in the same place as the issuer itself, with an independent obligation to register the resale or find an applicable exemption.

Based on these facts, practitioners can reach dramatically different results as to what factors are required to justify the private nature of a resale. Because the affiliate stands in the shoes of the issuer, some practitioners would require that such a resale be analyzed by strict reference to all § 4(a)(2) factors. Others would reach the opposite result, concluding that, since there is no need to protect an original private placement exemption for the issuer, § 4(a)(2) and its historical multi-factor test do not apply.

Comment: These conceptual issues arise rarely in ABS transactions, in which § 4(1½) is normally used in a manner similar to Rule 144A. In these transactions, an institutional initial purchaser ordinarily will resell securities solely to institutional accredited investors (as opposed to QIBs), and the transaction documents will require compliance with all elements that would be required of a § 4(a)(2)

---

[50] Eliminating the Prohibition Against General Solicitation and General Advertising in Rule 506 and Rule 144A Offerings, 78 Fed. Reg. 44,771 (July 24, 2013).

[51] 15 U.S.C. § 77d(a)(1).

[52] 15 U.S.C. § 77b(a)(11).

[53] Securities Act § 2(a)(11), 15 U.S.C. § 77b(a)(11).

private placement for both the initial resale and for any future resales.

C. Resales Under Rule 144

Because of the difficulty in applying § 4(1½), the SEC adopted Rule 144.[54] Rule 144 provides a safe harbor for sales of securities, whether restricted or unrestricted, by or for the account of an affiliate of the issuer, as well as for sales of restricted securities by anyone.[55] The requirements of Rule 144 differ depending on whether the seller is an affiliate of the issuer and whether the issuer is subject to the periodic reporting requirements of the Securities Exchange Act of 1934 (Exchange Act).

1. Restricted securities of an issuer subject to reporting requirements

With respect to restricted securities of an issuer that is (and has been for at least 90 days before the sale) subject to the periodic reporting requirements of the Exchange Act, any non-affiliate of the issuer (which must not have been an affiliate during the preceding three months), is subject to a six-month holding period before it may resell those restricted securities under Rule 144. After the expiration of the six-month holding period, and until the expiration of a one-year holding period, the non-affiliate may resell those restricted securities under Rule 144 upon compliance with only its current public information requirement. After the expiration of the one-year holding period, may resell those restricted securities without compliance with any other Rule 144 requirements.

Any affiliate of the issuer (or a person or entity that was an affiliate during the preceding 90 days) or any person or entity selling on its behalf will be subject to a six-month holding period before it may resell those restricted securities under Rule 144. After the expiration of the six-month holding period, it may resell those restricted securities under Rule 144 only upon compliance with all of its requirements.

2. Restricted securities of an issuer not subject to reporting requirements

With respect to restricted securities of an issuer that is not (and has not been for at least 90 days before the sale) subject to the periodic reporting requirements of the Exchange Act, any non-affiliate of the issuer (which must not have been an affiliate during the preceding three months) will be subject to a one-year holding period before it may resell those restricted securities under Rule 144. After the expiration of the one-year holding period, it may resell those restricted securities under Rule 144 without compliance with any other requirements.

Any affiliate of the issuer (or a person or entity that was an affiliate during the preceding 90 days) or any person or entity selling on its behalf will be subject to a one-year holding period before it may resell those restricted securities under Rule 144. After the expiration of the one-year holding period, it may resell those restricted securities under Rule 144 only upon compliance with all of its requirements.

3. Unrestricted securities of an issuer subject to reporting requirements

With respect to unrestricted securities of an issuer that is (and has been for at least 90 days before the sale) subject to the periodic reporting requirements of the Exchange Act, any non-affiliate of the issuer generally need not rely on Rule 144, as it will have the exemption of § 4(a)(1).

Any affiliate of the issuer (or a person or entity that was an affiliate during the preceding 90 days) or any person or entity selling on its behalf will be subject to a six-month holding period before it may resell those unrestricted securities under Rule 144. After the expiration of the six-month holding period, it may resell those unrestricted securities under Rule 144 only upon compliance with all of its requirements.

4. Unrestricted securities of an issuer not subject to reporting requirements

With respect to unrestricted securities of an issuer that is not (and has not been for at least 90 days before the sale) subject to the periodic reporting requirements of the Exchange Act, any non-affiliate of the issuer generally need not rely on Rule 144, as it will have the exemption of § 4(a)(1). Any affiliate of the issuer (or a person or entity that was an affiliate during the preceding 90 days) or any person or entity selling on its behalf will be subject to a one-year holding period before it may resell those unrestricted securities under Rule 144. After the expiration of the one-year holding period, it may resell those unrestricted securities under Rule 144 only upon compliance with all of its requirements.

5. Other Rule 144 requirements

The other requirements of Rule 144 (which may or may not apply to any particular resale, as described above) are as follows.

There must be adequate current public information about the issuer. This requirement is deemed satisfied for an issuer that is (and has been for at least 90 days before the sale) subject to the periodic reporting requirements of the Exchange Act, if:

- it has filed all required reports for the preceding 12 months (or such shorter period as it has been required to file those reports) other than Form 8-K reports; and

- it has submitted and posted on its website any required interactive data files required to be submitted and posted under Rule 405 of Regulation S-T during the preceding 12 months (or such shorter period as it has been required to file those reports).[56]

For an issuer that is not subject to the periodic reporting requirements of the Exchange Act, then there must be publicly available information as specified in Exchange Act Rule 15c2-11(a)(5).[57] The seller may rely on a reporting issuer's statement in its most recent Exchange Act filing or a written statement from the issuer as to the currency of its filings and submissions,

---

[54] 17 C.F.R. § 230.144.
[55] 17 C.F.R. § 230.144(b).

[56] 17 C.F.R. § 232.405.
[57] 17 C.F.R. §§ 240.15c2-11(a)(5)(i)–(xiv), 240.15c2-11(a)(5)(xvi).

unless it knows or has reason to believe that the statement is inaccurate.[58]

Any required holding period for a purchased security does not begin to run until the securities have been fully paid for. A promissory note does not constitute full payment unless it is full recourse and fully secured by collateral other than the securities purchased. There are special rules allowing "tacking" in calculating the holding period in a variety of specific circumstances, including stock dividends, stock splits, recapitalizations, conversions, foreclosure on pledged securities, gifts, trusts, and estates.[59]

For securities solely for the account of an affiliate, sales within the three months preceding the transaction in question are aggregated with that transaction and cannot exceed the greater of:

- one percent of the issued and outstanding units of the same class of the issuer, as shown in its most recent published report or statement;

- the average weekly reporting trading volume through all national securities exchanges for the four weeks preceding the filing of the required notice of sale with the SEC; or

- the average weekly trading volume reported through an effective transaction reporting plan or effective national market system plan as defined in Item 600 of Regulation NMS during the same four-week period.[60]

With respect to sales of "debt securities," which are defined to include any ABS within the meaning of Regulation AB,[61] aggregate sales of the same tranche within the three months preceding the transaction in question cannot exceed the greater of the foregoing and 10 percent of the principal amount of the tranche.[62]

Again, there are special rules dealing with the determination of the amount of securities that have been sold in several specific situations, including conversions, foreclosure on pledged securities, gifts, trusts, and estates. When two or more persons act "in concert" for the purposes of selling securities, their sales are aggregated for purposes of determining whether they have met the volume limitations,[63] and there are rules regarding the aggregation of sales by certain related parties.[64]

Rule 144 sales generally must be effected in "brokers' transactions" or in transactions directly with a market maker, and the seller may not solicit orders or make a payment other than to the broker executing the sell order.[65] A "brokers' transaction" includes transactions by a broker who does no more than execute the customer's orders as his agent, receives no more than the customary commission, and (with certain exceptions) neither solicits nor arranges the solicitation of orders to buy the securities in anticipation of the transaction.

Additionally, the broker must not, after reasonable inquiry, be aware of circumstances indicating that the seller is an "underwriter" or that the transaction is part of a "distribution" of securities of the issuer; the broker is deemed to be aware of the contents of the seller's Form 144.[66] The manner-of-sale requirements do not apply to ABS and other debt securities.[67]

If the relevant sales exceed 5000 units or $50,000 in aggregate sales price in any three-month period, a Notice of Proposed Sale on Form 144 must be filed with the SEC (and transmitted to the principal national securities exchange, if any, on which the securities are listed). The seller must have a bona fide intention to sell the securities specified within a reasonable time after filing.[68]

> **Comment:** Rule 144 provides a clear, clean exception for resales of restricted securities by a non-affiliate after a holding period of six months (for a reporting issuer) or one year (for a non-reporting issuer) in these circumstances. Perhaps most importantly, this permits resales of securities of private issuers (which otherwise generally would not qualify for Rule 144, as they will not meet the public information test). However, privately issued ABS are likely to be subject to a variety of other restrictions on transfer pursuant to the terms of their transaction documents.

D. Regulation S and Extraterritoriality

Regulation S provides a safe harbor for offers and sales outside of the United States,[69] which are not within the jurisdictional scope of § 5 of the Securities Act.[70] There are two basic rules for any issuer or "distributor" (meaning an underwriter, dealer, or any other contractual participant in a Regulation S offering).[71]

First, the offer or sale must be made in an "offshore transaction." An "offshore transaction" is an offer and sale in which no offer is made to anyone in the U.S., so long as either the buyer is (or is reasonably believed by the seller to be) outside of the U.S. at the time the buy order is originated or the transaction is executed through the facilities of an offshore securities market specified in the regulation.[72]

Second, no "directed selling efforts" may be made in the U.S. by the issuer, any distributor, any of their affiliates, or anyone acting on their behalf.[73] "Directed selling efforts" generally means any activity that is intended to, or could reasonably be expected to, condition the U.S. market for the securities, including any advertisement in a publication printed primarily for U.S. distribution with a circulation of 15,000 or more. There are a variety of specific exceptions to this definition, including advertisements required by law and certain "tombstone" advertisements in publications with a primarily

---

[58] Securities Act Rule 144(c)(1), 17 C.F.R. § 230.144(c)(1).

[59] 17 C.F.R. § 230.144(d).

[60] 17 C.F.R. § 242.600.

[61] 17 C.F.R. § 230.144(a)(4).

[62] 17 C.F.R. § 230.144(e)(2).

[63] 17 C.F.R. § 230.144(e).

[64] 17 C.F.R. § 230.144(a)(2).

[65] 17 C.F.R. § 230.144(f).

[66] Securities Act § 4(a)(4), 15 U.S.C. § 77d(a)(4); Securities Act Rule 144(g), 17 C.F.R. § 230.144(g).

[67] 17 C.F.R. § 230.144(f)(3)(ii).

[68] 17 C.F.R. § 230.144(h).

[69] 17 C.F.R. §§ 230.901–05.

[70] Securities Act Rule 901, 17 C.F.R. § 230.901.

[71] Securities Act Rule 902(d), 17 C.F.R. § 230.902(d).

[72] 17 C.F.R. §§ 230.902(h), 230.902(b)(1).

[73] Securities Act Rule 903(a), 17 C.F.R. § 230.903(a).

206   SPS   1/14   A - 41

foreign circulation.[74] An internet posting may constitute directed selling efforts in the U.S. unless the issuer takes "adequate measures" to preclude U.S. persons from purchasing the securities.

Whether "adequate measures" have been taken depends on the facts and circumstances, but a prominent disclaimer that the offer is directed only to countries other than the U.S., combined with procedures reasonably designed to prevent sales to U.S. persons, should suffice.[75] A concurrent U.S. registered public offering or exempt private offering will not constitute directed selling efforts[76] and will not be integrated with the Regulation S offering.[77]

There are no additional requirements for a foreign issuer that meets certain tests that make it clear it has little U.S. presence and the offering clearly is not directed to U.S. interests (Category 1).[78] An intermediate group of additional requirements applies to offerings of equity securities of a foreign issuer that files Exchange Act reports, and to "debt securities" (which, for purposes of Regulation S, includes most ABS)[79] of any issuer that files Exchange Act reports or of a non-reporting foreign issuer (Category 2).[80] The most stringent group of additional requirements applies to all other issuers, including any non-reporting U.S. issuer (Category 3).[81]

Those additional requirements for ABS and other debt securities are as follows (equity securities being subject to even more stringent requirements).

First, the issuer must implement "offering restrictions."[82] This means that:

- each distributor must agree that all sales during a specified "distribution compliance period" must be made in accordance with Regulation S, or pursuant to registration or an applicable exemption; and

- all offering materials must contain prominent statements that, among other things, the securities have not been registered and may not be offered or sold in the U.S. or to "U.S. persons" without registration or an applicable exemption.[83]

The "distribution compliance period" begins when the securities are first offered to persons other than a distributor (or the closing of the offering, whichever is later) and ends (for Category 2 securities and Category 3 debt securities, including

ABS) 40 days later.[84] A "U.S. person" includes, with certain exceptions, a natural person residing in the U.S., a business entity organized under U.S. law, an estate of which any administrator is a U.S. person, an agency or branch of a foreign entity located in the U.S., a nondiscretionary account held for the benefit of a U.S. person, a discretionary account held by a fiduciary organized or resident in the U.S., and certain foreign entities formed by a U.S. person for the purpose of investing in unregistered securities.[85]

Second, offers and sales made prior to the end of the distribution compliance period must not be made to or for the benefit of a U.S. person other than a distributor. Category 3 debt securities must be represented by a temporary global security that is not exchangeable for definitive securities until conclusion of the distribution compliance period and (for a non-distributor) certification of beneficial ownership by non-U.S. person or person who purchased in a transaction exempt from the registration requirements of the Securities Act.[86]

Third, each distributor, dealer, or other person receiving a sales commission before the end of the distribution compliance period must send a notice to the purchaser noting that the purchaser is subject to the same restrictions on offers and sales that apply to the distributor.[87]

A resale by anyone other than an issuer, a distributor or one of their affiliates (except for an officer or director who is an affiliate solely for that reason, who may rely on the resale safe harbor) meets the requirements of Regulation S if made in an offshore transaction, and no directed selling efforts are made in the U.S. by the seller, an affiliate, or anyone acting on their behalf.[88] For an officer or director, no selling concession, fee, or other remuneration may be paid other than a customary brokerage commission.[89] Additional requirements apply to resales by dealers and others receiving selling concessions.[90]

Securities acquired in a Regulation S transaction are restricted securities, which cannot be resold except in compliance with Regulation S or pursuant to registration or exemption.[91]

Regulation S was significantly less restrictive when first adopted, but the SEC quickly adopted changes because it viewed many of the transactions that relied on the rule as abusive. One of the preliminary notes to Regulation S still states that:

> In view of the objective of these rules and the policies underlying the [Securities] Act, Regulation S is not available with respect to any transaction or series of transactions that, although in technical compliance with these rules, is part of a play or scheme to evade the registration provisions of the [Securities] Act. In such cases, registration under the Act is required.[92]

Comment: An issuer should be cautious in relying on

---

[74] Securities Act Rule 902(c), 17 C.F.R. § 230.902(c).

[75] Statement of the Commission Regarding Use of Internet Web Sites to Offer Securities, Solicit Securities Transactions or Advertise Investment Services Offshore, 63 Fed. Reg. 14,806, 14,808–09 (Mar. 27, 1998).

[76] Offshore Offers and Sales, 55 Fed. Reg. 18,306, 18,312 (May 2, 1990).

[77] 55 Fed. Reg. at 18,320.

[78] *See* 17 C.F.R. § 230.903(b)(1).

[79] *See* 17 C.F.R. § 230.902(a).

[80] *See* 17 C.F.R. § 230.903(b)(2).

[81] *See* 17 C.F.R. § 230.903(b)(3).

[82] *Id.*

[83] 17 C.F.R. § 230.902(g).

---

[84] 17 C.F.R. §§ 230.902(f), 230.903(b)(2)(ii), 230.903(b)(3)(ii).

[85] 17 C.F.R. § 230.902(k).

[86] 17 C.F.R. §§ 230.903(b)(2)(ii), 230.903(b)(3)(ii)(A).

[87] 17 C.F.R. §§ 230.903(b)(2)(iii), 230.903(b)(3)(iii).

[88] Securities Act Rule 904(a), 17 C.F.R. § 230.904(a).

[89] 17 C.F.R. § 230.904(b)(2).

[90] 17 C.F.R. § 230.904(b)(1).

[91] Securities Act Rule 905, 17 C.F.R. § 230.905.

[92] *Id.*

Regulation S if the offered securities are expected to flow quickly back into the U.S., regardless of technical compliance with the rule. For this reason, Regulation S is somewhat less "safe" a safe harbor than it might otherwise appear.

VI.
Periodic and Other Reporting Requirements

A. When Exchange Act Periodic Reporting Is Required

Periodic reporting under the Exchange Act is required whenever an issuer registers a class of securities under Exchange Act § 12.[1] Section 12 requires registration whenever a class of an issuer's securities is listed on a national securities exchange,[2] or when an issuer has assets of more than $10 million and a class of non-exempted equity securities held of record by either 2000 persons (or 500 persons who are not accredited investors).[3] Asset-backed securities (ABS) are virtually never required to be registered under these tests.

Periodic reporting also is required whenever an issuer files a registration statement under the Securities Act and that registration statement becomes effective.[4] It is under this rule that issuers of publicly offered ABS generally are required to file periodic Exchange Act reports.

B. Identifying the Reporting Entity

As under the Securities Act,[5] for purposes of the Exchange Act, the depositor in an ABS transaction, acting solely in its capacity as depositor to the trust for a particular transaction, is the "issuer" of the ABS in that transaction. When the depositor acts as a depositor in a separate ABS transaction (or issues its own securities), it is a different "issuer."[6] The effectiveness of a shelf registration statement does not by itself result in reporting obligations until the time of the first takedown, each new takedown results in a new reporting requirement, and each "issuer" has a separate reporting obligation.[7] Securities and Exchange Commission (SEC) staff generally takes the view that a depositor's trust may not file combined periodic reports, each must report separately.[8]

In some structures, the pool assets are represented by a separate security formed specifically for purposes of the transaction. While the offer and sale of these intermediate securities may be required to be registered under the Securities Act,[9] separate periodic reports need generally not be filed for these securities.[10]

C. Distribution Reports on Form 10-D

1. General requirements for Form 10-D

Form 10-D is a special periodic report for ABS that is required to be filed monthly,[11] within 15 calendar days after the date that distributions are required to be made on the ABS.[12] In general, information need not be reported in a distribution report on Form 10-D if it already has been disclosed in a periodic report or registration statement.[13]

Much of the information required by Form 10-D is tied to the "distribution period," a term that is not defined by the SEC.

Comment: Generally, the distribution period is the period that is designated by the transaction documents as the "collection period," or the period during which amounts collected on the pool assets are to be used to make payments on the ABS on a related distribution date.

Form 10-D must be signed by the depositor or on behalf of the issuing entity by an authorized representative of the servicer (or the master servicer, or entity performing similar functions, if there are multiple servicers).[14]

2. Distribution and pool performance information

Item 1 of Form 10-D requires reporting of distribution and pool performance information pursuant to Item 1121 of Regulation AB.[15] Among the items required to be reported are:

- the amount and disposition of excess cash;
- amounts drawn on credit support and amounts remaining;
- updated information on the asset pool, including weighted average interest rate, weighted average remaining term and pool factors;
- material changes in the determination of delinquencies, charge-offs and uncollectible amounts;
- the amount and purpose of any advances;
- material modifications to pool assets;
- disclosure regarding material breaches of representations, warranties or covenants;
- disclosure regarding any new ABS backed by the same asset pool;
- changes in the asset pool due to pre-funding or revolving period mechanisms, repurchases or substitutions

---

[1] Exchange Act § 13, 15 U.S.C. § 78m. *See* Exchange Act § 12, 15 U.S.C. § 78*l*

[2] 15 U.S.C. § 78*l*(b).

[3] 15 U.S.C. § 78*l*(g).

[4] Exchange Act § 15(d), 15 U.S.C. § 78o(d).

[5] *See* 206 SPS § I-B, *Structure of a "Plain Vanilla" Securitization.*

[6] Exchange Act Rule 3b-19, 17 C.F.R. § 240.3b-19.

[7] Exchange Act Rule 15d-22, 17 C.F.R. § 240.15b-22.

[8] Asset-Backed Securities, 70 Fed. Reg. 1506, 1564 n.457 (Jan. 7, 2005), SEC Release No. 33-8518 (Dec. 22, 2004).

[9] *See* 206 SPS § II-D3, *Resecuritizations, repacks and registration of underlying or separate securities.*

[10] So long as both the issuing entity for the ABS and the intermediate financial asset were both established by the same depositor or sponsor, the intermediate asset is created solely to satisfy legal requirements or otherwise facilitate the securitization, both the ABS and the intermediate financial asset are registered under the Securities Act, and the intermediate financial asset is not created as a scheme to evade

securities law requirements. Exchange Act Rule 15d-23(a), 17 C.F.R. § 240.15d-23(a).

[11] SEC, Form 10-D: Asset-Backed Issuer Distribution Report Pursuant to Section 13 or 15(d) of the Securities Exchange Act of 1934.

[12] Exchange Act Rule 12b-25 may provide a five-day extension under certain circumstances. 17 C.F.R. § 240.12b-25. *See* 206 SPS § VI-H2, *Extensions under Rule 12b-25.*

[13] SEC Form 10-D, at 1 (General Instruction C(3): Preparation of Report).

[14] SEC Form 10-D, at 2 (General Instruction E: Signature and Filing of Report).

[15] 17 C.F.R. § 229.1121.

arising from breaches of representations or warranties, and amounts remaining in any pre-funding account.

- disclosures required by Rule 15Ga-1[16] regarding demands to repurchase or replace pool assets for breach of representations or warranties; and

- for transactions with a revolving or pre-funding period, for the last distribution date in each fiscal year and on which that period ends, updated disclosure regarding originators, pool assets and significant obligors, if there have been material changes since the last report.

Perhaps most importantly, the distribution report for the related distribution period, as required to be provided pursuant to the transaction documents, must be filed as an exhibit.

3. Legal proceedings

Item 2 of Form 10-D requires disclosure regarding legal or governmental proceedings against the sponsor, depositor, issuing entity, trustee, master servicer, any significant servicer, or an originator that originated (or is expected to originate) 20 percent or more of the pool assets, if material and not previously disclosed. Material information regarding an insolvency proceeding involving any of these parties must be disclosed, as must information regarding insolvency of a 20-percent originator.

4. Sales of securities and use of proceeds

Item 3 of Form 10-D requires disclosure of "the information required by Item 2 of Part II of Form 10-Q" with regard to "any sale of securities . . . backed by the same asset pool or . . . otherwise issued by the issuing entity," whether registered or issued privately. This portion of Form 10-Q by its terms applies only to equity securities, but as required under Form 10-D is generally interpreted to apply to all ABS that fall within its scope. Among the required information is:

- the date of sale;

- the name or class of the buyer (for privately offered securities);

- whether they were sold for cash, and if so, the aggregate offering price and underwriting discounts;

- the exemption from registration relied upon (for privately offered securities); and

- the use of proceeds.

Where the issuer is a master trust, the required information also includes, to the extent material, the relative priority of the new securities, the new securities' rights to pool assets, and the allocation of cash flows, expenses and losses among all classes.

> **Comment:** Some issuers routinely file this information in a Form 8-K shortly after completion of the offering, so that it doesn't get missed when the time comes for disclosure on Form 10-D.

Item 3 requires updated information regarding the use of proceeds of the offering pursuant to Item 701(f) of Regulation S-K,[17] if required pursuant to Securities Act Rule 463 (reporting regarding use of proceeds required on first periodic report filed after the offering, and thereafter until application of all the offering proceeds or disclosure of the termination of the offering).[18] Also required is disclosure regarding purchases of equity securities, a requirement that generally is inapplicable to ABS.

5. Defaults upon senior securities

Item 4 of Form 10-D requires disclosure of "the information required by Item 3 of Part II of Form 10-Q" for the reporting period. This entails reporting regarding—

> any material default in the payment of principal, interest, a sinking or purchase fund installment, or any other material default not cured within 30 days, with respect to any indebtedness of the registrant or any of its significant subsidiaries exceeding 5 percent of the total assets of the registrant and its consolidated subsidiaries.[19]

In that case, the registrant must identify the indebtedness, state the nature of the default, and, in the case of a principal, interest, or sinking or purchase fund installment, the amount of the default and the total arrearage.

> **Comment:** For ABS, the references to consolidated subsidiaries generally are inapplicable—the report should relate to defaults by the issuing entity. Where the ABS are pass-through certificates without specific required principal payment amounts, the applicability of this item is unclear, but in any event the registrant should report the failure to pay the principal amount on the scheduled final distribution date.

Item 4 of Form 10-D also requires certain disclosures regarding arrearages in payment of preferred stock dividends, which are irrelevant to ABS.

6. Submission of matters to a vote of security holders

Item 5 of Form 10-D requires disclosure of "the information required by Item 4 of Part II of Form 10-Q" for the reporting period. Item 5 of Form 10-D is headed "Submission of Matters to a Vote of Security Holders," but that item was deleted from Item 4 of Part II of Form 10-Q in 2009 and moved to Item 5.07 of Form 8-K in 2009 as a current disclosure item.[20] Item 4 of Part II of Form 10-Q now relates to mine safety disclosures, a topic that generally is irrelevant to ABS issuers.

> **Comment:** If matters submitted to a vote or consent of the ABS holders, and the resulting votes or consents already have been described in a Form 8-K, there should be no need to disclose them in a subsequent Form 10-D.

---

[16] 17 C.F.R. § 240.15Ga-1; *see* 206 SPS § VI-I, *Repurchase Demand Reporting on Form ABS-15G* (discussing Rule 15Ga-1).

[17] 17 C.F.R. § 229.701(f).

[18] 17 C.F.R. § 230.463.

[19] SEC Form 10-Q: Quarterly or Transition Report Pursuant to Section 13 or 15(d) of the Securities Exchange Act of 1934, at 6 (Item II(3): Defaults Upon Senior Securities).

[20] *See* 206 SPS § VI-D8, *Submission of matters to a vote of security holders.*

7. Significant obligors of pool assets

Item 6 of Form 10-D requires disclosure of the mattes required by Item 1112(b) of Regulation AB, the same significant obligor financial information that is required in the registration statement. It may be incorporated by reference from Exchange Act reports of the significant obligor in the same circumstances as it may be incorporated by reference in the registration statement.[21]

Whether an obligor meets the 10-percent significance threshold must be re-calculated at the end of every distribution period. If a formerly significant obligor falls below the 10-percent threshold, it will no longer be a significant obligor and reporting will no longer be required, even if it later exceeds that threshold.[22]

8. Significant enhancement provider information

Item 7 of Form 10-D requires disclosure of the matters required by the information required by Items 1114(b)(2) and 1115(b) of Regulation AB, the same financial information that is required regarding providers of derivatives that are primarily for credit support or not primarily for credit support. It may be incorporated by reference from the Exchange Act reports of the provider in the same circumstances as it may be incorporated by reference in the registration statement.[23]

The instruction to this item notes that the information need only be reported in the report filed for the distribution period in which updated information regarding the enhancement provider is required pursuant to Regulation AB.

> **Comment:** Quarterly or annual financial information should only be provided in the Form 10-D for the period including the date on which the provider was required to file (or would have been required to file, if it was a reporting entity) its Forms 10-Q or 10-K, respectively.

Whether a derivative provider meets the applicable significance percentage must be re-calculated at the end of every distribution period. Unlike with significant obligors, this calculation must be made anew at the end of every distribution period, even if the provider fell below the applicable significance percentage for a prior period.[24]

> **Comment:** If Forms 10-D are incorporated by reference into the registration statement,[25] the written consent of the auditors to include any required audited financial statements must be obtained. Otherwise, the auditors' consent is not required.

9. Other information

Information that was required to be reported on Form 8-K during the reporting period but was not must be reported in response to this item. The information need not then be repeated in a Form 8-K.

D. Current Reports on Form 8-K

1. General requirements for Form 8-K

Generally, a current report on Form 8-K is required to be filed within four business days of a reportable event.[26]

Form 8-K is required to be signed by the depositor or on behalf of the issuing entity by an authorized representative of the servicer (or the master servicer, or entity performing similar functions, if there are multiple servicers).[27]

Not every disclosure item under Form 8-K is required for ABS issuers. A chart detailing which items are required and which may be omitted is included as Practice Tool 3.[28]

2. Entry into a material definitive agreement

This item requires disclosure of the entry of a material definitive agreement not in the ordinary course of business, or an amendment to such an agreement, including the date of the agreement or amendment, the parties, a brief description of any material relationship between the registrant or its affiliates and any of the parties, and a brief description of the material terms and conditions of the agreement or amendment. For ABS transactions, this item covers any agreement that is material to the transaction, even if the depositor is not a party.[29]

> **Comment:** The agreement or amendment itself must not be filed as an exhibit to Form 8-K, but generally would have to be filed as an exhibit to the next required Form 10-D or 10-K.[30] In order not to forget to file material definitive agreements and amendments, it is wise to consider voluntarily filing them early with the Form 8-K that requires the initial disclosure.

3. Termination of a material definitive agreement

This item requires disclosure regarding the termination of a material definitive agreement that was not made in the ordinary course of business, other than by expiration or completion of all of the parties' obligations. The required disclosure covers the date of termination, the parties, a brief description of any material relationship between the registrant or its affiliates and any of the parties, and a brief description of the material terms and conditions of the agreement or amendment. For ABS trans-

---

[21] See 206 SPS § IV-A8, *Significant obligors.*

[22] DIV. OF CORP. FIN., SEC, MANUAL OF PUBLICLY AVAILABLE TELEPHONE INTERPRETATIONS—REGULATION AB AND RELATED RULES § 19.01 (2005) (covering Items 6 and 7 of Form 10-D); 17 C.F.R. § 229.1100.

[23] See 206 SPS § IV-A8, *Significant obligors;* 206 SPS § IV-A10, *Credit support.*

[24] DIV. OF CORP. FIN., REGULATION AB TELEPHONE INTERPRETATIONS, at § 19.01.

[25] See 206 SPS § II-D4, *Incorporation by reference* (discussing when Forms 10-D and 10-K need not be incorporated by reference into a shelf registration statement on Form S-3).

[26] SEC, Form 8-K: Current Report Pursuant to Section 13 or 15(d) of the Securities Exchange Act of 1934, at 2 (General Instruction B(1): Events to Be Reported and Time for Filing of Reports). Extensions pursuant to Rule 12b-25 are not available for Form 8-K. 17 C.F.R. § 240.12b-25.

[27] SEC Form 8-K, at 4 (General Instruction G(3): Signatures).

[28] See 206 SPS Practice Tool 3, *Form 8-K Disclosure Items for ABS Issuers.*

[29] SEC Form 8-K, at 4 (Item 1.01: Entry into a Material Definitive Agreement, Instruction 3).

[30] Regulation S-K Item 601(b)(i), 17 C.F.R. § 229.601(b)(i).

actions, this item covers any agreement that is material to the transaction, even if the depositor is not a party.[31]

4. Triggering events that accelerate or increase a direct financial obligation under an off-balance sheet arrangement

The actual text of Item 2.04 appears to have little relevance to ABS issuers, but an instruction adds specific disclosure requirements that apply only to ABS issuers. Upon an early amortization, performance trigger or other event—including an event of default—that would materially alter the payment priority or distribution of cash flows or the amortization schedule for the ABS, disclosure is required regarding the resulting changes to the payment priorities, flow of funds or ABS. Again, disclosure is required whether or not the depositor is a party to the agreement in question.[32]

5. Material modifications to rights of security holders

Item 3.03 requires disclosure if the transaction documents that define the security holders' rights are materially modified, in which case the date of the modification, the title of the class of securities involved and the general effect of the modification must be described. If the issuance of other securities materially limits or qualifies the registered securities, then additional disclosure is required.

6. Amendments to articles of incorporation of bylaws; Change in fiscal year

The text of Item 5.03 appears to have little relevance for ABS issuers. However, an instruction requires disclosure regarding any amendment to the governing documents of the issuing entity, whether material or not.[33]

7. Change in shell company status

While not among the items that specifically may be omitted by ABS issuers,[34] Item 5.06 is generally irrelevant to ABS issuers.

8. Submission of matters to a vote of security holders

If any matter was submitted to a vote or consent of security holders, then Item 5.07 requires several disclosure, including a brief description of each matter voted upon and votes cast for, against or withheld. Much of the rest of the text of this item will have little relevance to ABS issuers.

9. Shareholder director nominations

While not among the items that specifically may be omitted by ABS issuers,[35] Item 5.08 is generally irrelevant to ABS issuers.

10. ABS informational and computational material

Item 6.01 is used for filing, when required, of ABS informational and computational materials (ABSICM). The general four business day deadline does not apply to this item. Rather, the ABSICM rules govern the required timing of a filing under this item.[36]

11. Change of servicer or trustee

If a servicer for which disclosure is required under Item 1108(a)(2) of Regulation AB,[37] or a trustee has resigned or has been removed, or has been replaced or substituted, or if a new such servicer or trustee has been appointed, then Item 6.02 requires the date of the event to be stated and the circumstances surrounding the change to be described. The material terms regarding the servicer's removal, replacement, resignation or transfer must be summarized, as required by Item 1108(d) of Regulation AB.[38] All of the required disclosures regarding a new servicer or trustee must be provided.[39] If any of this information is unavailable when filing is required, then this may be noted in the filing and the required information provided in an amendment filed within four business days after the information becomes available.[40]

> **Comment:** Servicing transfers may present difficult disclosure issues. Servicing may be transferred in many different ways, all of which must be monitored. The rules do not distinguish between transfers made by a servicer that is in contractual privity with the issuer and one that is not. The transfer of servicing rights without the actual transfer of reportable servicer to another reportable servicer, so long as the transferring servicer retains some servicing. However, if servicing is transferred between two existing servicers and the transferee crosses a servicing threshold beyond which additional disclosure would be required,[41] then most practitioners would advise reporting under this item. Transfers from an interim servicer to a permanent successor servicer should be disclosed, even if information regarding both servicers is described in the prospectus.

The SEC staff has provided additional helpful guidance regarding this item. A change in the identity of a reportable servicer for a particular servicing must be disclosed if the new servicer is reportable. There is no specific requirement to dis-

---

[31] SEC Form 8-K, at 5 (Item 1.02: Termination of a Material Definitive Agreement, Instruction 3).

[32] SEC Form 8-K, at 10 (Item 2.04: Triggering Events that Accelerate or Increase a Direct Financial Obligation or an Obligation under an Off-Balance Sheet Arrangement, Instruction 5).

[33] SEC Form 8-K, at 17 (Item 5.03: Amendments to Articles of Incorporation or Bylaws; Change in Fiscal Year, Instruction 2).

[34] See 206 SPS § VI-D1, General requirements for Form 8-K.

[35] Id.

[36] See 206 SPS § III-D4, ABS informational and computational materials.

[37] 17 C.F.R. § 229.1108(a)(2). See 206 SPS § IV-A5, Servicers.

[38] 17 C.F.R. § 229.1108(d).

[39] See 206 SPS § IV-A5, Servicers (discussing required disclosures regarding servicers); 206 SPS § IV-A13, Other requirements (discussing required disclosures regarding trustees).

[40] SEC Form 8-K, at 20 (Item 6.02: Change of Servicer or Trustee, Instruction).

[41] See 206 SPS § IV-A5, Servicers.

close a material change in a reportable servicer's procedures, but such a change should be disclosed if it relates to the distribution and pool performance information that Form 10-D requires or if the disclosure is of a material fact necessary to make the rest of the disclosure not misleading.[42]

12. Change in credit enhancement or other external support

If any reportable material external credit enhancement or support, or derivative not primarily for credit support,[43] terminates other than by expiration or completion of all of the parties' obligations, then Item 6.03 requires a variety of specific disclosures. The date of the termination, the parties to the enhancement, and material terms of the enhancement must be described, as must the material circumstances surrounding the termination and any material early termination penalties.

If the depositor (or servicer signing the depositor's Form 10-K) becomes aware of any new such enhancement or derivative, then the date of the addition must be specified, as well as all of the required disclosures regarding the new enhancement or derivative.[44] If the depositor or such a servicer becomes aware of any material change to an existing reportable enhancement or derivative, then the date of the change, the parties to the enhancement and material terms of the enhancement must be described.[45] If any of this information is unavailable when filing is required, then this may be noted in the filing and the required information provided in an amendment filed within four business days after the information becomes available.[46]

13. Failure to make a required distribution

If a required distribution to ABS holders is not made as of the distribution date and the failure is material, then Item 6.04 requires the failure to be identified and its nature described. Therefore, both late and incorrect distributions are required to be disclosed, if material.

Comment: While the subsequent correction of an error does not necessarily mitigate its materiality, as a practical matter ABS issuers may be able to conclude that even a substantial error is not material when they compensate investors for losses incurred in receiving an incorrect or late payment.

14. Securities Act updating disclosure

For a shelf offering on Form S-3, if any material characteristic of the asset pool at issuance differs by 5 percent or more

(other than as a result of the pool assets converting into cash in accordance with their terms) from the description of the pool in the prospectus, then updated information regarding pool assets and significant obligors must be provided pursuant to Item 6.05.[47] Also, if applicable, information regarding new servicers and originators is required.[48]

15. Regulation FD disclosure

Information required by Regulation FD that the registrant determines to disclose via Form 8-K is provided under this Item.[49]

E. Annual Reports on Form 10-K

1. General requirements for Form 10-K

Reporting issuers must file an annual report on Form 10-K within 90 days after the end of the fiscal year.[50]

Form 10-K must be signed on behalf of the depositor by the senior officer in charge of securitization or on behalf of the issuing entity by the senior officer in charge of the servicing function of the servicer (or the master servicer, or entity performing the equivalent function, if there are multiple servicers).[51]

Most of the disclosure items under Form 10-K are not required for ABS issuers. A chart detailing which items are required and which may be omitted is included as Practice Tool 4.[52] Most of the other required disclosure items are identical to required disclosure items under Form 10-D or Form S-3:

- Regulation AB Item 1112(b), significant obligor financial information;[53]

- Regulation AB Items 1114(b)(2) and 1115(b), significant enhancement and derivative provider financial information;[54]

---

[42] DIV. OF CORP. FIN., SEC, MANUAL OF PUBLICLY AVAILABLE TELEPHONE INTERPRETATIONS—REGULATION AB AND RELATED RULES § 7.02 (2005) (covering Item 1108(a) and related disclosures); 17 C.F.R. § 229.1108(a).

[43] *See* 206 SPS § IV-A10, *Credit support* (discussing disclosures related to credit support); 206 SPS § IV-A11, *Derivatives not primarily for credit support* (discussing disclosures related to derivatives that are not primarily for credit support).

[44] *Id.*

[45] *See* 206 SPS § IV-A5, *Servicers* (discussing required disclosures regarding servicers); 206 SPS § IV-A13, *Other requirements* (discussing required disclosures regarding trustees).

[46] SEC Form 8-K, at 21 (Item 6.03: Change in Credit Enhancement or Other External Support, Instruction 2).

[47] *See* 206 SPS § IV-A7, *Pool assets, including disclosures regarding the issuer's review of the pool assets* (discussing required disclosures regarding pool assets); 206 SPS § IV-A8, *Significant obligors* (discussing required disclosures regarding significant obligors).

[48] *See* 206 SPS § IV-A5, *Servicers* (discussing required disclosures regarding servicers); 206 SPS § IV-A6, *Originators* (discussing required disclosures regarding originators).

[49] *See generally* 206 SPS § VI-J, *Regulation FD and Selective Disclosure.*

[50] SEC, Form 10-K: Annual Report Pursuant to Section 13 or 15(d) of the Securities Exchange Act of 1934. These requirements may not apply to certain "accelerated filers," as defined in Exchange Act Rule 12b-2 or pursuant to an extension under Exchange Act Rule 12b-25. *See* 17 C.F.R. §§ 240.12b-2, 240.12b-25; 206 SPS § VI-H2, *Extensions under Rule 12b-25*. However, ABS issuers are highly unlikely to be accelerated filers.

[51] SEC Form 10-K, at 5 (General Instruction J(3): Signatures).

[52] *See* 206 SPS Practice Tool 4, *Form 10-K Disclosure Items for ABS Issuers.*

[53] 17 C.F.R. § 229.1112(b). *See* 206 SPS § IV-A8, *Significant obligors.*

[54] 17 C.F.R. §§ 229.1114(b)(2), 229.1115(b). *See* 206 SPS § IV-A10, *Credit Support*; 206 SPS § IV-A11, *Derivatives not primarily for credit support.* Note that the auditors' consent will be required for the inclusion of audited financial information if Forms 10-K are incorpo-

- Regulation AB Item 1117, information regarding legal proceedings;[55] and

- Regulation AB Item 1119, information regarding affiliations and certain relationships and related transactions.[56]

2. Compliance with applicable servicing criteria

Item 1122 of Regulation AB requires reports, to be filed as exhibits from "each party participating in the servicing function" (PPSF),[57] on each PPSF's assessment of compliance with certain specific servicing criteria,[58] as well as an accountant's attestation report on each PPSF assessment,[59] as required by Rule 13a-18 or Rule 15d-18.[60]

The required servicing criteria, which are set forth in item 1122(d),[61] are very broad, but they cannot be modified. If a PPSF's procedures differ from those in Item 1122, it must report that it is not in compliance and describe why its procedures are different.[62]

Compliance is measured at the end of the fiscal year, with respect to all ABS transactions involving the party in question that are backed by assets of the same asset type, including the transaction in question. In other words, compliance is measured on a platform-wide basis, so isolated instances of noncompliance in the servicing of any particular asset pool are not necessarily required to be reported.[63] The platform may be limited to "mirror actual servicing practices of the servicer" so long as they are not "artificially designed." For example, a PPSF that segregates its operations by geographic location or computer system may use those factors in determining the scope of its servicing platform.[64]

Each assessment of servicing compliance must be accompanied by an independent accounting firm's attestation, stating that the assessment is fairly stated in all material respects, or the reasons why the accountants cannot express this opinion.[65] If the Form 10-K is incorporated by reference into the registration statement, the accountants' consent also must be obtained for this incorporation.

If an assessment of servicing compliance or related attestation identifies any material instance of noncompliance with the servicing criteria, that instance must be identified in the text of the Form 10-K.

Comment: It is good practice, and may help to avoid SEC staff comment, to describe any steps that have been or are being taken to correct any identified material instance of noncompliance.

3. Identifying parties participating in the servicing function

The phrase "party participating in the servicing function" (PPSF) is broadly defined as "any entity (e.g., master servicer, primary servicers, trustees) that is performing activities that address the criteria in paragraph (d) of [Item 1122 of Regulation AB], unless such entity's activities relate only to 5 [percent] or less of the pool assets."[66] The scope of this phrase is clearly broader than the definition of "servicer," because "the fact that a party, such as a trustee, may perform an aspect of the servicing function covered by the criteria for purposes of requiring an assessment and attestation report does not mean that the party is included in the definition of 'servicer' . . . for purposes of other requirements."[67]

SEC staff has provided some helpful guidance. A trustee or administrator that calculates distribution amounts is a PPSF, but a party that makes distributions based on another party's calculations is not.[68] A vendor engaged by a servicer to perform specific and limited activities or to perform activities scripted by the servicer is not a separate PPSF if:

- the vendor is not a "servicer" as defined in Regulation AB;

- the servicer elects to take responsibility for assessing compliance with the servicing criteria applicable to the vendor in its assessment of compliance;

- the servicer has policies and procedures designed to provide reasonable assurance that the vendor's activities comply in all material respects with applicable servicing criteria; and

- the servicer's report on its assessment of compliance discloses:

- the vendor's servicing criteria for which the servicer is assuming responsibility;

- any material instance of noncompliance by the vendor that the servicer identifies or of which it is aware; and

- any material deficiency that is identified in the servicer's policies and procedures to monitor the vendor's compliance.[69]

However, in many other cases, determining whether a party is a PPSF is likely to involve difficult interpretive questions. Among the other parties that may be considered to be PPSFs, depending upon the facts and circumstances, are document custodians, credit risk managers, subcontractors that re-

---

rated by reference into the registration statement.

[55] 17 C.F.R. § 229.1117. *See* 206 SPS § VI-C3, *Legal proceedings.*

[56] 17 C.F.R. § 229.1119. *See* 206 SPS § IV-A13, *Other requirements.*

[57] *See* 206 SPS § VI-E3, *Identifying parties participating in the servicing function.*

[58] 17 C.F.R. § 229.1122(a).

[59] 17 C.F.R. § 229.1122(b).

[60] 17 C.F.R. §§ 240.13a-18, 240.15d-18.

[61] 17 C.F.R. § 229.1122(d).

[62] Div. of Corp. Fin., SEC, Manual of Publicly Available Telephone Interpretations—Regulation AB and Related Rules § 11.01 (2005) (covering Item 1122(d)); 17 C.F.R. § 229.1122(d).

[63] Div. of Corp. Fin., Regulation AB Telephone Interpretations, at § 17.05.

[64] Div. of Corp. Fin., Regulation AB Telephone Interpretations, at § 17.03.

[65] 17 C.F.R. § 210.2-02(g).

[66] Regulation AB Item 1122, 17 C.F.R. § 229.1122 instruc. 2.

[67] Asset-Backed Securities, 70 Fed. Reg. 1506, 1574 (Jan. 7, 2005).

[68] Div. of Corp. Fin., Regulation AB Telephone Interpretations, at § 17.01.

[69] Div. of Corp. Fin., Regulation AB Telephone Interpretations, at § 17.06.

possess or dispose of collateral, lockbox banks and collection agencies. On the other hand, a party that owns the servicing rights to assets may not be a PPSF if it does not perform any servicing functions. Even a nominal servicer may not be a PPSF if it completely subcontracts and does not monitor the performance of its servicing obligations.

4. Servicer compliance statement

Pursuant to Item 1123 of Regulation AB, each master servicer, affiliated servicer, or servicer that services 10 percent or more of the pool assets must provide a statement of compliance,[70] signed by an authorized officer, to the effect that:

- a review of the servicer's activities during the reporting period and of its performance under the applicable servicing agreement has been made under the officer's supervision; and

- to the best of the officer's knowledge, based on that review, the servicer has fulfilled all of its obligations under the agreement in all material respects throughout the reporting period (or specifying each failure to fulfill any such obligation in any material respect that is known to the officer, and the nature and status of the failure).[71]

Each such certification is then filed as an exhibit to the Form 10-K.

This certification is not required of servicers falling under Regulation AB Item 1108(a)(2)(iv), which covers "[a]ny other material servicer responsible for calculating or making distributions to holders of the asset-backed securities, performing work-outs or foreclosures, or other aspect of the servicing of the pool assets or the asset-backed securities upon which the performance of the pool assets or the asset-backed securities is materially dependent."[72] Therefore, while a trustee that calculates distribution amounts may be a "servicer," it will not be required to provide a servicer compliance statement unless it performs some other servicing function.[73]

> **Comment:** Other purely administrative servicers that do not directly manage pool assets are generally considered to be similarly exempt from providing a servicer compliance statement.

F. Sarbanes-Oxley Act Certification

Section 302 of the Sarbanes-Oxley Act of 2002 (Sarbanes-Oxley Act) requires that the principal executive officer or principal financial officer of a registrant certify, in each annual and quarterly report, as to the accuracy of the report and the included financial statements and the adequacy of certain internal controls, to the best of the officer's knowledge.[74] This statute has been implemented by Exchange Act Rules 13a-14(d) and

15d-14(d),[75] and by Item 601(b)(31) of Regulation S-K, which provides a special form of this certification for use by ABS issuers.[76] The ABS form of certification focuses on the servicer compliance requirements[77] and other information required to be provided by ABS registrants rather than financial statements of the registrant, which are not included in ABS periodic reports. Since ABS registrants do not file Quarterly Reports on Form 10-Q, this certification only is required in Annual Reports on Form 10-K.

The criminal certification required by § 906 of the Sarbanes-Oxley Act, as codified at 13 U.S.C. § 1350, is not required for ABS periodic reports, because they do not contain financial statements.[78] Similarly, asset-backed issuers are not required to comply with the requirements of § 404 of the Sarbanes-Oxley Act with regard to internal control over financial reporting.[79]

G. No Suspension of Periodic Reporting for ABS

Before enactment of the Dodd-Frank Wall Street Reform and Consumer Protection Act (Dodd-Frank Act), an ABS issuer's period reporting obligations under § 15(d) of the Exchange Act were automatically suspended for any fiscal year after the year in which the registration statement became effective (or, for offerings of ABS registered in a takedown from a shelf registration statement,[80] the fiscal year after the takedown) if the securities of each relevant class were held of record by fewer than 300 persons.[81] Most ABS issuers (other than master trusts) were able to take advantage of this suspension, as they ordinarily have fewer than 300 record holders of a class of securities. ABS issuers can no longer suspend periodic reporting in this manner.

Section 943(a) of the Dodd-Frank Act specifically removed the statutory exemption for issuers of ABS and authorized the SEC to prescribe by rule the ability of ABS issuers to suspend or terminate periodic reporting under the Exchange Act. In response, the SEC amended Exchange Act Rule 15d-22(b) to provide that an ABS issuer's reporting obligation for any class of publicly registered ABS is suspended as to any semi-annual fiscal period, other than a period in the fiscal year in which the relevant Securities Act registration statement became effective (or, for ABS issued in a takedown from a shelf registration statement, in which the takedown occurred),[82] if at the beginning of that fiscal period there are no securities of that class that were sold in the registered transaction held by non-

---

[70] *See* Regulation AB Item 1108(a)(2), 17 C.F.R. § 229.1108(a)(2); 206 SPS § IV-A5, *Servicers*.

[71] 17 C.F.R. § 229.1123.

[72] 17 C.F.R. § 229.1108(a)(2)(iv).

[73] Div. of Corp. Fin., Regulation AB Telephone Interpretations, at § 12.01; 17 C.F.R. 229.1108(a)(2)(iv).

[74] 15 U.S.C. § 7241.

[75] 17 C.F.R. §§ 240.13a-14(d), 240.15d-14(d).

[76] 17 C.F.R. § 229.601(b)(31).

[77] *See* 206 SPS § VI-E2, *Compliance with applicable servicing criteria.*

[78] *See* 17 C.F.R. §§ 240.13a-14(d), 240.15d-14(d).

[79] 17 C.F.R. §§ 229.308 instruc. 2, 240.13a-15(a), 240.15d-15(a).

[80] Exchange Act Rule 15d-22(b), 17 C.F.R. § 240.15d-22(b) (2009) (rule in effect prior to enactment of the Dodd-Frank Act).

[81] *See* 15 U.S.C. § 78o(d) (governing ABS issuer period reporting obligations).

[82] The SEC also amended Rule 15d-22(a) to more generally codify the rule that the starting and suspension dates for reporting for ABS issued in a takedown from a shelf registration statement will continue to be determined separately for each takedown. *See* 17 C.F.R. § 240.15d-22(a).

affiliates of the depositor, and if a certification on Form 15 has been filed.[83] Further, when there are no ABS of a class sold in a registered transaction still outstanding, the issuer's reporting obligations with respect to that class will be suspended immediately upon filing a certification on Form 15, if the issuer has filed all required reports for the shorter of its most recent three fiscal years (and the portion of the current year preceding the filing of its Form 15) or the period since the issuer became required to report. In either case, the filing of Form 15 will be a prerequisite to the suspension of any reporting requirements.[84]

Explanatory notes to the rule clarify that securities held of record by a broker, dealer, bank or nominee for the accounts of customers are considered held by the separate accounts for which they are held, so if an investment bank holds ABS that were issued by an affiliate for the benefit of nonaffiliated investors, the issuer of those ABS cannot suspend reporting.

H. Failure to Comply with Periodic Reporting Requirements

1. Consequences

The SEC has the authority to impose a wide range of civil penalties on issuers that do not comply with their periodic reporting requirements under the Exchange Act, and criminal prosecution also is a possibility (albeit a remote one).[85]

The most immediate impact of a failure to file is likely to be the loss of the ability to file a new shelf registration statement or to add capacity to an existing shelf. It is a registrant eligibility condition for filing Form S-3 that:

> to the extent the depositor or any issuing entity previously established, directly or indirectly, by the depositor or any affiliate of the depositor . . . are or were at any time during the twelve calendar months and any portion of a month immediately preceding the filing of the registration statement on this Form subject to the requirements of section 12 or 15(d) of the Exchange Act . . . with respect to a class of asset-backed securities involving the same asset class, such depositor and each such issuing entity must have filed all material required to be filed regarding such asset-backed securities pursuant to section 13, 14 or 15(d) of the Exchange Act . . . for such period (or such shorter period that each such entity was required to file such materials). In addition, such material must have been filed in a timely manner, other than a report that is required solely pursuant to Item 1.01, 1.02, 2.03, 2.04, 2.05, 2.06, 4.02(a), 6.01, 6.03 or 6.05 of Form 8-K . . . .[86]

These eligibility requirements are determined at the time the registration statement is filed.[87] If there has been a failure to file timely, a waiver from the SEC staff will be required.

Comment: The staff takes periodic reporting failures very seriously. Even if a waiver ultimately is granted, the failure to timely file a required report could result in a significant delay in a depositor's ability to file a shelf registration statement.

An ABS issuer that has not filed all reports and other materials required under § 13, § 14 or § 15(d) of the Exchange Act is an "ineligible issuer" and therefore generally may not use free writing prospectuses in the offering process.[88] This requirement is somewhat less troublesome than the shelf eligibility requirement described above, because there is no timeliness requirement. An issuer that has failed to file timely may simply file the delinquent report, rather than needing to approach the SEC staff for a waiver.

2. Extensions under Rule 12b-25

A short extension of the filing deadline for a Form 10-D or 10-K (but not 8-K) may be available under Rule 12b-25.[89] If the issuer is unable to file all or any portion of the required report "without unreasonable effort or expense," then the report will be deemed to have been filed timely so long as:

- a Form 12b-25 is filed no more than one business day after the due date,[90] which (1) discloses in detail the reasons for the inability to file timely, (2) represents that the cause of the late filing could not be eliminated without unreasonable effort or expense, and (3) represents that the report will be filed no later than the 15th day after the due date for Form 10-K, or the fifth day after the due date for Form 10-D; and

- the late report is actually filed by the 15th or fifth day after the due date, as applicable.

3. Omission of unavailable information under Rule 12b-21

Exchange Act Rule 12b-21 provides a limited exemption for the omission of information that is not "known or reasonably available."[91] If any required information is unknown and not reasonably available to the registrant, either because obtaining it would involve unreasonable effort or expense, or because it rests peculiarly within the knowledge of a nonaffiliate, the rule permits omission of that information, so long as the registrant:

- provides all information on the subject that it possesses or can acquire without unreasonable effort or expense (including the source of the information); and

- shows that unreasonable effort or expense would be involved, or indicates the absence of any affiliation with

---

[83] 17 C.F.R. § 240.15d-22(b). *See* SEC, Form 15: Certification and Notice of Termination of Registration under Section 12(G) of the Securities Exchange Act of 1934 or Suspension of Duty to File Reports under Sections 13 and 15(D) of the Securities Exchange Act of 1934.

[84] Before the amendment of § 15(d) to exclude ABS, the suspension of filing obligations was automatic if an ABS issuer met the requirements of the statute. The SEC's rules required that Form 15 be filed, but it was not a condition to the suspension of reporting obligations.

[85] *See, e.g.*, Exchange Act §§ 21, 21C, 15 U.S.C. §§ 78u, 78u-3.

[86] SEC Form S-3: Registration Statement under the Securities Act

of 1933, at 3 (General Instruction I(A)(4): Registrant Requirements).

[87] Asset-Backed Securities, 70 Fed. Reg. 1506, 1526.

[88] *See* 206 SPS § III-D5, *Free writing prospectuses.*

[89] 17 C.F.R. § 240.12b-25.

[90] SEC, Form 12b-25: Notification of Late Filing.

[91] 17 C.F.R. § 240.12b-21.

the knowledgeable person and states the results of the request to that person for the information.

Comment: Similar to the application of Rule 409 in the context of registration statements,[92] SEC staff historically has viewed Rule 12b-21 as setting a very high bar, so it should not be relied upon lightly.

I. Repurchase Demand Reporting on Form ABS-15G

Exchange Act Rule 15Ga-1,[93] which was adopted by the SEC as required by § 943 of the Dodd-Frank Act, requires the filing of Form ABS-15G with respect to all Exchange Act ABS,[94] whether publicly or privately offered, for which the transaction documents provide a covenant to repurchase or replace underlying assets for breach of a representation or warranty (Reportable ABS). Each "securitizer,"[95] which generally includes sponsors and depositors, is required to file Form ABS-15G.[96] However, for transactions where the sponsor and depositor are affiliated, only the sponsor or the depositor (but not both) is required to file the form.

Each Form ABS-15G must include a tabular summary of all rejected, disputed, withdrawn, fulfilled and pending repurchase requests made during the applicable reporting period. The required disclosure is not to be limited to repurchase requests made by the securitization trustee or another party having a contractual right to request repurchase; repurchase requests made by investors also must be disclosed. Rule 15Ga-1 requires reporting with respect to all Reportable ABS transactions by securitizers in the U.S., including ABS sold outside the U.S.. Rule 15Ga-1 also covers offerings of Reportable ABS in the U.S. by foreign securitizers.

For each calendar quarter, each securitizer that issued Reportable ABS or organized a relevant Reportable ABS transaction by securitizing assets or had any outstanding Reportable ABS held by nonaffiliates must file Form ABS-15G to reflect any repurchase request activity for all of the securitizer's Reportable ABS, no matter when issued, during the reporting period. The securitizer may prospectively suspend its duty to file quarterly updates if no repurchase request activity occurred during the reporting period by checking a box on the Form. Unless and until the quarterly reporting obligation is reinstated by the receipt of a repurchase demand during a reporting period, the securitizer is only required to file on an annual basis, no later than 45 days after the end of each calendar year.

The requirements of Form ABS-15G are not limited to successful demands for repurchase, but also include disclosure of both pending and unfulfilled repurchase requests by the trustee, as well as repurchase requests made by a securityholder even if the trustee did not make a demand for repurchase. Form ABS-15G requires disclosure in a tabular format by asset class, listing the names of all of the relevant issuing entities of Reportable ABS by date of formation of the issuing entity. The table also must include an indication as to whether any Reportable ABS of the relevant issuing entity were registered under the Securities Act and requires the securitizer to detail the repurchase statistics for each originator of underlying assets, without regard to concentration.

For each originator and for each issuing entity, Form ABS-15G requires disclosure of the number, outstanding principal balance,[97] and percentage by principal balance,[98] for the applicable period, of:

- assets originated by each originator in the pool at the time of securitization for each issuing entity;
- assets that were the subject of a repurchase demand for breach of representations and warranties;
- assets that were actually repurchased or replaced;
- assets that are pending repurchase or replacement due to the expiration of a cure period;
- assets that are pending repurchase or replacement where the demand currently is in dispute;
- assets that were not repurchased or replaced because the demand was withdrawn; and
- assets that were not repurchased or replaced because the demand was rejected.

Each of these number and principal amount disclosures must be totaled by asset class.

Securitizers are permitted to omit information that is unknown or not reasonably available to the securitizer without unreasonable effort or expense if they include a statement describing why unreasonable effort or expense would be required.[99]

Exchange Act Rule 15Ga-1 and Form ABS-15G present a number of significant interpretive and practical difficulties for which the SEC staff has declined to provide additional guidance. Market practice regarding many of these issues is reflected in the American Securitization Forum's *Market Guide to Questions Regarding Implementation of SEC Rule 15Ga-1*,[100] a copy of which is included as Practice Tool 5.[101] For example, the rule does not provide definitions for each of the column headings, so market participants may construe the data fields differently, so long as the position taken is meaningful and consistent with the purposes of the rule.

---

[92] *See* 206 SPS § IV-A2, *Static pool information.*

[93] 17 C.F.R. § 240.15Ga-1.

[94] *See* 206 SPS § I-C, *Definition Under Regulation AB.*

[95] A "securitizer" is "(A) an issuer of an asset-backed security; or (B) a person who organizes and initiates an asset-backed securities transaction by selling or transferring assets, either directly or indirectly, including through an affiliate, to the issuer." Securities Act § 15G(a)(3), 15 U.S.C. § 78o-11(a)(3).

[96] SEC, Form ABS-15G: Asset-Backed Securitizer Report Pursuant to Section 15G of the Securities Exchange Act of 1934.

[97] "Outstanding principal balance" means the principal balance as of the reporting end date.

[98] "Percentage by principal balance" means the outstanding principal balance of the assets subject to the repurchase request divided by the outstanding principal balance of the asset pool as of the reporting period end date.

[99] This is a difficult standard to meet, as described in 206 SPS § VI-H3, *Omission of unavailable information under Rule 12b-21.*

[100] AM. SECURITIZATION FORUM, MARKET GUIDE TO QUESTIONS REGARDING IMPLEMENTATION OF SEC RULE 15GA-1 (2011).

[101] *See* 206 SPS Practice Tool 5, *ASF Market Guide to Questions Regarding Implementation of SEC Rule 15Ga.*

Market participants differ in their interpretations as to what constitutes reportable repurchase activity, with some viewing an asset subject to repurchase demand as having reportable activity every period until the demand is resolved, and others viewing an asset subject to repurchase demand as having reportable activity only when an event requires a change in the column in which it is reported. Also, many market participants are of the view that transactions with no reportable repurchase activity in a reporting period need not be included in the table.

J. Regulation FD and Selective Disclosure

"Selective disclosure" is the practice of disclosing material nonpublic information "such as advance warnings of earnings results, to securities analysts or selected institutional investors or both, before making full disclosure of the same information to the general public."[102] The SEC adopted Regulation FD to address perceived abuses in this area.[103] In the SEC's view, the recipient of selectively disclosed information profits at the expense of others, leading to a loss of investor confidence.[104] However, prior to Regulation FD, it was unclear whether this practice was illegal.[105]

Regulation FD applies only to issuers that are required to file periodic Exchange Act reports. Whenever such an issuer, or any person acting on its behalf, discloses any material nonpublic information regarding that issuer or its securities to certain identified persons, the issuer is required to make public disclosure of that information simultaneously (in the case of an intentional disclosure) and promptly (in the case of a non-intentional disclosure). Parties to whom disclosure triggers Regulation FD obligations include broker-dealers (and their associated persons), investment advisers (and their associated persons) investment companies (and their affiliated persons), and holders of the issuer's securities (if reasonably foreseeable that they will purchase or sell on the basis of the selectively disclosed information).

Regulation FD provides exemptions for disclosures made:

- to a person who owes a duty of trust or confidence to the issuer (such as an attorney, investment banker, or accountant);

- to a person who expressly agrees to maintain the disclosed information in confidence; and

- in connection with most securities offerings registered under the Securities Act, whether or not underwritten, for capital formation purposes for the account of the issuer, if the disclosure is by means of, among other things, a registration statement or prospectus, a free writing prospectus, or oral communications made after filing the registration statement.

A confidentiality agreement need not be in writing and need not prohibit trading on the basis of the selectively disclosed information in order to qualify for the confidentiality exemption.

Comment: Nevertheless, it is advisable for evidentiary purposes that any confidentiality agreement be in writing.

Regulation FD used to contain a specific exemption for disclosures made to credit rating agencies, but § 942(a) of the Dodd-Frank Act repealed that exemption. This has not resulted in significant practical difficulties, as rating agencies generally are not among the parties to whom selective disclosure triggers Regulation FD obligations.

The public disclosures required by Regulation FD may be made by filing a Form 8-K,[106] or by "another method . . . that is reasonably designed to provide broad, non-exclusionary distribution of the information to the public."[107] A broadly disseminated press release is one method that has long been recognized as being sufficient for purposes of Regulation AB.[108] The SEC more recently has indicated that a company's website posting may be sufficient if the website is a "recognized channel of distribution," the posting disseminates the information in a manner making it available to the market in general, and there has been a reasonable waiting period for investors and the market to react to the information. The determination of whether information has been sufficiently disseminated focuses on the manner of posting and whether it is timely and ready accessibility to investors and the markets.[109]

Comment: Because of the continued lack of certainty afforded by the SEC's standards for website postings, it remains preferable to use a Form 8-K or a press release to satisfy Regulation FD disclosure obligations.

---

[102] Selective Disclosure and Insider Trading, 65 Fed. Reg. 51,716 (Aug. 24, 2000), SEC Release No. 33-7881 (Aug. 21, 2000).

[103] 17 CFR §§ 243.100–03, 240.10b5-1, 240.10b5-2, 249.308.

[104] 65 Fed. Reg. at 51,716.

[105] 65 Fed. Reg. at 51,716 n.7. The same lack of clarity still applies to selective disclosure in contexts other than those regulated by Regulation FD, such as for privately placed securities that are not subject to Exchange Act reporting.

[106] *See* 206 SPS § VI-D15, *Regulation FD disclosure.*

[107] 17 C.F.R. § 243.101(c)(2).

[108] 65 Fed. Reg. at 51,723.

[109] Commission Guidance on the Use of Company Websites, 73 Fed. Reg. 45,862, 45,868 (Aug. 7, 2008), SEC Release No. 34-58288 (Aug. 1, 2008).

VII.

Rulemaking in Progress Regarding the Offering Process and Periodic Disclosure

A. Regulation AB II

1. *Regulation AB II, generally*

In 2010, the Securities and Exchange Commission (SEC) proposed a comprehensive set of amendments to Regulation AB and other rules affecting the offering process for asset-backed securities (ABS), commonly known as Regulation AB II.[1] If adopted as proposed, Regulation AB II would substantially change the offering, disclosure and reporting requirements for ABS. In explaining the genesis of its proposal, the SEC stated that "[t]he recent financial crisis highlighted that investors and other participants in the securitization market did not have the necessary tools to be able to fully understand the risk underlying those securities and did not value those securities properly or accurately."[2] According to the SEC, even "[i]n the private markets, . . . in many cases, investors did not have the information necessary to understand and properly analyze structured products . . . that were sold in transactions in reliance on exemptions from registration."[3] Therefore, the SEC for the first time proposed to heavily regulate offerings of ABS and other structured finance products made in reliance on the most commonly used exemptions from registration under the Securities Act, including Rule 144A.[4]

Regulation AB II would effectively create three distinct regulatory regimes for ABS offerings: stand-alone registration on Form SF-1, shelf registration on Form SF-3, and private offerings in reliance on Rule 144A or Rule 506(d).[5] A summary comparison of these regimes is provided as Practice Tool 6.[6]

In response to the subsequent enactment of the Dodd-Frank Wall Street Reform and Consumer Protection Act (Dodd-Frank Act) and extensive comments on its original proposal, the SEC re-proposed some aspects of Regulation AB II in 2012.[7] This section describes the significant changes to the ABS offering process that would be made by Regulation AB II, as re-proposed.

According to the SEC, it expects that once Regulation AB II is finally adopted, the transition period will extend for no more than a year.[8]

> **Comment:** The importance of Regulation AB II appears to have slipped somewhat in the SEC's regulatory agenda since the enactment of the Dodd-Frank Act, as the SEC still has not finished all of the rulemaking that is required under that law. Over three years after its initial proposal, the path to effectiveness of Regulation AB II is still unclear.

2. *Definition of asset-backed security under Regulation AB*

Regulation AB II would significantly limit the permitted exemptions from the "discrete pool" requirement of the definition of "asset-backed security" in Regulation AB, reflecting the SEC's belief that the current rules do not necessarily require that asset pools be sufficiently fixed at the time of an offering, "which may result in investors not receiving appropriate information about the securities being offered."[9] Currently, the maximum amount of prefunding is 50 percent of the offering proceeds (or the aggregate principal balance of the total asset pool whose cash flows support the ABS, in the case of a master trust).[10] This maximum amount would be reduced to 10 percent.[11]

The revised definition of "asset-backed security" would permit master trust structures to be used to securitize only assets arising out of revolving accounts.[12] Also, the maximum length of a revolving period in a securitization of non-revolving assets would be reduced from three years to one year.[13]

3. *New registration forms and shelf registration criteria*

a. *Forms SF-1 and SF-3*

In lieu of permitting the use of Forms S-1 and S-3 for registration of ABS,[14] the proposal would create two new forms tailored specifically for ABS offerings: Form SF-3, for shelf registration of ABS, and Form SF-1, for individual registrations by ABS issuers not eligible to use Form SF-3.[15]

b. *New shelf registration criteria, generally*

Currently, the transactional shelf offering criteria for ABS include a requirement that the securities will be rated investment grade by at least one nationally recognized statistical rating organization (NRSRO).[16] The new rules would eliminate this requirement for new Form SF-3 and replace it with the following new requirements:

- a certification filed at the time of each takedown by the chief executive officer of the depositor or executive officer in charge of securitization of the depositor, addressing the prospectus disclosure and the design of the securitization;

- transaction document provisions requiring that the trustee appoint a credit risk manager which would review assets when certain trigger events occur and man-

---

[1] Asset-Backed Securities, 75 Fed. Reg. 23,328 (May 3, 2010).

[2] 75 Fed. Reg. at 23,329.

[3] 75 Fed. Reg. at 23,330.

[4] 17 C.F.R. § 230.144A.

[5] 17 C.F.R. § 230.506(d).

[6] *See* 206 SPS Practice Tool 6, *Comparison of Regulatory Regimes under Proposed Regulation AB II.*

[7] Re-Proposal of Shelf Eligibility Conditions for Asset-Backed Securities, 76 Fed. Reg. 47,948 (Aug. 5, 2011).

[8] 76 Fed. Reg. 47,971.

[9] 75 Fed. Reg. 23,328, 23,389.

[10] *See* 206 SPS § I-C4, *"Discrete pool" requirement.*

[11] 75 Fed. Reg. at 23,390.

[12] *See* 75 Fed. Reg. at 23,389; 206 SPS § I-C4, *"Discrete pool" requirement.*

[13] *Id.*

[14] SEC, Form S-1: Registration Statement under the Securities Act of 1933; SEC, Form S-3: Registration Statement under the Securities Act of 1933. *See* 206 SPS § II-B1, *Shelf registration and Form S-3.*

[15] However, Form S-1 could still be used for offerings of ABS that do not meet the definition of "asset-backed security" in Regulation AB.

[16] *See* 206 SPS § II-B1, *Shelf registration and Form S-3.*

dating dispute resolution for failure to comply with requests to repurchase assets;

- transaction document provisions requiring the inclusion in distribution reports on Form 10-D of requests by investors to communicate with other investors;[17] and

- an annual evaluation of compliance with these requirements.[18]

c.   *Officer certification*

The required certification would be filed at the time of each takedown and would have to be signed by the depositor's chief executive officer or executive officer in charge of securitization. The certification would state that:

- the certifying officer has reviewed the prospectus and is familiar with the structure of the securitization, including the characteristics of the pool assets, internal credit enhancements, and the material terms of transaction documents and other arrangements;

- based on the officer's knowledge, the prospectus does not contain any untrue statement of a material fact or omit to state a material fact necessary to make the statements made, in light of the circumstances under which such statements were made, not misleading;

- based on the officer's knowledge, the prospectus and registration statement fairly present in all material respects the characteristics of the pool assets and the risks of ownership of the offered ABS, including all credit enhancements and risk factors that would affect whether cash flows from the pool assets are sufficient to service the offered ABS; and

- based on the officer's knowledge, taking into account the characteristics of the pool assets, the structure of the securitization (including internal credit enhancements) and any other material features of the transaction, the securitization is designed (but not guaranteed) to produce cash flows at times and in amounts sufficient to service expected payments on the offered ABS.[19]

Comment: It is not clear whether officers of depositors would be willing to sign a certification in the form in which it has been proposed, due to concerns that include the possibility of personal liability for expressing a view on the future performance of the pool assets and the lack of a definition of "fairly presents."

d.   *Credit risk manager and repurchase dispute resolution*

The transaction documents for the offered ABS would have to require the trustee to appoint a credit risk manager. The

role of the credit risk manager would be to review the pool assets when certain trigger events occur. The credit risk manager would be unaffiliated with the sponsor, depositor and servicer and would have access to copies of the underlying loan documents for the asset pool. The transaction documents would have to set defined events that would trigger the credit risk manager's review of the pool assets for compliance with representations and warranties. These trigger events would have to include when any credit enhancement requirements (such as required reserve amounts and target overcollateralization percentages) are not met and the direction of investors pursuant to processes agreed upon by the transaction parties and described in the transaction documents and the prospectus.[20]

The prospectus would be required to disclose the name of the credit risk manager, its form of organization, the extent of its experience and details about its compensation. Further disclosure would be required regarding the credit risk manager's duties, any limitations on its liability under the transaction documents, any indemnification provisions, any provisions regarding its removal or replacement, and how its expenses would be paid. The re-proposed rules also would require disclosure, if material, about any relationships between the credit risk manager and any other transaction parties.[21]

The credit risk manager would be required to report to the trustee on its findings and conclusions with regard to any review of the pool assets,[22] and the trustee could use the report to determine whether to make a repurchase request. If the credit risk manager is required to review assets during any distribution period, the Form 10-D for that period would have to disclose the event that triggered the review. If the credit risk manager provides a report to the trustee during a distribution period, the report would have to be filed as an exhibit to the Form 10-D for that period. Additional Form 10-D disclosures would be required regarding the date and circumstances of any resignation, removal or replacement of the credit risk manager, together with all of the disclosures described above with respect to any new credit risk manager.[23]

> **Comment:** In asset classes other than residential mortgage-backed securities, and in transactions without asset-level representations and warranties, many industry participants question the need to impose the cost and complexity of engaging an independent third party to police breaches of representations and warranties. Where the individual underlying assets are significantly larger (e.g., commercial mortgages) the assets generally are much more transparent, and where the assets are significantly smaller (e.g., automobile loans and credit cards), this approach may not be cost-effective.

As re-proposed, the rules also would require the transaction documents to include dispute resolution procedures. If an

---

[17] *See* SEC, Form 10-D: Asset-Backed Issuer Distribution Report Pursuant to Section 13 or 15(d) of the Securities Exchange Act of 1934.

[18] *See* 76 Fed. Reg. at 47,981 (Proposed Form SF-3, General Instruction I(B)(1): Transaction Requirements).

[19] *See* 76 Fed. Reg. at 47,977–78 (Proposed Item 601(b)(36) of Regulation S-K).

[20] *See* 76 Fed. Reg. at 47,981–82 (Proposed Form SF-3, General Instruction I(B)(1)(b)).

[21] *See* 76 Fed. Reg. at 47,978 (Proposed Item 1109(b) of Regulation AB).

[22] *See* 76 Fed. Reg. at 47,982 (Proposed Form SF-3, General Instruction I(B)(1)(b)(D)).

[23] *See* 76 Fed. Reg. at 47,984 (Proposed Item 1B of Form 10-D); 76 Fed. Reg. at 47,978 (Proposed Item 1121(f) of Regulation AB).

asset is subject to a repurchase request made pursuant to the terms of the transaction documents but is not repurchased within 180 days after notice is received of the repurchase request, the party submitting the repurchase request could refer the matter to either mediation or arbitration. The party with repurchase obligations would be required to agree to the dispute resolution mechanism selected by the party requesting the repurchase.[24]

e.   Investor communications

The transaction documents for the offered ABS would have to require the party responsible for making periodic filings on Form 10-D to include any request from an investor to communicate with other investors relating to their rights under the ABS that is received during the reporting period. The disclosure would include the name of the requesting investor, the date the request was received and a description of the method by which other investors may make contact. Investors could not use these mechanisms for purposes other than communicating with regard to rights under the registered ABS.[25]

An instruction to Form SF-3 would allow transaction parties to specify limited procedures for verifying the identities of beneficial owners making use of these mechanisms. If the investor is a record holder, the investor would not have to provide verification of ownership; if the investor is not a record holder, the transaction documents could require a written statement from the record holder that the investor beneficially held the ABS at the time of the request.[26]

f.   Registrant requirements and annual compliance check

Currently, the limited registrant requirements for shelf eligibility for ABS issuers are tested only at the time the registration statement is filed or amended.[27] As re-proposed,[28] these requirements would be significantly expanded, and would be tested annually.

To the extent that the depositor or any issuing entity previously established by the depositor or an affiliate of the depositor was required to comply with the transaction requirements of Form SF-3 during a 12-month look-back period with respect to an offering of ABS involving the same asset class, the depositor and each such issuing entity would be required to have timely filed all the required certifications and transaction documents containing the required provisions relating to the credit risk manager, repurchase request disputes and investor communications. In order to conduct a takedown, an ABS issuer would be required to conduct a periodic evaluation as to whether it was in compliance with these registrant requirements, as of a date 90 days after the end of the depositor's previous fiscal year. The depositor or issuing entity could cure

any deficiency by subsequently filing the missing information, and it would be deemed to again meet the registrant requirements after a 90-day waiting period.

In order to conduct a takedown, an ABS issuer also would be required to evaluate, as of a date 90 days after the end of the depositor's previous fiscal year, whether the depositor or any affiliated issuing entity that was required to file periodic Exchange Act reports during the previous 12 months had filed those reports, and filed them in a timely manner (other than reports required only by certain specified Form 8-K items).[29]

Comment: Many in the industry view this as a draconian standard. Because much of the information that is reportable by an ABS issuer comes from third parties, such as servicers, even an issuer's best efforts are sometimes insufficient to prevent late filings. As proposed, even a single late filing would result in the loss of shelf eligibility for an entire year.

g.   Signing the registration statement

Among the required signatories for an ABS registration statement is the controller or principal accounting officer of the depositor.[30] However, because "[a]sset-backed issuers are not required to file financial statements . . . and [their depositors] do not employ a principal accounting officer or controller," the SEC has concluded that "such signatures appear to serve no purpose . . . ."[31] The proposed rules would replace this required signature with that of the depositor's senior officer in charge of securitization.[32]

4.   Shelf registration mechanics

a.   Integrated prospectus, rather than base and supplement

Currently, the required disclosure in a shelf offering is accomplished primarily by means of a base prospectus that contemplates future takedowns, with specific information regarding the offered securities and the offering set forth in a final prospectus supplement that is filed at the time of the takedown.[33] According to the SEC, this practice "has resulted in unwieldy documents with excessive and inapplicable disclosure" that is "often overwhelming and is burdensome for investors to navigate."[34]

The proposed rules would instead require that the registrant file a single form of prospectus before a registration statement becomes effective, and file a single preliminary prospectus and a single final prospectus for each shelf takedown

---

[24] *See* 76 Fed. Reg. at 47,982 (Proposed Form SF-3, General Instruction I(B)(1)(b)(E)).

[25] *See* 76 Fed. Reg. at 47,984 (Proposed Item 1B of Form 10-D); 76 Fed. Reg. at 47,978–79 (Proposed Item 1121(g) of Regulation AB).

[26] *See* 76 Fed. Reg. at 47,982 (Proposed Form SF-3, General Instruction I(B)(1)(c)).

[27] *See* 206 SPS § II-B1, *Shelf registration and Form S-3.*

[28] *See* 76 Fed. Reg. at 47,981 (Proposed Form SF-3, General Instruction I(A): Registrant Requirements).

[29] *See* 76 Fed. Reg. at 47,981 (Proposed Form SF-3, General Instruction I(A)). *See also* SEC, Form 8-K: Current Report Pursuant to Section 13 or 15(d) of the Securities Exchange Act of 1934; 206 SPS § II-B1, *Shelf registration and Form S-3* (discussing the filings that are required to be made timely).

[30] *See* 206 SPS § II-D5, *Signing the registration statement.*

[31] 75 Fed. Reg. 23,328, 23,354.

[32] *See* 76 Fed. Reg. at 47,984 (Proposed Form SF-3, Signatures Instruction 1); 75 Fed. Reg. at 23,443 (Proposed Form SF-1, Signatures Instruction 1).

[33] This process is described further in 206 SPS § II-C1, *Base prospectus and prospectus supplements.*

[34] 75 Fed. Reg. at 23,352.

that includes all required disclosure in one integrated document.[35]

b. Single asset class, single depositor and "pay as you go" fees

Shelf issuers would no longer be permitted to include multiple base prospectuses to register offerings of different asset classes in a single registration statement. Multiple depositors sharing a single registration statement would also no longer be permitted.[36] Each separate asset class would require a separate registration statement filed by a single depositor.[37]

Comment: Currently, the main reason for including multiple asset classes within a single shelf registration statement is to permit ABS offerings backed by multiple types of assets to draw from the same pool of registered securities for which the filing fee has been paid, known colloquially as the "shelf capacity." This reduces the risk that registered (and paid for) shelf capacity ends up unused if conditions become unfavorable for offerings of a particular type of ABS.

"To alleviate some of the burden of managing multiple registration statements" for different asset classes,[38] the SEC has proposed allowing ABS shelf issuers to pay filing fees at the time of each offering, rather than paying in advance at the time the registration statement becomes effective as is currently required. The fee would be paid at the time that the preliminary prospectus is filed, at the then-current fee rate.[39]

c. Required preliminary prospectus and waiting period before sale

Currently, the use of a preliminary prospectus is not required in shelf offerings of ABS.[40] The proposed rules would require a preliminary prospectus that contains all required disclosure other than pricing-related information to be filed with the SEC at least five business days before the first contract of sale is entered into with an investor (or, if used earlier, by the second business day after first use).[41] While this is not entirely clear, the SEC presumably intends that the filing must be made on the earlier of the date that is five business days before the first sale or two business days after first use.[42] A free writing prospectus could not be used to satisfy this obligation.

Any material change in the information contained in the preliminary prospectus would require a new preliminary prospectus to be filed and, after that, another five business days to elapse before the first contract of sale.[43]

The exemption of most ABS shelf offerings of ABS from the requirement that a preliminary prospectus be delivered at least 48 hours before sending a confirmation of sale[44] would be repealed.[45]

Comment: Currently, changes to transaction structures are made—often in response to investor comments and concerns—all the way through the offering process. If adopted as proposed, these provisions would require structures to be finalized significantly earlier than they generally are today.

d. Timing for filing final transaction documents

As noted above, final transaction documents traditionally have been filed under cover of Form 8-K no later than 15 days after the closing date, though the SEC staff more recently has required the depositor to commit to file them by the time of the takedown.[46] As proposed to be revised, Regulation AB would explicitly require the material transaction documents to be filed as exhibits to the registration statement, in substantially final form, no later than the date on which the preliminary prospectus is required to be filed.[47] If the proposed preliminary prospectus filing requirements are adopted, this deadline would be five business days before pricing. The rules then would require that final transaction documents be filed no later than the date the final prospectus is required to be filed. Only if the documents remain unchanged from the "substantially final" filing could the requirement of a new filing be avoided.[48]

Comment: For the same reasons as discussed above with regard to the preliminary prospectus proposals, a change of this magnitude in the timing of the required filing of transaction documents would require that structures be finalized much sooner than often occurs today.

5. Disclosure requirements in public offerings of ABS

a. Asset-level disclosure

One of the most significant changes that would be wrought by the Regulation AB II proposals would be to require, for the first time, detailed asset-level disclosures regarding the asset

---

[35] *See* 75 Fed. Reg. at 23,437 (Proposed Rule 430D of Regulation C).

[36] *See* 206 SPS § II-C1, *Base prospectus and prospectus supplements.*

[37] *See* 76 Fed. Reg. at 47,981 (Proposed Form SF-3, General Instruction IV); *see also* 75 Fed. Reg. at 23,352.

[38] 75 Fed. Reg. at 23,353–54.

[39] *See* 75 Fed. Reg. at 23,438–39 (Proposed Rule 456(c)(1) of Regulation C); 75 Fed. Reg. at 23,439 (Proposed Rule 457(s) of Regulation C).

[40] *See* 206 SPS § III-D3, *The preliminary prospectus.*

[41] A preliminary prospectus could omit information with respect to the offering price, underwriting discounts or commissions, discounts or commissions to dealers, amount of proceeds, or other matters dependent upon the offering price.

[42] *See* 75 Fed. Reg. at 23,439 (Proposed Rule 424(h) of Regulation C); 75 Fed. Reg. at 23,437 (Proposed Rule 430D(a)(1) of Regulation

C).

[43] *See* 75 Fed. Reg. at 23,437 (Proposed Rule 430D(a)(2) of Regulation C).

[44] *See* 206 SPS § III-D3, *The preliminary prospectus.*

[45] *See* 75 Fed. Reg. at 23,450 (proposed amendment to Exchange Act Rule 15c2-8(b)).

[46] *See* 206 SPS § II-C2, *Takedowns.*

[47] *See* 76 Fed. Reg. at 47,978 (proposed amendment to Item 1100(f) of Regulation AB).

[48] 76 Fed. Reg. at 47,964. The final filed transaction documents could still omit prices, signatures and similar matters. Any change to a transaction document would have to be minor to avoid the need to re-file it. 76 Fed. Reg. at 47,964 n.120.

pool.[49] These new disclosures, which would be required both at the time of the initial offering and on an ongoing basis, are intended to provide more information about the borrower's ability to pay, as the characteristics of the receivable and the characteristics of any collateral.

New Schedule L would specify general data requirements for most asset classes. Among the general data requirements would be a unique identifying number, an indication as to whether the asset was originated under an exception to applicable underwriting criteria, the identity of the servicer and any servicing advance methodology. Schedule L also would impose tailored data requirements for residential mortgage loans, commercial mortgage loans, auto loans, auto leases, equipment loans, equipment leases, student loans, floor plan financings, corporate debt and resecuritizations. If Schedule L does not prescribe specific data points for an asset type, the issuer would need to meet the general data requirements.

For an offering of residential mortgage-backed securities, for example, the required asset-level data points would include: for a refinancing, the amount of cash received by the borrower; for a senior mortgage, the amount of any junior loan; for a junior mortgage, information on the senior loan; the borrower's credit score and income; and the amount of the borrower's monthly non-mortgage debt. The required data points for commercial loans would include: detailed information regarding the mortgaged property and its revenues, operating expenses, net operating income and net cash flow; when a defeasance option is available; and the identity of the three largest tenants and their lease expiration dates. For auto and equipment leases, the residual value of the leased property would be required. For floorplan financing ABS issued by a master trust, detailed performance information would be required for assets that were part of the asset pool prior to the offering.

In an effort to address privacy concerns, some data would be provided only in the form of codes, categories or ranges. Information regarding the debtor's credit score, debt and income would be shown in ranges, for example, while geographic location information would be provided only by Metropolitan or Micropolitan Statistical Area.

According to the SEC, "some [credit card and charge card ABS asset pools] may contain as many as 20 to 45 million accounts," an "overwhelming volume of data." For that reason, the SEC concluded that "granular asset-level information would be as useful for investors and the provision of asset-level data may be cost-prohibitive for issuers."[50] The SEC instead proposed to require that grouped account data be filed for these asset classes, as set forth in a new Schedule CC.[51] "[G]rouped account data would be created by compressing the underlying asset-level data into combinations of standardized distribu-

tional groups using asset-level characteristics and providing specified data about these groups."[52]

Issuers of utility stranded cost ABS would be exempt from the asset-level and grouped account data requirements.[53]

In a resecuritization, all of the required asset-level data for the pool assets collateralizing the underlying ABS would have to be disclosed, just as if it were primary securitization of those assets.[54] There is no de minimis test, so all of this information would be required no matter how many ABS are in the asset pool or how small the concentration of a particular class of ABS is in that pool.

Asset-level data in a Form S-1 filing or preliminary prospectus would be as of a "measurement date" pegged to a recent practicable date. The final prospectus would provide asset-level data as of the cut-off date. Grouped account data would be provided only as of the applicable measurement date.[55] Updated delinquency information would be required to address activity between the measurement date and the cut-off date.[56]

Comment: Because many of the proposed asset-level data fields are not currently captured by originators during the underwriting process or by servicers after origination, many originators and servicers would need to update their origination and servicing platforms and guidelines. Both originators and servicers also may need to review the additional required data to ensure that any required disclosure or use of that information does not violate privacy laws.

All required asset-level or grouped account data would have to be filed in Extensible Mark-Up Language, or XML.[57] This would permit prospective investors to download the data and analyze and manipulate it using their own models.

b. Static pool information

The SEC has proposed a variety of changes to the existing static pool information requirements.[58] Because of perceived inconsistencies among ABS issuers in disclosure of static pool information, the proposed changes are "designed to increase clarity, transparency and comparability."[59] The proposed changes include the following disclosures:

- a narrative description of the static pool information presented, the methodology used in the calculations, a description of terms or abbreviations used and a descrip-

---

[49] *See* 75 Fed. Reg. at 23,422 (Proposed Item 1111(h) of Regulation AB); 75 Fed. Reg. at 23,422–28 (Proposed Item 1111A (Schedule L) of Regulation AB); 75 Fed. Reg. at 23,447 (Item 8(a) of the first proposed Form SF-3).

[50] 75 Fed. Reg. at 23,360.

[51] *See* 75 Fed. Reg. at 23,422 (Proposed Item 1111(h) of Regulation AB); 75 Fed. Reg. at 23,428–29 (Proposed Item 1111B (Schedule CC) of Regulation AB); 75 Fed. Reg. at 23,447 (Item 8(a) of the first proposed Form SF-3).

[52] 75 Fed. Reg. at 23,372.

[53] *See* 75 Fed. Reg. at 23,422 (Proposed Item 1111(h) of Regulation AB).

[54] *See* 75 Fed. Reg. at 23,428 (Item 11(b) of proposed Item 1111A of Regulation AB).

[55] The required data would be filed on Form 8-K and incorporated by reference into the prospectus. *See* 75 Fed. Reg. at 23,422 (Proposed Items 1111(h) and 1111(i) of Regulation AB); 75 Fed. Reg. at 23,451 (Item 6.06(a) of proposed Form 8-K).

[56] *See* 75 Fed. Reg. at 23,423 (Item 1(b) of proposed Item 1111A of Regulation AB).

[57] *See* 75 Fed. Reg. at 23,439 (proposed amendment to Rule 11 of Regulation S-T).

[58] *See* 206 SPS § IV-A2, *Static pool information.*

[59] 75 Fed. Reg. at 23,384.

tion of how the static pool assets differ from the assets included in the securitized pool;

- if an issuer has not provided static pool information or has provided alternative disclosure, an explanation of why it has done so;

- for amortizing pools, a calculation of delinquencies and losses in accordance with a specified standard; and

- also for amortizing pools, a graphic presentation of delinquency, loss and prepayment data.[60]

Proposed changes to Item 312 of Regulation S-T would remove the references to the former temporary accommodation permitting the use of Internet websites to provide static pool information, and would codify an accommodation permitting static pool data to be filed in .pdf format.[61]

c. Servicers

While material instances of noncompliance with the servicing criteria that are identified by each party participating in the servicing function (PPSF) in its platform level of assessment must be disclosed in the text of the Form 10-K,[62] the platform-level nature of the assessment means that the relevance of these instances to the particular issuer or its ABS may be unclear. The proposed revisions to Item 1122 of Regulation AB would address this concern by requiring disclosure of whether identified instances of noncompliance involved the servicing of the pool assets for the transaction in question. The revisions also would codify the requirement to disclose information regarding any steps taken to remedy a material instance of noncompliance, and codify the SEC staff's existing interpretive guidance,[63] which permits a servicer to narrow the scope of its assessed platform to take into account "divisions among transactions that are consistent with actual practices."[64]

d. Originators

If the cumulative amount of assets originated by parties other than the sponsor represents 10 percent or more of the asset pool, every originator would be required to be identified in the prospectus,[65] even if it falls below the 10-percent threshold currently required for disclosure.[66]

e. Pool assets

In addition to the proposed asset-level disclosure requirements, Regulation AB II would expand the scope of the required disclosure regarding the pool assets as a whole. Among other things, the following additional disclosures would be required:

- specific data regarding the amount and characteristics of pool assets that were originated under exceptions to credit underwriting standards;

- if compensating factors regarding pool assets underwritten as exceptions to credit underwriting standards are disclosed, a description of those compensating factors and disclosure of the amount of assets in the pool not meeting those compensating factors;

- steps taken by originators to verify information used in credit underwriting of pool assets;

- a description of the transaction document provisions governing modification of the terms of pool assets; and

- whether or not a representation and warranty as to fraud is provided.[67]

The Commission also reiterated its view that because "existing Item 1111 calls for statistical information in the prospectus regarding an originator's 'risk-layering practices' that demonstrates the manner and extent to which multiple non-traditional features of a loan are bundled into one instrument, issuers should already be providing this disclosure," including risks related to the geographic location of the property.[68]

f. Other proposed disclosure requirements

Regulation AB II includes several other proposed disclosure requirements, some of which have been (or are likely to be) overtaken by subsequent developments.

The SEC proposed to require the creation and filing of a computer program of the flow of funds known as the "cash flow waterfall" using the Python programming language.[69] In the Regulation AB II Re-Proposing Release, the SEC noted that it had received many negative comments on its waterfall computer program proposal, so it intends to revise and re-propose this requirement.[70]

The SEC proposed to require disclosure, for the sponsor and each originator that originated 20 percent or more of the pool assets, of the amount (if material), on a pool-by-pool basis, of publicly securitized assets originated or securitized by that party that were the subject of a demand to repurchase or replace over the preceding three years, together with the percentage of that amount not then repurchased or replaced.[71] Substantially similar prospectus disclosure is already required if the transaction documents for the securitization contain a covenant to repurchase or replace an underlying asset for breach of a representation or warranty, pursuant to Exchange Act Rule 15Ga-

---

[60] See 75 Fed. Reg. at 23,421 (proposed amendments to Item 1105 of Regulation AB).

[61] See 75 Fed. Reg. at 23,440 (proposed amendments to Item 312 of Regulation S-T).

[62] SEC, Form 10-K: Annual Report Pursuant to Section 13 or 15(d) of the Securities Exchange Act of 1934; see 206 SPS § VI-E2, Compliance with applicable servicing criteria.

[63] See 206 SPS § VI-E2, Compliance with applicable servicing criteria.

[64] See 75 Fed. Reg. at 23,435 (proposed amendments to Item 1122 of Regulation AB).

[65] See 75 Fed. Reg. at 23,421 (proposed amendments to Item 1110(a) of Regulation AB).

[66] See 206 SPS § IV-A8, Significant obligors.

[67] See 75 Fed. Reg. at 23,421–22 (proposed amendments to Item 1111 of Regulation AB).

[68] See 75 Fed. Reg. at 23,377.

[69] See 75 Fed. Reg. at 23,429 (Proposed Item 1113(h)(5) of Regulation AB).

[70] 76 Fed. Reg. at 47,971.

[71] See 75 Fed. Reg. at 23,420–21 (Proposed Items 1104(f) and 1110(c) of Regulation AB).

1.[72] Information regarding the financial condition of the sponsor or any 20-percent originator also would be required if there is a material risk that the party's financial condition could materially affect its ability to repurchase defective assets or, in the case of an originator, its origination of pool assets.[73]

The SEC originally proposed a shelf eligibility criterion for credit risk retention, which was abandoned in the re-proposal[74] as a result of the Dodd-Frank Act provision requiring the adoption of rules to require credit risk retention for all "asset-backed securities," as defined by the Dodd-Frank Act (Exchange Act ABS).[75] As a corollary of the originally proposed shelf eligibility requirement for credit risk retention, the SEC also proposed to require disclosure of the nature and amount of the risk retained by the sponsor or its affiliate (or, in a stand-alone registration on Form SF-1, that no credit risk retention was required). This proposal may be superseded by more specific disclosure requirements adopted in the final credit risk retention rules. The Regulation AB II proposals also would mandate disclosure of any interest retained in the transaction by the sponsor, servicer, or 20-percent originator.[76]

6. Disclosure requirements in exempt transactions

a. Generally

Regulation AB II would substantially revise the rules of the road for most unregistered private offerings of ABS by applying the same disclosure requirements as for registered offerings to offerings made under Rule 144A,[77] the most active private ABS market, as well as to offerings made in reliance on Rule 506 of Regulation D under the Securities Act.[78] These dramatically expanded disclosure requirements would apply not only to ABS and Exchange Act ABS, but to an even broader category of "structured finance products."

The new disclosure requirements would not apply to private sales of ABS made in reliance on the statutory exemption provided by § 4(a)(2) of the Securities Act,[79] or the so-called "§ 4 (1½)" private resale exemption.[80] Unfortunately, the applicability of these facts-and-circumstances exemptions is much less certain than the regulatory exemptions; they require much stricter restrictions on transfer of the offered securities, and the offered securities cannot be in book-entry format.

b. What is a "structured finance product"?

"Structured finance product" would be defined very broadly "in order to reflect the wide range of securitization products that are sold in the private markets,"[81] and would include:

- a synthetic asset-backed security; or

- a fixed-income or other security collateralized by any pool of self-liquidating financial assets, such as loans, leases, mortgages, and secured or unsecured receivables, which entitles the security holders to receive payments that depend on the cash flow from the assets, including:

- an asset-backed security as defined in Regulation AB;

- a collateralized mortgage obligation;

- a collateralized debt obligation (CDO), including a CDO of ABS;

- a collateralized bond obligation; or

- a security that at the time of the offering is "commonly known as" ABS or a structured finance product.[82]

It is not clear whether covered bonds would be a "structured finance product," as they were not mentioned by the SEC, though the SEC did state its view that asset-backed commercial paper (ABCP) would be covered.[83]

c. Information requirements in Rule 144A and Rule 506 offerings and Rule 144 resales

As described above, a holder or prospective purchaser of Rule 144A securities must have the right to obtain certain specified financial and other basic information regarding the securities and the underlying assets.[84] If all purchasers of securities in a Rule 506 offering are accredited investors, there are no specific disclosure requirements.[85] According to the SEC, purchasers in these types of transactions "may receive only a minimal amount of information regarding the securities."[86]

As proposed by the SEC, for an offering of a structured finance product to rely on the Rule 144A safe harbor for its exemption from registration under the Securities Act, the transaction documents would have to grant to security holders and prospective purchasers of securities the right to obtain from the issuer, upon request, the same information that would be required to be provided in an offering registered on Form SF-1 or Form S-1, together with the ongoing information that an issuer would be required to provide in filed periodic reports under the

---

[72] See 206 SPS § VI-I, *Repurchase Demand Reporting on Form ABS-15G.*

[73] See 75 Fed. Reg. at 23,429 (proposed amendments to Item 1112 of Regulation AB).

[74] 76 Fed. Reg. at 47,950.

[75] These rules, which are not yet effective, have been proposed and then re-proposed. Credit Risk Retention, 78 Fed. Reg. 57,928 (Sept. 20, 2013); Credit Risk Retention, 76 Fed. Reg. 24,090 (Apr. 29, 2011).

[76] See 75 Fed. Reg. at 23,442 (Item 6 of proposed Form SF-1); 75 Fed. Reg. at 23,447 (Item 6 of proposed Form SF-3); 75 Fed. Reg. at 23,420–21 (Proposed Item 1104(e) of Regulation AB); 75 Fed. Reg. at 23,421 (Proposed Items 1108(e) and 1110(b)(3) of Regulation AB).

[77] See 206 SPS § V-B3, *Rule 144A*; 17 C.F.R. § 230.144A.

[78] See 206 SPS § V-B2, *Regulation D.*

[79] See 206 SPS § V-B1, *Section 4(a)(2).*

[80] See 205 SPS § V-B4, *Private resales and "§ 4(1½)".*

[81] 75 Fed. Reg. at 23,395.

[82] See 75 Fed. Reg. at 23,435–36 (Proposed Securities Act Rule 144A(a)(8)); 75 Fed. Reg. at 23,439 (Proposed Securities Act Rule 501(i)).

[83] 75 Fed. Reg. at 23,395 n.467. Some offerings of ABCP rely on Rule 144A, but many other offerings rely on a statutory exemption from registration.

[84] See 206 SPS § V-B3, *Rule 144A.*

[85] See 206 SPS § V-B2, *Regulation D.*

[86] 75 Fed. Reg. at 23,395.

Exchange Act.[87] The issuer would have to covenant to provide the same set of initial information in connection with a sale of structured finance products under Rule 506,[88] though the ongoing information would not be required. In addition, the transaction documents for securities being resold in reliance on Rule 144[89] would have to contain a covenant by the issuer to provide the same initial and ongoing information as in a Rule 144A offering, but only in the case of a resale by an affiliate of the issuer or a resale by a non-affiliate within the first year after the initial sale by the issuer.[90]

For a structured finance product that qualifies as an "asset-backed security" under Regulation AB and would be registrable on Form SF-1, and for which there would be prescribed asset-level data points, the information that would be required to be disclosed is relatively clear. For other types of structured finance products that may only be registered on Form S-1, one would expect the required disclosures to be negotiated with the SEC staff during its review of the registration statement, so it is not clear exactly what disclosures would be required in a private offering relying on Securites Act Rules 144A or 506. Initially, the SEC gave little guidance on this point, other than stating:

> For a managed CDO offering, we would expect disclosure regarding the asset and collateral managers, including fees and related party transaction information, their objectives and strategies, any interest that they have retained in the transaction or underlying assets, and substitution, reinvestment and management parameters. For a synthetic CDO offering, we would expect, among other things, disclosure of the differences between the spreads on synthetic assets and the market prices for the assets, the process for obtaining the credit default swap or other synthetic assets, and the internal rate of return to equity if that was a consideration in the structuring of the transaction.[91]

Many commenters expressed concerns about the scope of information that would be required for structured finance products that are not typically offered in registered offerings under Regulation AB. Recognizing these concerns, in the re-proposal the SEC requested comment on whether the rules should require asset-level data disclosure only where a privately offered structured finance product is backed by an asset class for which there are prescribed asset-level data requirements in Regulation AB.[92]

> **Comment:** Historically, one of the primary reasons to undertake a private offering, rather than a registered public offering, has been the increased flexibility regarding disclosure. Broad federal regulation of the required disclosure in exempt private offerings of ABS made to the most

sophisticated institutional investors would represent a historic shift in the way securities offerings have been regulated. Many industry participants believe that there remains an important role for negotiated transactions in which securities are purchased by institutional investors that have the resources and experience to fend for themselves.

d. Form 144A-SF and Form D

In Rule 144A offerings of structured finance products, the issuer would be required to file a public notice with the SEC on new Form 144A-SF. Among other thing, in the notice the issuer would identify the principal transaction parties, describe the type of securities being offered and their structure, briefly describe the asset pool, state the date of the initial sale and resale, state the amount of securities offered or sold in the initial offering, and undertake to provide a copy of the offering materials to the SEC upon request. The filing deadline for the notice would be 15 days after the initial sale of securities. Failure to file the notice would not jeopardize the 144A safe harbor for the offering in question, but future offerings of structured finance products by the issuer or its affiliates would be ineligible for Rule 144A until filing of the delinquent notice.[93]

Form D, an existing notice that is required to be filed in any offering under Rule 506 or any other exemption under Regulation D, would be amended to capture substantially the same information as Form 144A-SF.[94]

e. Enforcement

Proposed Securities Act Rule 192 would mandate that the issuer comply with any required covenants to provide information included in its transaction documents and would specify that a failure to comply "would constitute an engagement in a transaction, practice, or course of business which operates or would operate as a fraud or deceit upon the purchaser of the securities."[95] This rule would allow the SEC to bring an enforcement action for a compliance failure.

B. Disclosure of Findings and Conclusions of Third-Party Diligence Reports

1. Required disclosure by issuers and underwriters

Section 932 of the Dodd-Frank Act added Section 15E(s)(4)(A) to the Exchange Act.[96] This provision requires an issuer or underwriter of Exchange Act ABS to make publicly available the findings and conclusions of any third-party due diligence report obtained by the issuer or underwriter. The SEC has proposed rules to implement this requirement.[97]

---

[87] See 75 Fed. Reg. at 23,436 (Proposed Securities Act Rule 144A(d)(4)(iii)).

[88] See 75 Fed. Reg. at 23,439 (proposed amendments to Rule 502(b) of Regulation D).

[89] See 206 SPS § V-C, Resales Under Rule 144; 17 C.F.R. § 230.144.

[90] See 75 Fed. Reg. at 23,435 (Proposed Securities Act Rule 144(c)(ii)).

[91] 75 Fed. Reg. at 23,396.

[92] 76 Fed. Reg. at 47,971.

[93] See 75 Fed. Reg. at 23,436 (Proposed Securities Act Rule 144A(f)); 75 Fed. Reg. at 23,449 (Proposed Form 144A-SF).

[94] See 75 Fed. Reg. at 23,449–50 (proposed amendments to Form D).

[95] See 75 Fed. Reg. at 23,436 (Proposed Securities Act Rule 192).

[96] 15 U.S.C. § 78o-7(s)(4)(A).

[97] Proposed Rules for Nationally Recognized Statistical Rating Organizations, 76 Fed. Reg. 33,420 (June 8, 2011). The SEC originally

Proposed Rule 15Ga-2 would implement this provision by generally requiring an issuer,[98] or underwriter,[99] of Exchange Act ABS that is to be rated by a nationally recognized statistical ratings organization (NRSRO) to furnish[100] a Form ABS-15G,[101] which as amended by these rules would have a new section requiring disclosure of the findings and conclusions of any third-party due diligence report obtained by the issuer or underwriter. The form would have to be furnished to the SEC via EDGAR five business days before the first sale in the offering.

The issuer or underwriter would not need to furnish Form ABS-15G for this purpose if it obtains a representation from each NRSRO engaged to produce a credit rating for the Exchange Act ABS that the NRSRO will publicly disclose the findings and conclusions of any third-party due diligence report together with the publication of its credit rating at least five business days before the first sale in the offering. If the NRSRO fails to timely comply with its representation, the issuer or underwriter would be required to furnish the required information on Form ABS-15G no later than two business days before the first sale in the offering.

The SEC acknowledged that "public disclosure of information relating to an unregistered offering could raise concerns regarding an issuer's or underwriter's reliance on the private offering exemptions and safe harbors under" the Securities Act of 1933, but went on to state the SEC's view that the required information can be disclosed—

> without jeopardizing reliance on those exemptions and safe harbors, provided that the only information made publicly available is that which is required by the proposed rule, and the issuer does not otherwise use Form ABS-15G

---

had proposed third-party diligence rules together with the Dodd-Frank Act rules regarding issuer review of assets. 206 SPS § IV-A7, *Pool assets, including disclosures regarding the issuer's review of the pool assets*. However, in adopting the final issuer review rules, the SEC deferred consideration of the third-party diligence report disclosure rules.

[98] For these purposes, the term "issuer" means the sponsor of the transaction as well as the depositor. 76 Fed. Reg. at 33,468 n.42.

[99] The term "underwriter" generally is not used in connection with private offerings, but in its earlier proposal the SEC indicated that "underwriter" refers to parties that perform functions in private offerings of Exchange Act ABS that are similar those performed by underwriters in public offerings of Exchange Act ABS, such as initial purchasers and placement agents. Issuer Review of Assets in Offerings of Asset-Backed Securities, 75 Fed. Reg. 64,182, 64,188 n.53 (Oct. 19, 2010). Presumably, the term "underwriter" should continue to be interpreted in the same manner.

[100] Information that is "furnished" rather than "filed" is not subject to the liability provisions of § 18 of the Exchange Act. However, this is of little practical moment, as § 18 is used only infrequently as a basis for securities fraud claims due to the difficulty of proving all of its elements and the various procedural obstacles. Information that is "furnished" remains subject to Rule 10b-5 under the Exchange Act, which is much more commonly used as a basis for securities fraud claims.

[101] Form ABS-15G has already been adopted for purposes of disclosures regarding fulfilled and unfulfilled repurchase requests for alleged breaches of representations and warranties. *See* 206 SPS § VI-I, *Repurchase Demand Reporting on Form ABS-15G*.

to offer or sell securities or in a manner that conditions the market for offers or sales of its securities.[102]

Comment: This concern may be of somewhat less moment to ABS issuers, since general solicitation is no longer a disqualifying factor in a Rule 144A offering.[103]

In connection with its earlier proposal of Rule 15Ga-2, the SEC had noted that § 15E(s)(4)(A) of the Exchange Act does not specify how it is to apply to offshore transactions, but Rule 15Ga-2 would require issuers and underwriters to disclose information about Exchange Act ABS sold in unregistered transactions outside the U.S. The SEC also wondered if Rule 15Ga-2 might "result in foreign issuers seeking to avoid the . . . requirement [to file Form ABS-15G] by excluding U.S. investors from purchasing portions of ABS primarily offered outside the United States . . . ," implying that the rule would apply to private offerings of Exchange Act ABS in the U.S. by foreign issuers.[104] The SEC did not address these matters again, so its views on these issues appear to remain unchanged.

2. What is a "third-party diligence report"?

A "due diligence report" would be any report containing findings and conclusions relating to specified "due diligence services."[105] The SEC intends for "due diligence services" to cover only services typically provided by third-party due diligence service providers in the securitization market, not every entity that might perform type of diligence function in the offering process. The SEC intends for the definition of "due diligence report" to cover only reports from specialized due diligence services providers that are relevant to the determination of a credit rating of Exchange Act ABS,[106] and "believes that the third-party due diligence reports referenced in Section 15E(s)(4) of the Exchange Act are not the same as the review required by . . . Rule 193" by the issuer with regard to the pool assets.[107] However, the SEC also states that an issuer might engage a third party to assist it in its required review of the assets under Securities Act Rule 193 and states in the Proposing Release that the issuer might obtain a third-party due diligence report from that third party.[108]

Comment: As proposed, the dividing line between a Rule 193 issuer review and a due diligence report under proposed Rule 15Ga-2 is quite unclear.

Proposed Exchange Act Rule 17g-10 would define "due diligence services" as a review of the assets underlying Ex-

---

[102] 75 Fed. Reg. at 64,188.

[103] *See* 206 SPS § V-B3, *Rule 144A*. General solicitation would still be an issuer in "true" private placements under § 4(a)(2) of the Securities Act. 15 U.S.C. § 77d(a)(2). *See* 206 SPS § V-B1, *Section 4(a)(2)*.

[104] 75 Fed. Reg. at 64,189.

[105] *See* 76 Fed. Reg. at 33,538 (Proposed Exchange Act Rule 15Ga-2(c)).

[106] 76 Fed. Reg. at 33,472.

[107] 76 Fed. Reg. at 33,468; *see* 206 SPS § IV-A7, *Pool assets, including disclosures regarding the issuer's review of the pool assets* (discussing the Securities Act Rule 193 issuer review requirements).

[108] 76 Fed. Reg. at 33,468; *see* 206 SPS § IV-A7, *Pool assets, including disclosures regarding the issuer's review of the pool assets*.

change Act ABS for the purpose of making findings with respect to four specific categories of due diligence services, as well as a "catchall" for services that may in the future be provided for other asset classes but that do not fall within one of the enumerated categories. In order to understand how the SEC derived those proposed categories, it is important to note that the SEC derived them from its perception of current practices in the marketplace and that the SEC believes that "providers of third-party due diligence services most commonly are hired by issuers and underwriters to perform reviews of pools of mortgages that will be securitized into [residential mortgage-backed securities]."[109]

> **Comment:** Many industry participants question the appropriateness of basing rules that apply to the entire ABS market on practices that were developed for residential mortgages.

The first category of due diligence services enumerated by proposed Rule 17g-10 is a review of the underlying assets for the purpose of making findings with respect to the quality or integrity of the information or data about the assets provided by the securitizer or originator. The SEC notes that this could include a comparison of the loan tape data with hard copy documentation in an underlying sampled loan file, or verification that the loan tape contains all the information about the assets required by an NRSRO for its rating process.[110]

> **Comment:** This category is a good example of the difficulty that would be involved in determining whether a particular report would constitute a due diligence report subject to proposed Exchange Act Rule 15Ga-2. For example, an accountant's agreed-upon procedures letter might fall within its scope, but such a letter generally is obtained by an underwriter for purposes of its own due diligence to protect against liability under § 11 and § 12(a)(2) of the Securities Act and Rule 10b-5 under the Exchange Act. Such a letter is not provided by a specialized due diligence services provider, and ordinarily is not required by or relevant to any NRSRO rating the securities.

The second category of due diligence services enumerated by proposed Exchange Act Rule 17g-10 is a review of the underlying assets for the purpose of determining whether the origination of the assets conformed to stated underwriting or credit standards. According to the SEC, this could entail reviewing whether a sampled loan meets the originator's underwriting guidelines or, if not, that the originator provided a reasonable and documented exception. This type of review also could encompass an examination of how the originator verified information in a sampled loan—such as, for residential mortgage-backed securities (RMBS), the borrower's occupancy status, income, assets, or employment status.[111]

The third category of due diligence services enumerated by proposed Rule 17g-10 is a review of the underlying assets for the purpose of making findings with respect to the value of collateral securing those assets. The SEC notes that this could entail analyzing how the originator verified the value of the asset—for example, for RMBS, an NRSRO might require that the review consider the quality of the appraiser of the property and the quality of the appraisal. It could include reviewing whether the appraiser used a valuation model, as well as the performance of a separate valuation by the provider if it believes that the original appraised value of the property is less than the value presented by the originator.[112]

The fourth category of due diligence services enumerated under proposed Rule 17g-10 is a review of the underlying assets for the purpose of making findings with respect to whether the originator of the assets complied with applicable laws and regulations. The Proposing Release notes that this could entail, for RMBS, analyzing the documentation in a sampled loan file to verify that the loan was made in conformance with "truth-in-lending" requirements.[113]

The fifth "catchall" category enumerated under proposed Rule 17g-10 would encompass any other review of the underlying assets for the purpose of making findings with respect to any other factor or characteristic that would be material to the likelihood that the issuer will pay interest and principal timely (i.e., the likelihood of default or delinquency). The SEC believes that findings relevant to the likelihood of default would be relevant to determining a credit rating (because the statutory definition of "credit rating" is "an assessment of the creditworthiness of an obligor as an entity or with respect to specific securities"), and that reviews designed to generate findings irrelevant to a credit rating would be outside the scope of the rule.[114]

3. Form ABS Due Diligence 15-E

Whenever third-party due diligence services are provided to an NRSRO, issuer[115] or underwriter, § 15E(s)(4)(B) of the Exchange Act (as added by § 932 of the Dodd-Frank Act) requires the due diligence services provider to provide to any NRSRO rating any of Exchange Act ABS to which those services "relate" a written certification in a format to be prescribed by rule.[116] Section 15E(s)(4)(C) requires the SEC to "establish the appropriate format and content . . . to ensure that providers of due diligence services have conducted a thorough review of data, documentation, and other relevant information necessary for an NRSRO to provide an accurate rating."[117] To implement this requirement, proposed Exchange Act Rule 17g-10 would require the mandated written certification to be made on Form ABS Due Diligence-15E.

Among other things, proposed Form ABS Due Diligence-15E would require the provider to identify the issuer, underwriter or NRSRO that engaged it, as well as the identity of each NRSRO whose published criteria were satisfied by the performance of the provider's due diligence services. The provider would be required to provide a variety of prescribed details regarding the scope and manner of due diligence that it performed and, most importantly, to summarize the findings and

---

[109] 76 Fed. Reg. at 33,471.
[110] 76 Fed. Reg. at 33,472.
[111] *Id.*

[112] *Id.*
[113] 76 Fed. Reg. at 33,472–73.
[114] 76 Fed. Reg. at 33,473.
[115] Defined by proposed Rule 17g-10 as either the sponsor or the depositor.
[116] 15 U.S.C. § 78o-7(s)(4)(B).
[117] 76 Fed. Reg. at 33,474.

conclusions of its due diligence review. The certification would have to be signed by an individual duly authorized by the provider who would represent that the provider conducted a "thorough review" and that the information in the certification is "accurate in all significant respects."

The proposed rule would require that the certification be provided to any NRSRO producing a credit rating to which the due diligence services "relate." The term "relate" is not de-fined in Section 15E(s)(4)(B) of the Exchange Act or in pro-posed Rule 17g-10.

Comment: It is not clear to what extent due diligence services provided in connection with a transaction might be deemed to "relate" to a credit rating, if those services were not required by, and their results were not provided to, an NRSRO as a part of its rating process.

Practice Tool 1: Diagram of a "Plain Vanilla" Securitization

ABS Certificates

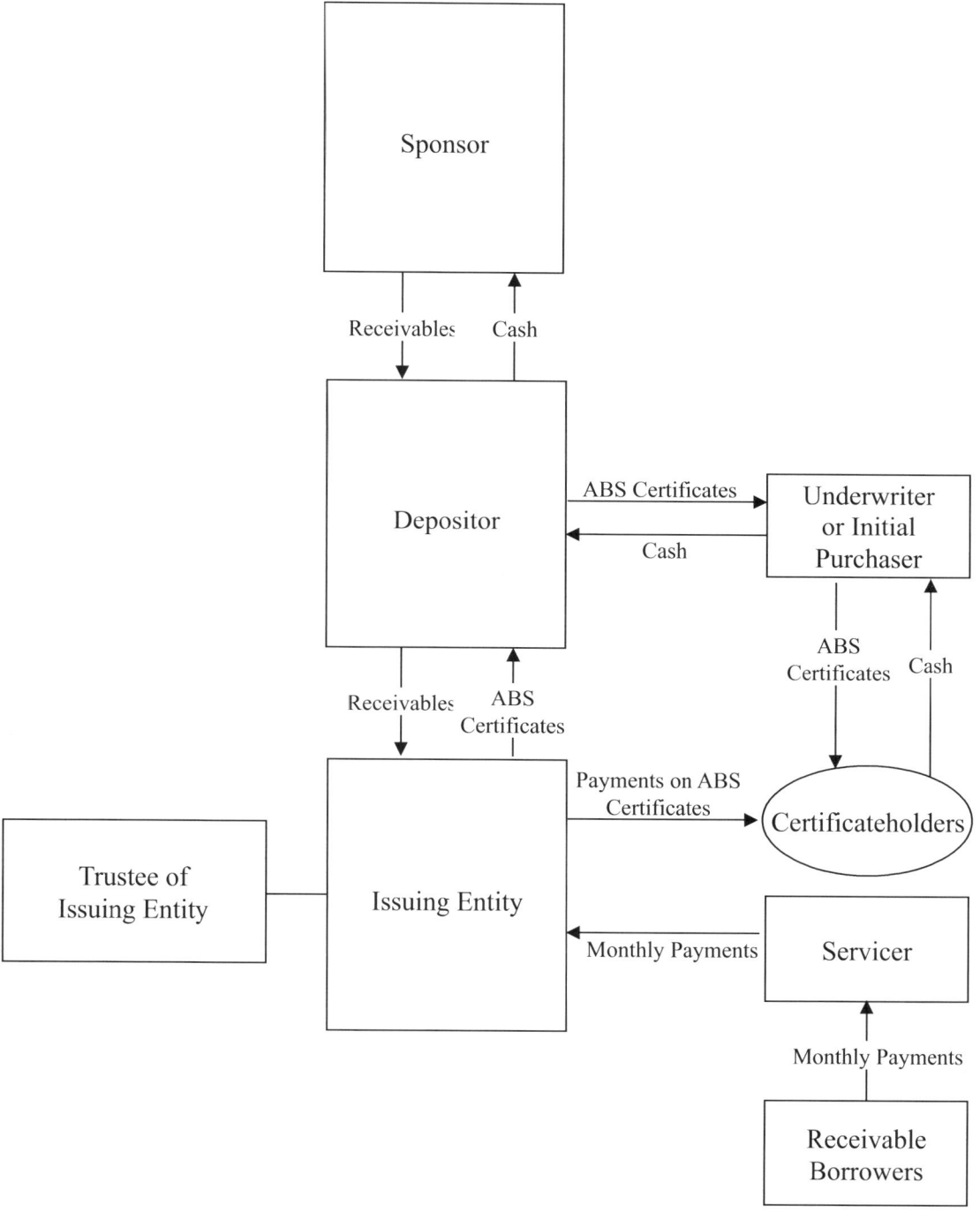

ABS Notes

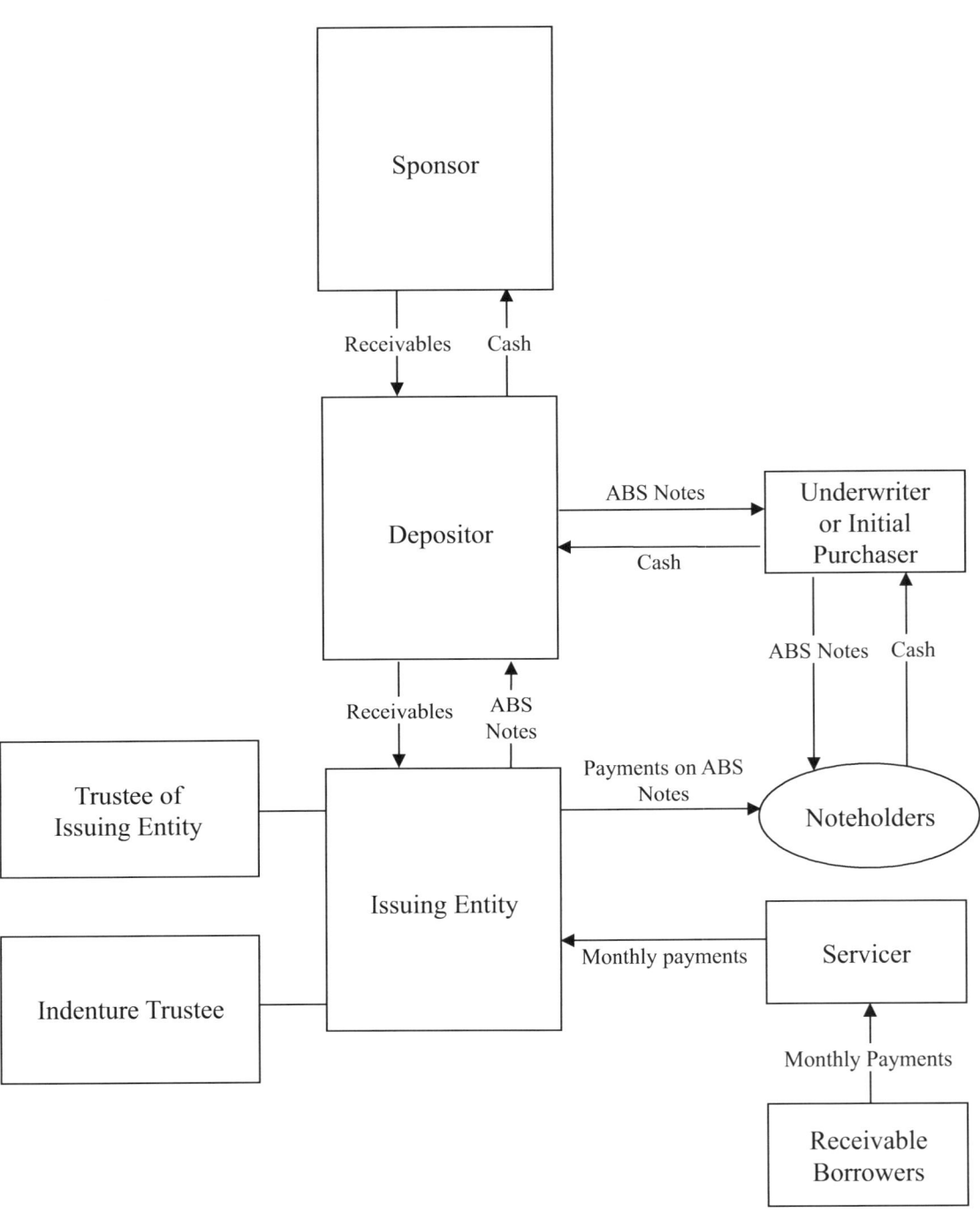

75846360

Practice Tool 2: Filing Requirements for Commonly Used Free Writing Prospectuses in ABS Transactions

Type of FWP	Filing Requirement

1. Any FWP that contains only information that constitutes ABS informational and computational materials (as defined in Item 1101(a) of Regulation AB) (ABSICM), other than
• Certain preliminary term sheets (*see* 3 below), and
• Certain final term sheets (*see* 4 below)
	• Required to be filed by the later of:
	  • The due date for filing the final prospectus (second business day after first use of the final prospectus); and
	  • two business days after first use
	Securities Act Rules 424(b) (instruction), 426(b)(2), 433(d)(6)(i). Generally, the applicable required filing date will be the due date for filing the final prospectus.

2. Any issuer FWP that contains information that does not constitute ABSICM	• Required to be filed on or before date of first use, unless does not contain substantive changes or additions to a previously filed FWP. Securities Act Rules 433(d)(1)(i)(A), 433(d)(3).
3. Preliminary term sheet	• If limited to information that constitutes ABSICM, and does not reflect the final terms, not required to be filed. Securities Act Rule 433(d)(5)(i). • If not limited to information that constitutes ABSICM, *see* 2 above. • If it reflects the final terms, *see* 4 below. • If no final term sheet is prepared, the latest version of the preliminary term sheet should be filed in the same manner as a final term sheet. *See* 4 below.

Type of FWP	Filing Requirement

4. Final term sheet, whether
• A complete final term sheet in the same form as a preliminary terms sheet (*see* 3 above), or
• An abbreviated description of the final terms if a full final term sheet is not filed
	• If limited to information that constitutes ABSICM, required to be filed within two days of the later of:
	  • the date of the establishment of final terms; and
	  • the date of first use. Securities Act Rule 433(d)(5)(ii). Generally, this is the same time frame as for any other FWP that contains only information that constitutes ABSICM. *See* 1 above.
	• If not limited to information that constitutes ABSICM, *see* 2 above.

5. Term sheet supplement (*i.e.,* portions of the prospectus disclosure that are presented in the form of a term sheet, which include risk factors or other information that does not constitute ABSICM)	• *See* 2 above.
6. "Virtual red" (*i.e.*, a preliminary offering document substantially in the form of a preliminary prospectus but filed as a free writing prospectus)	• *See* 2 above.
7. Information regarding the asset pool (*e.g.*, loan tables prepared or agreed to by the issuer, a loan schedule or other loan-level information), other than certain custom loan strats disseminated by underwriter (*see* 8 below)	• *See* 1 above.
8. Any issuer information contained in an FWP used by an underwriter, or by any other offering participant other than the issuer	• If included in (or incorporated by reference into) a statutory prospectus or FWP previously filed, not required to be filed. Securities Act Rule 433(d)(4). • Otherwise, required to be filed by the issuer on or before the date of first use. Securities Act Rule 433(d)(1)(i)(B).

B - 202   1/14   206 SPS

Type of FWP	Filing Requirement
9. Custom loan strats disseminated by underwriter	• If the underlying loan data (such as a loan tape) has been filed as an FWP, not required to be filed. *See* 8 above.
10. Underwriter information (and other information disseminated by an offering participant other than the issuer) that *is not* broadly disseminated	• Not required to be filed by the underwriter. Securities Act Rule 433(d)(1)(ii). • With regard to any issuer information contained therein, *see* 8 above.
11. Underwriter information (and other information disseminated by an offering participant other than the issuer) that *is* broadly disseminated	• Required to be filed by the underwriter on or before date of first use. Securities Act Rule 433(d)(1)(ii). • With regard to any issuer information contained therein, *see* 8 above.
12. "Derived" information disseminated by the underwriter (*e.g.*, yield, weighted average life, etc.)	• Not required to be filed by the issuer. Securities Act Rule 433(d)(1)(i)(B). • If not broadly disseminated, not required to be filed by the underwriter. *See* 10 above. • If broadly disseminated, required to be filed on or before date of first use. *See* 11 above.

Type of FWP	Filing Requirement

13. Electronic road show	• If includes a presentation by "management involved in the securitization or servicing function" of the sponsor, depositor, or servicer, not required to be filed. Securities Act Rules 433(d)(8)(i), 433(h)(4).
	• With regard to accompanying visual aids:
	  • if provided simultaneously and "in a manner designed" to make them "available only as part of the road show and not separately," not required to be filed, Securities Act Rule 433(d)(8) (accompanying note); and
	  • otherwise, treat as any other FWP, *see* 1 or 2 above, as applicable.

14. Media publication disseminated by unaffiliated media outlet, which issuer or another offering participant authorized or for which it approved information	• If paid for by issuer or another offering participant:
	  • if substance was previously filed with SEC in any manner, not required to be filed, Securities Act Rule 433(f)(2)(i); and
	  • otherwise, required to be filed by the issuer or other offering participant within four days of discovery, Securities Act Rule 433(f)(1)(ii).
	• If not paid for by an issuer or other offering participant, must be filed on or before date of first use. Securities Act Rule 433(f); *see also* 2, 8 or 11 above, as applicable.

Practice Tool 3: Form 8-K Disclosure Items for ABS Issuers

Disclosure Items		Required (If Applicable)[1]	Omission Specifically Permitted[2]
Item 1.01	Entry into a Material Definitive Agreement	✔	
Item 1.02	Termination of a Material Definitive Agreement	✔	
Item 1.03	Bankruptcy or Receivership	✔	
Item 1.04	Mine Safety – Reporting of Shutdowns and Patterns of Violations	✔	
Item 2.01	Completion of Acquisition or Disposition of Assets		✔
Item 2.02	Results of Operations and Financial Condition		✔
Item 2.03	Creation of a Direct Financial Obligation or an Obligation under an Off-Balance Sheet Arrangement of a Registrant		✔
Item 2.04	Triggering Events That Accelerate or Increase a Direct Financial Obligation or an Obligation under an Off-Balance Sheet Arrangement	✔	
Item 2.05	Costs Associated with Exit or Disposal Activities		✔
Item 2.06	Material Impairments		✔

Disclosure Items		Required (If Applicable)[1]	Omission Specifically Permitted[2]
Item 3.01	Notice of Delisting or Failure to Satisfy a Continued Listing Rule or Standard; Transfer of Listing		✔
Item 3.02	Unregistered Sales of Equity Securities		✔
Item 3.03	Material Modifications to Rights of Security Holders	✔	
Item 4.01	Changes in Registrant's Certifying Accountant		✔
Item 4.02	Non-Reliance on Previously Issued Financial Statements or a Related Audit Report or Completed Interim Review		✔
Item 5.01	Changes in Control of Registrant		✔
Item 5.02	Departure of Directors or Principal Officers; Election of Directors; Appointment of Certain Officers; Compensatory Arrangements of Certain Officers		✔
Item 5.03	Amendments to Articles of Incorporation or Bylaws; Change in Fiscal Year	✔	
Item 5.04	Temporary Suspension of Trading Under Registrant's Employee Benefit Plans		✔
Item 5.05	Amendments to the Registrant's Code of Ethics, or Waiver of a Provision of the Code of Ethics		✔
Item 5.06	Change in Shell Company Status	✔	

Disclosure Items		Required (If Applicable)[1]	Omission Specifically Permitted[2]
Item 5.07	Submission of Matters to a Vote of Security Holders	✔	
Item 5.08	Shareholder Director Nominations	✔	
Item 6.01	ABS Informational and Computational Material	✔	
Item 6.02	Change of Servicer or Trustee	✔	
Item 6.03	Change in Credit Enhancement or Other External Support	✔	
Item 6.04	Failure to Make a Required Distribution	✔	
Item 6.05	Securities Act Updating Disclosure	✔	
Item 7.01	Regulation FD Disclosure	✔	
Item 8.01	Other Events	✔	
Item 9.01	Financial Statements and Exhibits	✔	

[1] Only the applicable items triggered by a reportable event must be included. All other items may be completely omitted. Form 8-K, General Instruction D.

[2] An ABS issuer need not file a Form 8-K upon the occurrence of any of these events. Also, the names of the depositor and sponsor must be included on the cover page after the name of the issuing entity. *See* Form 8-K, General Instruction G.

Practice Tool 4: Form 10-K Disclosure Items for ABS Issuers

Disclosure Items		Required (If Applicable)[1]	Omission Specifically Permitted[2]
Item 1	Business		✔
Item 1A	Risk Factors		✔
Item 1B	Unresolved Staff Comments	✔	
Item 2	Properties		✔
Item 3	Legal Proceedings		✔
Item 4	Mine Safety Disclosures		✔
Item 5	Market for Registrant's Common Equity, Related Stockholder Matters and Issuer Purchases of Equity Securities		✔
Item 6	Selected Financial Data		✔
Item 7	Management's Discussion and Analysis of Financial Condition and Results of Operations		✔
Item 7A	Quantitative and Qualitative Disclosure About Market Risk		✔
Item 8	Financial Statements and Supplementary Data.		✔
Item 9	Changes in and Disagreements with Accountants on Accounting and Financial Disclosure		✔
Item 9A	Controls and Procedures		✔

Disclosure Items		Required (If Applicable)[1]	Omission Specifically Permitted[2]
Item 9A(T)	Controls and Procedures		✔
Item 9B	Other Information	✔	
Item 10	Directors, Executive Officers and Corporate Governance		✔[3]
Item 11	Executive Compensation.		✔[3]
Item 12	Security Ownership of Certain Beneficial Owners and Management and Related Stockholder Matters		✔[3]
Item 13	Certain Relationships and Related Transactions, and Director Independence		✔[3]
Item 14	Principal Accounting Fees and Services		✔
Item 15	Exhibits, Financial Statement Schedules.	✔	
Additional Information Required for ABS Issuers[4]			
	Item 1112(b) of Regulation AB, Significant Obligor Financial Information	✔	
	Items 1114(b)(2) and 1115(b) of Regulation AB, Significant Enhancement Provider Financial Information	✔	
	Item 1117 of Regulation AB, Legal Proceedings	✔	

Disclosure Items		Required (If Applicable)[1]	Omission Specifically Permitted[2]
	Item 1119 of Regulation AB, Affiliations and Certain Relationships and Related Transactions	✔	
	Item 1122 of Regulation AB, Compliance with Applicable Servicing Criteria	✔	
	Item 1123 of Regulation AB, Servicer Compliance Statement	✔	

[1] The numbers and captions of all items must be included, but if any item is not applicable or the answer is negative, then that may be the sole response. Exchange Act Rule 12b-13, 17 CFR 240.12b-13.

[2] ABS issuers may omit the information called for by each of these items. Form 10-K, General Instruction J(1).

[3] May be omitted by ABS issuers if they do not have any executive officers or directors.

[4] This additional information must be included by all ABS issuers. Also, the names of the depositor and sponsor must be included on the cover page after the name of the issuing entity. *See* Form 10-K, General Instruction J(2).

Practice Tool 5: ASF Market Guide to Questions Regarding Implementation of SEC Rule 15Ga

The American Securitization Forum is helping facilitate the identification of issues that require interpretation or clarification under the Rule 15Ga-1 and Rule AB (the Repurchase Disclosure Regulations). Reproduced below is the ASF Market Guide to Questions Regarding Implementation of SEC Rule 15Ga.

Reprinted with permission of the AMERICAN SECURITIZATION FORUM. All Rights Reserved.

AMERICAN SECURITIZATION FORUM
MARKET GUIDE TO
QUESTIONS REGARDING IMPLEMENTATION OF
SEC RULE 15Ga-1

December 22, 2011

This market guide is intended for ASF members only.

ASF Rule 15Ga-1 Market Guide
Page i

TABLE OF CONTENTS

ASF Rule 15Ga-1 Market Guide
Page ii

ASF Rule 15Ga-1 Market Guide
Page iii

ASF Rule 15Ga-1 Market Guide
Page 1

I. Introduction

On January 20, 2011, the Securities and Exchange Commission (the "Commission") released "Disclosure for Asset-Backed Securities Required by Section 943 of The Dodd-Frank Wall Street Reform and Consumer Protection Act" (Release Nos. 33-9175; 34-63741) (the "Final Release"), which enacted Rule 15Ga-1 (the "Rule") and certain Items under Regulation AB (the "Repurchase Disclosure Regulations").[1] With the adoption of the Repurchase Disclosure Regulations, market participants have been working toward implementing appropriate processes to prepare for them. As a part of those efforts, market participants continue to identify and discuss issues arising in the context of these regulations that require interpretation or clarification. ASF seeks to facilitate that process by distributing to our members this guide of market views on interpretive questions arising under these regulations.

This market guide is limited to issues relating to the scope and basic terms of the Repurchase Disclosure Regulations and is not intended to address all implementation issues, particularly those where the facts and circumstances surrounding a particular transaction or security may bear on the issue. The views set forth below do not constitute legal advice but instead reflect industry views and consensus positions on the questions presented based on various resources, including the Repurchase Disclosure Regulations, the Commission's August 25, 2011 correcting amendment to Rule 15Ga-1 (the "Correcting Amendment").[2] the Commission's commentary in the October 2010 Proposing Release and the Final Release, and ASF's meeting with Commission staff on March 17, 2011 and follow-up conference call on March 28, 2011 (collectively, the "ASF SEC Meeting"). All of the views set forth herein are subject to change as market practices develop and/or if additional guidance from the Commission and its staff becomes available. **This market guide is intended for ASF members only.**

---

[1] http://www.sec.gov/rules/final/2011/33-9175fr.pdf.

[2] http://www.sec.gov/rules/final/2011/33-9175a.pdf

ASF Rule 15Ga-1 Market Guide
Page 2

II. Disclosure Requirements for Securitizers

Rule 15Ga-1 requires securitizers to file new Form ABS-15G periodically to disclose, on an aggregated basis, certain information concerning assets that were the subject of a demand to repurchase or replace for breach of a representation and warranty concerning the pool assets. Item 1121 of Regulation AB was also amended to cause individual issuers to report the same information regarding their particular asset pool on each Form 10-D filing.

A. Covered Parties and Transactions

(1) <u>What is an asset-backed security for purposes of the Rule?</u> ABS is defined more broadly for purposes of Rule 15Ga-1 than it is under existing Regulation AB. *Final Release, p. 4491.* The applicable statutory definition of an ABS under Rule 15Ga-1 is found at Section 3(a)(77) of the Securities Exchange Act of 1934 (as amended by Section 943 of the Dodd-Frank Wall Street Reform and Consumer Protection Act ("<u>Dodd-Frank</u>"), the "<u>Exchange Act</u>"). This Exchange Act ABS definition ("<u>Exchange Act ABS</u>" or for purposes of this Guide, "<u>ABS</u>") includes all fixed-income or other securities collateralized by any type of self-liquidating financial asset or cash flow from those assets. CDOs, CLOs, GSE-issued or -guaranteed securities (such as Fannie Mae and Freddie Mac) and ABS issued by municipalities are all included despite their general exclusion from the definition of ABS under Regulation AB and/or their exemption from the registration requirements of the Securities Act of 1933 (the "Securities Act"). *Final Release, p. 4491.* In addition, at the ASF SEC Meeting, Commission staff indicated their belief that Dodd-Frank does not provide the Commission with exemptive authority as it relates to Rule 15Ga-1 and that Ginnie Mae securities are, in fact, within the scope of the Rule.[3]

(2) <u>Are unregistered securities covered?</u> Yes. The Final Release expressly states that all securities meeting the definition of Exchange Act ABS are covered "whether or not sold in Securities Act registered transactions." *Final Release, p. 4491.* The Commission has confirmed that "filing proposed Form ABS-15G would not foreclose the reliance of an issuer on the private offering exemption in the Securities Act of 1933 and the safe harbor for offshore transactions from the registration provisions in Section 5." *Final Release, p. 4499.*

(3) <u>For which Exchange Act ABS must data be presented in a Form ABS-15G report?</u> The only Exchange Act ABS for which data must be presented in a given period are those (i) for which the underlying transaction agreements contain a covenant to repurchase or replace an underlying asset for breach of a representation or warranty ("<u>R&W Repurchase Provisions</u>"),[4] (ii) for which underlying assets were the subject of a demand

---

[3] While the Commission believes that Ginnie Mae securities are Exchange Act ABS and thus within the scope of the Rule, market participants do not expect a voluminous amount of reportable activity will be required to be disclosed under the Rule regarding those securities due to their federal guaranty and the limited instances under the Ginnie Mae programs in which communications are made that could be characterized as a demand to repurchase or replace an asset.

[4] Market participants interpret "underlying transaction agreements" to be the pooling and servicing agreement, asset purchase agreement, trust agreement, indenture or other operative document controlling the rights of securitization parties and investors.

ASF Rule 15Ga-1 Market Guide
Page 3

to repurchase or replace for breach of representations and warranties concerning pool assets, and (iii) that were held by a non-affiliate of the securitizer during the related period. *Rule 15Ga-1(a)*. If an Exchange Act ABS is repaid in full or is purchased in whole by affiliates of the securitizer during a reporting period then activity within the period with respect to that ABS would still be required on the Form ABS-15G relating to that period but it would not be included in future reports.

Furthermore, Regulation AB issuers of Exchange Act ABS for which the underlying transaction agreements contain R&W Repurchase Provisions must provide certain information required by Rule 15Ga-1 on each Form 10-D filing and in a prospectus. See Section II.D and Part III below.

(4)   What entities are "securitizers" for purposes of this Rule? Under Section 15G(a)(3) of the Exchange Act, a "securitizer" is defined as either (A) an issuer of an ABS or (B) a person who organizes and initiates an ABS transaction by selling or transferring assets, either directly or indirectly, including through an affiliate, to the issuer. *Final Release, p. 4491*. The Commission has stated that the "issuer" under this definition would be the entity that meets the definition of "Depositor" under Regulation AB. *Final Release, n. 22, p. 4491*. A typical two-step ABS transaction would therefore include two securitizers: the depositor (which is the deemed "issuer") and the sponsor (which sells the securitized assets to the depositor/issuer).[5] *Final Release, p. 4491*.

For Exchange Act ABS issued by Fannie Mae or Freddie Mac, the "securitizer" would be the applicable GSE and not a financial institution that merely transfers loans for securitization by Fannie Mae or Freddie Mac. The Commission explained in the Final Release that it revised the text of the Rule to refer to the assets "securitized" by a securitizer instead of the assets "originated or sold"[6] as originally proposed to address commentators' concerns that the requirement should apply solely to Fannie Mae or Freddie Mac and not the institution transferring loans for securitization by Fannie Mae or Freddie Mac. Market participants believe this change makes clear that Fannie Mae and Freddie Mac are the sole securitizers in GSE transactions that do not include any third-party depositor or sponsor. *Final Release, n. 81, p. 4496*.

(5)   How are securitizers located outside the United States affected by the Rule? At the ASF SEC Meeting, Commission staff reiterated the view expressed in the Final Release that securitizers subject to the Commission's jurisdiction are required to file the

---

[5] Clause (B) of the definition of "securitizer" set forth in Dodd-Frank generally tracks the definition of "sponsor" under Regulation AB. Footnote 42 of the risk retention proposing release concludes (without explanation) that "in the context of collateralized loan obligations (CLOs), the CLO manager generally acts as the sponsor by selecting the commercial loans to be purchased" by the issuer. Market participants disagree with this conclusion because managers of CLOs or CDOs that purchase syndicated commercial loans or bonds in the open market do not "sell" or "transfer" assets to the issuing entity and believe that the Commission's interpretation of a securitizer in the footnote- i.e., that it includes an entity that merely selects assets rather than selling or transferring them- is inconsistent with the definitions of Sponsor and securitizer. Market participants have voiced these concerns in numerous comment letters to the joint regulators. See the joint regulators' risk retention proposing release at http://www.sec.gov/rules/proposed/2011/34-64148fr.pdf and ASF's comment letter at http://www.americansecuritization.com/uploadedFiles/ASF_Risk_Retention_Comment_Letter.pdf.

[6] The Commission refers to this language in the commentary of the Final Release as "originated and transferred" or "originated and sold," however the actual language of the proposed rule was "originated or sold."

ASF Rule 15Ga-1 Market Guide
Page 4

disclosures prescribed by the Rule. Final Release, n. 21, p. 4491. Commission staff believe that Dodd-Frank does not provide the Commission with exemptive authority as it relates to Section 943 and Rule 15Ga-1, whether for ABS offered outside the U.S. or for ABS sold in the U.S. by foreign securitizers. Unlike the Dodd-Frank risk retention rules under Section 941, Rule 15Ga-1 does not contain a de minimus exception for non-U.S. transactions and the staff did not take, and made clear that they do not intend to take, an interpretive position as to specific jurisdictional scenarios. Instead, the staff indicated that securitizers and their counsel would have to make their own determinations as to the limits of the Commission's jurisdiction in the context of the Rule. Because of the lack of guidance on these jurisdictional limits, securitizers should consider their specific facts and circumstances carefully with their counsel.

In the absence of another nexus with U.S. markets (including those of the type noted below), non-U.S. securitizers that have issued ABS exclusively on a "Regulation S only" basis may be comfortable concluding, on advice of their U.S. counsel, that they are outside the Commission's jurisdiction for purposes of the Rule. Non-U.S. securitizers that have issued some Exchange Act ABS in the United States (whether or not the ABS were registered under the Securities Act) may want to consider the following factors, among others, when determining whether or not they are within the Commission's jurisdiction for purposes of the Rule: (i) the principal amount of ABS issued by the securitizer in the U.S. relative to the principal amount of ABS issued outside the U.S.; (ii) the current outstanding principal amount of ABS issued by the securitizer in the U.S. relative to the current outstanding principal amount of ABS issued by the securitizer outside the U.S.; (iii) how recently the U.S. issuance activity occurred; and, (iv) for non-U.S. securitizers that have issued ABS in more than one asset class, whether there are differences in the above factors between the various asset classes issued (e.g., the securitizer has issued RMBS in both the 144A and Regulation S markets but issued auto ABS only in the Regulation S market).

In addition, while it is not clear whether and, if so, to what extent relevant to this analysis, all entities that are non-U.S. securitizers may want to consider the following factors (whether or not they have issued ABS in the 144A market): (x) whether the entity is a periodic reporting company in the U.S. in another capacity (e.g., in its corporate or organic capacity); (y) whether there is a "substantial U.S. market interest" (as defined in Regulation S) for any of the entity's debt or equity securities (whether or not ABS); and (z) whether an affiliate of the non-U.S. securitizer is clearly within the Commission's jurisdiction and the non-U.S. securitizer could be considered as acting for or on behalf of the affiliate (or there are other circumstances which the Commission might consider relevant under its "anti-avoidance" principles).

(6) <u>If a securitizer has gone out of business, filed for bankruptcy protection, etc. must it still file Forms ABS-15G?</u> At the ASF SEC Meeting, the Commission staff indicated that institutions that have succeeded by merger or otherwise to a predecessor securitizer would be subject to the Rule. However, the staff acknowledged that, in practical terms, a securitizer whose affairs have been wound down through bankruptcy, liquidation or other insolvency proceeding, while still technically subject to the Rule, may not be in a

ASF Rule 15Ga-1 Market Guide
Page 5

position to make the required filings and for this reason, the staff would not consider a blanket filing accommodation for such securitizers. The individual circumstances of each securitizer and its affiliated securitizers must be considered before a filing determination is made. For example, while a securitizer's affairs may have been wound down, the affairs of an affiliated securitizer may still be active.

(7)   Under which CIK number should the Form ABS-15G be filed? Each Form ABS-15G should be filed under the securitizer's Central Index Key ("CIK") number, which is the CIK number assigned to the relevant company in its standalone capacity as depositor or sponsor, as applicable. A CIK number is the unique identification number that the Commission assigns to individuals and corporations who file disclosure documents with the Commission electronically via its EDGAR system. A CIK number serves, among other things, to define a discrete database on the EDGAR system and all filings made under the same CIK number are archived in the same database. More information on CIK numbers, including how to obtain a new CIK number, can be found on the Commission's website and in the EDGAR Filer Manual.[7]

(8)   If there is more than one securitizer related to an ABS transaction and they are affiliates must they file separate Form ABS-15G reports that provide overlapping or identical information? Generally, no. For instance, the sponsor and the depositor in a typical two-step securitization are affiliates who are both securitizers for purposes of the Rule.[8] For this reason, both would have reporting obligations, but reporting by one company under the Rule generally excuses reporting by its affiliates. For example:

- Sponsor Makes Filings: If a sponsor were to make the required filings regarding all applicable Exchange Act ABS then each of its affiliated depositors would be excused from reporting on those same ABS. *Rule 15Ga-1(b): Final Release, p. 4491.*

- Single Depositor Makes Filings: If a sponsor utilizes a single depositor for all its ABS issuances and that depositor makes the required disclosure for all applicable Exchange Act ABS, the sponsor would be excused from reporting on those same ABS. *Rule 15Ga-1(b): Final Release at pp. 4491-4492.*

- Multiple Depositors Make Filings: If a sponsor utilizes more than one depositor, using different depositors for or within each asset class securitized (e.g., using one or two depositors for auto loan securitizations and one or two depositors for credit card securitizations), then disclosure by each such depositor regarding all applicable Exchange Act ABS would excuse the sponsor's reporting on those same ABS. *Rule 15Ga-1(a): Final Release, n. 25, p. 4492.*

---

[7] See https://www.filermanagement.edgarfiling.sec.gov/servlet/FilerMgmtServlet and http://www.sec.gov/info/edgar.shtml.

[8] For asset-backed securities transactions where there is not an intermediate transfer of the assets from the sponsor to the issuing entity (one-step securitizations), the term depositor refers to the sponsor. See Item 1101(e) of Regulation AB.

ASF Rule 15Ga-1 Market Guide
Page 6

(9)   If there is more than one securitizer related to an ABS transaction and they are not affiliates must they each file a Form ABS-15G? Yes, the exception excusing multiple filings covering the same disclosures in Rule 15Ga-1(b) only relates to affiliated securitizers. The Commission specifically indicated that a securitizer's obligation to file Form ABS-15G is not excused in the "rent-a-shelf" context if one securitizer (the renter) contractually assumes the obligation to make all filings on behalf of a second securitizer (the registrant) or in cases where an unaffiliated originator agrees with a securitizer to make its required filings. *Final Release, n. 26, p. 4492.*

(10) If there are multiple securitizers in a transaction that are unaffiliated sellers of assets to the depositor, for which assets should data be presented in each securitizer's Form ABS-15G? If multiple unaffiliated sellers have decided to securitize their assets together in one securitization transaction involving a sale by each seller of its assets to the depositor for the securitization (as is typical in many CMBS transactions), each seller will be a "securitizer" with respect to its own assets for purposes of Rule 15Ga-1. Pursuant to Section 15G(a)(3)(B) of the Exchange Act, a securitizer is "a person who organizes and initiates an asset-backed securities transaction *by selling or transferring assets,* either directly or indirectly...to the issuer" (emphasis added). Rule 15Ga-1(a) requires that a securitizer disclose in its Form ABS-15G filing "fulfilled and unfulfilled repurchase requests...concerning all assets *securitized by the securitizer* that were the subject of a demand..." (emphasis added). In this transaction, the depositor is a securitizer (pursuant to Section 15G(a)(3)(A) of the Exchange Act) of all the assets, because it is the "issuer" of the ABS and has sold all of the assets into the securitization trust, and each seller is the securitizer of the specific assets it sold to the depositor. Accordingly, with respect to this transaction, the Form ABS-15G filing of the depositor must present data with respect to the assets sold by all of the sellers and the Form ABS-15G filing of each seller must present data solely with respect to the assets sold by such seller to the depositor.

B. *Rule 15Ga-1 Reporting Data*

(11) What data must be presented in response to Rule 15Ga-1? Rule 15Ga-1(a) states that "a securitizer...shall disclose...repurchase requests...*by providing the information required in paragraph (a)(1) of this section concerning all assets...that were the subject of a demand to repurchase or replace* for breach of the representations and warranties concerning the pool assets for all asset-backed securities held by non-affiliates of the securitizer during the reporting period." (emphasis added). Therefore, the applicable tabular information set forth in paragraph (a)(1) is required to be disclosed for all assets that have previously been subject of a demand. The table must include the following items:

(i)   asset class;

(ii)   name of issuing entity;

(iii) indication of registration under the Securities Act and CIK number of issuing entity (if applicable);

ASF Rule 15Ga-1 Market Guide
Page 7

    (iv)   originator of pool assets;

    (v)   pool assets at the time of securitization;

    (vi)   pool assets subject to a demand to repurchase or replace for breach of a representation or warranty;

    (vii)   pool assets repurchased or replaced;

    (viii)   pool assets pending repurchase or replacement (within cure period);

    (ix)   pool assets subject to disputed demands for repurchase or replacement;

    (x)   pool assets subject to withdrawn demands for repurchase or replacement;

    (xi)   pool assets subject to rejected demands for repurchase or replacement; and

    (xii)   aggregations of certain of the data by asset class, issuing entity and all issuing entities.

Rule 15Ga-1(a)(1)(i)-(xii). This data is to be aggregated across ABS and periodically filed by securitizers on Form ABS-15G. This data is also to be presented on a pool-specific basis for publicly registered ABS and filed by issuers on Form 10-D.

The Rule does not provide definitions or instructions as to what constitutes, among other things, assets "pending repurchase or replacement," repurchase demands "in dispute" and repurchase demands "withdrawn." Market participants believe the Commission did not include rigid definitions in the Rule to accommodate the realities of reporting across transactions that may substantially differ based on vintage, structure, securitization program or asset class. Market participants also believe that the instruction encouraging securitizers to use explanatory footnotes provides further support that the Rule is intended to permit a variety of disclosures.[9] As such, securitizers intend to construe the various data fields in a way that is feasible and meaningful within the context of their particular circumstances but that is also consistent with the Rule's inherent focus on the incremental steps of the remedial process. Market participants intend to provide explanatory footnotes indicating exactly what each data field, or "bucket," is intended to capture.

While the applicable tabular information set forth in paragraph (a)(1) is required to be disclosed for all assets that have previously been subject of a demand, Instruction 1 to paragraph (a)(1) explains that "[t]he table should include any activity during the reporting period, including activity related to assets subject to demands made prior to the beginning of the reporting period." The Commission does not indicate what

---

[9] "Indicate by footnote and provide narrative disclosure in order to further explain the information presented in the table, as appropriate." *Instruction 2 to paragraph (a)(1).*

ASF Rule 15Ga-1 Market Guide
Page 8

constitutes "activity" for purposes of complying with this instruction, but it does make clear that the reporting should not be "cumulative," implying that data cannot remain in the table permanently.[10] Market participants believe there are different approaches by which securitizers can provide clear disclosure of repurchase demand "activity" that would not amount to cumulative reporting. Regardless of the approach employed, the securitizer should include within the report any information or explanation necessary for investors and other users of the data to understand the disclosure.

One example of such an approach would be to interpret "activity" as occurring only when there is a change in status of the loan from one reporting period to the next. For example, if a demand was in dispute in Q1, the securitizer would indicate such activity in the table. If the loan changes status in Q2, say, for example, if the loan was repurchased or the demand was withdrawn, then the securitizer would indicate that activity in the table. However, if the loan did not change status in Q2 and the only activity was the demand in dispute in Q1, there would be no reporting required on the loan until a change in status had occurred. Under this approach, the reporting would not be cumulative because only changes in status, or new activity, would be reported.

Another approach would be to interpret "activity" as occurring if a loan is in a particular status regardless of whether such status has changed from the previous reporting period. For example, if a demand was in dispute in Q1, the securitizer would indicate such activity in the report for Q1 and in each successive report until the loan changed status. If the loan did not change status until Q4, the securitizer would file reports in Q2 and Q3 that still reflected the demand being in dispute and then file a report in Q4 reflecting its new status. To ensure that this approach did not result in cumulative reporting, securitizers could consider certain statuses, such as demand withdrawn or demand rejected, as each representing a "final decision" on the asset, after which no further reporting would occur.

(12) <u>Is any explanatory disclosure permitted?</u> Yes, the securitizer is directed to "[i]ndicate by footnote and provide narrative disclosure in order to further explain the information presented in the table, as appropriate." *Instruction 2 to Rule 15Ga-1(a)(1), Final Release, p. 4514.*

(13) <u>May a securitizer omit any required information?</u> Yes, a securitizer may omit information that is unknown or not reasonably available to the securitizer without unreasonable effort or expense. *Rule 15Ga-1(a)(2).* The filing, however, must include a statement describing why unreasonable effort or expense would be involved in obtaining the omitted information. *Final Release, p. 4499.* If a securitizer filing a Form ABS-15G report is unable to obtain information regarding investor demands upon a trustee prior to July 22, 2010 (the effective date of Dodd-Frank) it may omit that information without having to assert that unreasonable effort or expense would be incurred in obtaining it but, again, it must provide a narrative description of the

---

[10] "Instead, we are adopting, as suggested by commentators, a requirement for securitizers to present only the information for the quarter in their quarterly filing because cumulative data may be cumbersome to manipulate and not be as useful to identify recent trends as information presented on a quarter by quarter basis." *Final Release, p. 4501.*

ASF Rule 15Ga-1 Market Guide
Page 9

omission in a footnote (the "Pre-Effective Date Omission Standard"). *Final Release pp. 4498-4499.* The Commission included the Pre-Effective Date Omission Standard because it recognized that "initially a securitizer may not be able to obtain complete information from a trustee because it may not have established systems to track investor demands." *Final Release, p. 4498.* Indeed, a trustee's obligation to provide the securitizer a record of investor demands made upon the trustee would currently exist only to the extent there is a contractual obligation to do so.

(14) <u>If a securitizer discloses repurchase demand activity on an ABS issuance must it also report on other issuances where there has been no repurchase demand activity during the applicable period?</u> No. By its terms, Rule 15Ga-1(a) requires disclosures to be made only in cases where demands to repurchase or replace have been made ("disclose fulfilled and unfulfilled repurchase requests...by providing the information required in paragraph (a)(1)...concerning all assets securitized by the securitizer that were the subject of a demand to repurchase or replace for breach of the representations and warranties concerning the pool assets..."). If there has been no repurchase demand activity for a particular transaction, there is no obligation to report that fact on Form ABS-15G. The Commission acknowledged this in the Final Release ("We also highlight the instruction to Rule 15Ga–1(a)(1)(ii) which specifies that the table should include *all issuing entities with activity* during the quarterly reporting period, including those that are no longer outstanding at the end of the calendar quarter") (emphasis added). *Final Release, n. 136, p. 4501.*[11]

This is consistent with a securitizer's comparable obligation to check the "no activity to report" box on the Form ABS-15G rather than disclose hundreds or even thousands of zeroes in the applicable columns on transactions where there has been no repurchase demand activity. Further, the Commission makes clear in the Final Release that if a securitizer that has suspended its obligation to report receives subsequent repurchase demand activity with respect to a transaction, it is then obligated to begin reporting only on such activity: "Thereafter, a securitizer would have suspended its obligation to report on a quarterly basis, until the time when a demand occurs during the quarterly reporting period. However, the securitizer would be required to file an annual Form ABS–15G to confirm that no demands were made during the entire year. If demands were made during a calendar quarter, *the securitizer would have to report that activity* for the calendar quarter by filing Form ABS–15G within 45 days of the end of the calendar quarter" (emphasis added). *Final Release, p. 4501.*

(15) <u>Must data included in a Form ABS-15G filing be organized by asset class?</u> Yes. Rule 15Ga-1 requires that the disclosure in each Form ABS-15G filing be organized by asset class. Additionally, Item 1104(e)(1) of Regulation AB requires that the prospectus for

---

[11] If disclosures are required for particular assets under Rule 15Ga-1(a), paragraph (a)(1) sets forth the particular information required to be included in such disclosures, including the name of the issuing entity pursuant to clause (ii). Additionally, the instruction to Rule 15Ga-1(a)(1)(ii) indicates that securitizers are to disclose "all issuing entities with outstanding asset-backed securities during the reporting period." However, consistent with Rule 15Ga-1(a) and the Commission's guidance in Footnote 136, this instruction applies only with respect to issuing entities for which information about their underlying assets is required to be disclosed (i.e., in the case where repurchase demand activity has occurred). In other words, if there is no disclosure required pursuant to Rule 15Ga-1(a), the information and instructions listed under paragraph (a)(1) are of no consequence.

ASF Rule 15Ga-1 Market Guide
Page 10

a Regulation AB-compliant ABS offering include Rule 15Ga-1 data for other ABS organized by the sponsor that are of the same asset class as the ABS being offered. *Final Release, n. 152, p. 4502.*

(16) <u>How are ABS to be organized within a given asset class?</u> In preparing a Form ABS-15G, the individual ABS in a single asset class are to be identified by the name of the related "issuing entity" (as defined in Item 1101(f) of Regulation AB) and presented in order of the date of formation of the issuing entity. *Rule 15Ga-1(a)(1)(xii); Final Release, p. 4498.*

(17) <u>If a master trust structure is used, is information provided separately for each ABS issuance by that master trust?</u> No, if multiple series of ABS are issued by a single issuing entity and backed by a single pool of receivables in a master trust structure (e.g., in a credit card receivables or automobile floorplan securitization) then (A) the data with respect to that issuing entity would be aggregated in the Form ABS-15G filing and (B) the issuing entity's placement in the Form ABS-15G would be based on its date of formation (and not, for example, based on the date of the trust's most recent ABS issuance). *Final Release, n. 84, p. 4498.*

(18) <u>Must the Form ABS-15G filing indicate whether ABS were registered under the Securities Act?</u> Yes, the securitizer must indicate whether the ABS were registered and, if so, provide the CIK number of the related issuing entity. *Final Release, p. 4498.*

(19) <u>If pool assets were originated by more than one party, how is data presented?</u> If the asset pool underlying an ABS contains assets originated by multiple originators and if repurchase demand activity occurred for the ABS, disclosure must be provided separately for each originator's subpool of pool assets supporting such ABS. *Instruction to Rule 15Ga-1(a)(1)(iv).* There is no *de minimis* exemption and data must be separately provided for every originator, regardless of how many of its assets were included in a pool underlying a particular ABS and regardless of whether there was any repurchase demand activity regarding those pool assets. ("In addition, originators with no repurchase request activity should be listed in the table also to provide comparable disclosures.") *Final Release, p. 4498.*

(20) <u>What is an "originator" for purposes of Rule 15Ga-1?</u> The term "originator" is not defined in the Final Release or Regulation AB ("As with trustees, we do not believe it is necessary to provide a separate definition for originators." *Regulation AB Final Release at 1538.*) While Dodd-Frank provides a definition of "originator" in Section 941, alongside the definition of "securitizer", Section 943 neither provides a separate definition of the term "originator" nor cross-references the definition that appears in Section 941 (as is done in Section 943 for the term "securitizer"). Because there is no definition provided in Section 943 for the term "originator," market participants believe it would be appropriate to interpret that term in a manner consistent with the disclosure provided when the Exchange Act ABS were originally issued. Market participants may disclose in a footnote the particular formulation of the term "originator" that was used for purposes of the Rule 15Ga-1 disclosure.

ASF Rule 15Ga-1 Market Guide
Page 11

For example, the market convention for Regulation AB offerings has been that even if a loan is originated in the name of a third-party, if there is another entity whose underwriting criteria were utilized in approving and funding the loan and if that other entity acquired the loan from the third-party, then that entity, rather than the third-party, would be the "originator." For instance, if a motor vehicle dealer worked with a finance company to apply that finance company's underwriting criteria to a proposed loan and then sold the loan to the finance company upon, or promptly following, origination, then the finance company, rather than the dealer, would be the "originator". If, however, the same motor vehicle dealer originated an asset based on its own underwriting guidelines but, nonetheless, later sold the loan to the same finance company, the dealer itself would then be treated as the "originator" of that loan. Other formulations of the term originator may be appropriate depending on the particular circumstances of the original offering and the availability of information.

(21) Can data for affiliated originators be consolidated? No. Although Item 1110 of Regulation AB requires issuers to aggregate a group of affiliated originators for purposes of identifying originators that originated 10% or more of the pool assets, Rule 15Ga-1 does not appear to allow for this type of aggregation. *Rule 15Ga-1(a)(iv)* ("all originators that originated assets in the asset pool for each issuing entity" must be disclosed.) Therefore, Form ABS-15G filings made by a securitizer, Rule 15Ga-1 information that is set forth in Regulation AB-compliant prospectuses and Form 10-D filings made by individual issuers in publicly registered transactions should present Rule 15Ga-1 data for every originator of assets in the related asset pool, regardless of whether disclosure regarding individual originators is otherwise required in the offering document for the related ABS.

(22) How are "outstanding principal balance" and "percentage by principal balance" to be calculated for Rule 15Ga-1 data presentations? The Instruction to paragraphs (a)(1)(vi)-(xi) of Rule 15Ga-1 provides that the "outstanding principal balance" of a pool asset is its principal balance as of the last day of the related reporting period and that each "percentage by principal balance" is to be calculated by dividing the outstanding principal balance of the pool asset by the outstanding principal balance of the entire asset pool as of the last day of the related reporting period. *Final Release, p. 4499; Correcting Amendment.* While these formulations may be appropriate for loans that are still part of a securitization pool, applying them to assets that are no longer in the pool, such as described below, may lead to illogical, and in some cases misleading, disclosure. ASF has discussed the below points with Commission staff in the hopes that the Commission would release formal guidance and provide clarity to the Rule. However, the Commission declined to provide guidance at this time, noting that securitizers have ample ability to provide explanatory footnotes in the disclosure to describe any relevant variations in disclosures brought on by the language of the Instruction. As such, market participants should take into consideration the below examples when making calculations pursuant to the Instruction and provide supplementary footnotes, as needed, to explain how such calculations were made and any related implications. Of course, a securitizer is also free to provide additional disclosures or calculations if it chooses.

ASF Rule 15Ga-1 Market Guide
Page 12

Paragraph (a)(1)(vii) relates to assets that were repurchased during the related period. By definition, those assets will have left the asset pool before the end of the period and it is unclear why the Instruction would provide that their "outstanding principal balance" as of a later date should be used, rather than using their principal balance as of the date of their removal from the asset pool. Indeed, the principal balance for purposes of making calculations for securitization trust distributions and reporting would be the principal balance on the date the asset left the pool. The principal balance on any later date would not be relevant for such purposes because the asset's principal balance as of a later date could reflect amortization that occurred after the asset left the asset pool. Market participants believe that the description of "outstanding principal balance" in the Instruction supports such an interpretation.[12] Market participants also believe it is appropriate to distinguish loans that have been liquidated so that the principal balance does not reflect any reductions for insurance payments or liquidation proceeds. Incorporating these amounts into the outstanding principal balance calculation required by the Rule would distort the principal amount actually repurchased.[13]

Assets that have left the pool during a reporting period will tend to distort the "percentage by principal balance" calculation. Measuring the pool balance (the denominator of the equation) as of the last day of the related reporting period would, as described above, reflect amortization that occurred after repurchased assets left the pool, which is not consistent with nor relevant to trust distributions and reporting. Unfortunately, the problems associated with this calculation would not be fixed simply by measuring the repurchased assets as of the date they were removed from the pool (as described in the preceding paragraph) because the assets remaining in the pool would still be measured as of the end of the reporting period. As a result, if a securitizer calculated "percentage by principal balance" for repurchases in this fashion, the resulting percentage would be overstated because the amortizing assets that remained in the pool would continue to amortize (for up to three months or, in the case of the initial reporting period, for up to three years) after the date on which any repurchased asset was removed.

Finally, by calculating the related percentages using the end-of-period balances it is possible that the percentages could be skewed if an ABS is not supported by a fixed, amortizing asset pool. For instance, a $10,000 asset may have been the subject of a demand for repurchase from an asset pool supporting an ABS issued in a revolving warehouse at a time when the asset pool totaled $100,000,000 (i.e., the asset

---

[12] The description of "percentage by principal balance" is instructive in this regard. The denominator in that calculation is the "outstanding principal balance of the *asset pool* as of the reporting period end date" (emphasis added). The term *asset pool* specifically relates to the pool of loans in the securitization trust and thus would not reflect amortization on assets that are no longer part of the pool. Market participants believe that "percentage by principal balance" and "outstanding principal balance" should be read consistently in this regard.

[13] In order to effectuate the items in this paragraph, "outstanding principal balance" could be calculated as (a) for any loan that has not been liquidated, the remaining outstanding principal balance of the loan at the earlier of the date on which it was repurchased or replaced from the pool or the end of the related reporting period, or (b) for any liquidated loan, the remaining outstanding principal balance of the loan at liquidation following application of all borrower payments, but not including any insurance payments or liquidation proceeds applied to principal.

ASF Rule 15Ga-1 Market Guide
Page 13

represented 0.01% ($10,000/$100,000,000) of the asset pool). If a "take-out" were effected (for example, for a term securitization) before the end of the period so that only $1,000,000 of assets remained in the asset pool at the end of the period, the prescribed calculation would suggest that 1.0% of the asset pool had been repurchased ($10,000/$1,000,000). In this case, a securitizer may wish to provide narrative disclosure in a footnote and consider providing the more accurate calculation that showed a 0.01% repurchase in the footnote.

(23) <u>What constitutes a demand?</u> The term "demand" is not defined in the Final Release. Market participants believe that a "demand" is a clear request for enforcement of a repurchase or replacement remedy on a specified asset or assets made by the trustee (or other party required under the transaction documents to enforce the obligation of the representing party to repurchase or replace assets) to the securitizer or other representing party, or made by an investor to the trustee or any other applicable party identified in Item 24. ("We continue to believe that disclosure should not be limited to only those demands, repurchases and replacements made pursuant to the transaction agreement alone. Investors have demanded that trustees enforce repurchase covenants because transaction agreements do not typically contain a provision for an investor to directly make a repurchase demand. Since Section 943(2) does not limit the required disclosures to those demands successfully made by the trustee, under our final rule, investor demands upon a trustee are required to be included in the table, irrespective of the trustee's determination to make a repurchase demand on a securitizer based on the investor request.") *Final Release, p. 4498.* As an example, even if the transaction documents provide that only a trustee may demand repurchase due to a breach, if an investor nonetheless makes such a demand to the trustee, that investor demand would give rise to the obligation to report.

Market participants believe that a clear request for enforcement of a repurchase or replacement remedy generally cannot be made through oral communications and that any oral communication that may be intended to be a repurchase demand must be reduced to writing so that it can be recorded and the substance of the communication can be verified. Oral communications in the context of a public disclosure requirement raise serious issues with respect to accuracy, verification and audit of the information, record-keeping, and compliance procedures. Market participants believe, therefore, that a simple process requiring a party that makes a request for enforcement through an oral communication to reduce that communication to writing should be consistent with the reporting requirements of the Rule, provided that such a process does not operate to preclude, discourage or significantly impede the party from making a demand. With regard to the initial three-year look-back period, market participants intend to make inquiry for purposes of complying with the Rule, but observe that these same accuracy, verification, compliance, record-keeping and audit considerations highlight practical impediments to comprehensive reporting in the case of oral communications that may or may not have intended to request enforcement.

ASF Rule 15Ga-1 Market Guide
Page 14

Market participants do not believe that mere "investor inquiries" about particular assets would constitute demands, as those are not clear requests for repurchase or replacement.

(24) <u>Must investor demands made upon transaction parties in addition to the trustee be disclosed?</u>

Market participants believe the Rule contemplates disclosure of investor demands made upon the securitizer, the trustee or any other party required under the transaction documents to enforce the obligation of the representing party to repurchase or replace assets. The Commission indicated in the Final Release that it made an accommodation for investor demands made upon trustees because transaction agreements have generally not provided for investors to make demands directly and because Dodd-Frank Section 943(2) does not limit the required disclosures to those demands successfully made by the trustee. ("We continue to believe that disclosure should not be limited to only those demands, repurchases and replacements made pursuant to the transaction agreement alone. Investors have demanded that trustees enforce repurchase covenants because transaction agreements do not typically contain a provision for an investor to directly make a repurchase demand. Since Section 943(2) does not limit the required disclosures to those demands successfully made by the trustee, under our final rule, investor demands upon a trustee are required to be included in the table, irrespective of the trustee's determination to make a repurchase demand on a securitizer based on the investor request.") *Final Release, p. 4498.* Market participants believe it is clear that this accommodation was made to supplement "those demands, repurchases and replacements made pursuant to the transaction agreement...." However, market participants believe that the Commission is under the mistaken impression that the trustee is always the party required under the transaction documents to enforce the obligation of the representing party to repurchase or replace assets. In fact, servicers, securities administrators and other parties are identified from time to time as the party required under the transaction documents to enforce the representing party's obligations. For this reason, market participants believe that the securitizer's obligation to report investor demands upon a trustee should also extend to any other party required under the transaction documents to enforce the obligation of the representing party to repurchase or replace assets.

(25) <u>Must demands that do not relate to a specific representation or warranty be reported?</u>
Yes, all demands should be reported, including demands that do not specifically allege a breach of any particular representation or warranty.

(26) <u>Reserved.</u>

(27) <u>Is disclosure required for all repurchases/replacements of assets in an ABS transaction?</u>
No, by its terms, Rule 15Ga-1(a) only requires disclosure concerning "assets securitized by the securitizer *that were the subject of a demand to repurchase or replace for breach of the representations and warranties* concerning the pool assets for all asset-backed securities held by non-affiliates of the securitizer during the period" (emphasis added). Two situations that would not give rise to reportable events would be (i) repurchases or

ASF Rule 15Ga-1 Market Guide
Page 15

replacements due to breaches that are discovered by the party obligated to repurchase or replace where no demand has been made and (ii) repurchases or replacements that are made for reasons other than a representation and warranty breach (e.g., a repurchase triggered due to a post-closing loan modification). Additionally, any activity in a transaction that is not subject to Rule 15Ga-1 (e.g., where transaction documents do not contain R&W Repurchase Provisions yet a securitizer nonetheless receives and honors a demand for repurchase) would not need to be reported.

(28) <u>What representations and warranties are covered</u>? A securitizer must report on repurchase demands due to any breach of a representation or warranty. Certain comment letters asked that the Rule be limited to breaches of representations and warranties regarding underwriting standards but the Commission rejected those requests. *Final Release, p. 4496.*

(29) <u>Reserved.</u>

C. *Timing of Filings – Form ABS-15G*

(30) <u>When is a securitizer first required to file Form ABS-15G?</u> Securitizers will need to file their initial Form ABS-15G at one of three times:

- For securitizers that issued ABS with R&W Repurchase Provisions between January 1, 2009 and December 31, 2011, an initial Form ABS-15G for the three year look-back period ended December 31, 2011 must be filed by February 14, 2012 if the securitizer has any ABS (issued at any time) outstanding on December 31, 2011 that are held by non-affiliates and contain underlying R&W Repurchase Provisions. For example, if a securitizer (i) issued credit card ABS with R&W Repurchase Provisions during the three year look-back period that are no longer outstanding at the end of such period and (ii) had previously issued RMBS with R&W Repurchase Provisions prior to the three year look-back period that are still outstanding and held by non-affiliates at the end of such period, the securitizer would be required to file the initial report. *Rule 15Ga-1(c)(1).* The securitizer must provide the required disclosures for all outstanding ABS (issued at any time) held by non-affiliates during the three year look-back period that contain underlying R&W Repurchase Provisions. Any repurchase demand activity that commenced prior to January 1, 2009, but that was completed during the three year look-back period (e.g., a repurchase demand that was made in November 2008 that resulted in a repurchase in February 2009), must also be reported on this initial report. *Instruction to Rule 15Ga-1(c)(1).*

- For securitizers that did not issue ABS with R&W Repurchase Provisions between January 1, 2009 and December 31, 2011, but who have older such ABS outstanding and held by non-affiliates after December 31, 2011, an initial Form ABS-15G will need to be filed within 45 days after completion of the calendar quarter ending on March 31, 2012. *Rule 15Ga-1(c)(2).* See Item 31 below for further information.

ASF Rule 15Ga-1 Market Guide
Page 16

- For securitizers that did not have any ABS with R&W Repurchase Provisions outstanding as of December 31, 2011, but who subsequently issue such ABS, their reporting obligation will commence for the quarter in which they first issue such ABS and the initial Form ABS-15G must be filed by no later than 45 days after the end of that calendar quarter. *Rule 15Ga-1(c)(2).*

(31) Is a securitizer that did not sponsor or issue ABS with R&W Repurchase Provisions during the three year look-back period required to make the quarterly filings if it has outstanding ABS with R&W Repurchase Provisions held by non-affiliates during the related period? Yes, (i) the initial filing requirement applies to those securitizers that sponsored or issued ABS with R&W Repurchase Provisions during the three-year look-back period and (ii) the quarterly filing requirement applies to those securitizers that sponsored or issued such ABS during the related quarter and also to any securitizer that had outstanding ABS (regardless of when they were issued) held by non-affiliates during the period. This means that a securitizer that did not sponsor or issue ABS with R&W Repurchase Provisions during the three year look-back period from January 2009 through December 2011 would not have to make the initial three-year look-back filing, but would have to make the quarterly filings for so long as any such ABS (i.e., from transactions issued prior to 2009) remained outstanding and held by non-affiliates. During the ASF SEC Meeting, Commission staff indicated that commentators wanted reporting under Rule 15Ga-1 to commence without a new-issuance trigger, and reasoned that the initial filing (with its historical focus) applies only to those securitizers that had been active during the three-year look-back period, while the quarterly filings (with their focus on current repurchase activity) apply to any securitizers with applicable outstanding ABS.

(32) Can a sponsor's reporting obligation be broader than the aggregate reporting obligations of the sponsor's depositors? Yes, at the ASF SEC Meeting, the Commission staff indicated that a sponsor's reporting obligation with respect to the "look-back" period is determined independently of the reporting obligations of the relevant depositors and therefore, may be broader than the aggregate reporting obligations of such depositors. In other words, if a single entity is the sponsor of securitization programs for different asset classes, and the sponsor was active in at least one such program during the "look-back" period, the sponsor (or the relevant depositors) must file an initial report covering all such programs, even if the other programs were dormant during the "look-back" period. For example, if a sponsor's depositor (Depositor A) issued auto ABS during the initial three-year look-back period, but the sponsor's other depositor (Depositor B) had not issued student loan ABS during the three-year look-back period, the sponsor (or both depositors) would still be obligated to file a report covering the three year look-back period for both auto and student loan ABS.

(33) Must repurchase demand activity on ABS issued before January 1, 2009 be reported? Yes, whenever a securitizer is required to file a Form ABS-15G it must report on all outstanding ABS held by non-affiliates during the reporting period for which the

ASF Rule 15Ga-1 Market Guide
Page 17

underlying transaction documents include R&W Repurchase Provisions. *Instruction to Rule 15Ga-1(c)(1)*. See Items 30 and 31, above.

(34) <u>Is an initial filing required if there is no activity to report?</u> Yes, a securitizer is required to file an initial Form ABS-15G in the manner described in Item 30, above, even if there is no repurchase demand activity to report. If there is no activity to report during the related reporting period, however, the securitizer may check the appropriate "no activity to report" box on the cover page of the Form ABS-15G, which will suspend its duty to file subsequent quarterly forms in the manner described in Item 37, below. *Final Release, pp. 4500, 4501 and n. 140.*

(35) <u>Which securitizers must make subsequent quarterly filings on Form ABS-15G?</u> Once a securitizer files an initial Form ABS-15G it is obligated to file subsequent, quarterly Forms ABS-15G unless and until either (i) it no longer has ABS with R&W Repurchase Provisions[14] outstanding and held by non-affiliates or (ii) its duty to file quarterly forms has been suspended in the manner described in Item 37, below (although an annual report would then be required). *Rule 15Ga-1(c)(2) and (3).*

(36) <u>When are subsequent Form ABS-15G filings due?</u> Subsequent quarterly filings are due within 45 days of the end of the related reporting quarter. *Rule 15Ga-1(c)(2).* Each quarterly report shows activity only during the related quarter (i.e., data is not to be aggregated with data from prior periods), including activity related to a demand that was made during a prior quarter. For what constitutes "activity", see Item 11, above. *Instruction 1 to Rule 15Ga-1(a)(1).*

(37) <u>Can filing of Form ABS-15G be suspended?</u> Only quarterly reporting can be suspended. If during a securitizer's initial filing period or during any subsequent quarterly reporting period there is no activity to report (consistent with Item 11), the securitizer may check the "no activity to report" box on Form ABS-15G and it will then only be obligated to file an annual report (no later than 45 days after each calendar year) confirming there was no activity for the prior year for so long as it has ABS with R&W Repurchase Provisions (see FN 14 of this Guide) outstanding and held by non-affiliates. *Rule 15Ga-1(c)(2)(i) and (ii) and (c)(3); Final Release, p. 4501.* If at any time after a securitizer's obligation to report has been suspended there is activity to report during a calendar quarter, then the securitizer's obligation to file quarterly Form ABS-15G will restart and will continue unless and until there is a subsequent quarter for which the securitizer reports "no activity." *Id.*

(38) <u>When does the obligation to file quarterly or annual reports terminate?</u> Once a securitizer has no outstanding ABS with R&W Repurchase Provisions (see FN 14 of this Guide) held by non-affiliates, the duty to file the periodic disclosures is terminated immediately upon the filing of a notice on Form ABS-15G. *Rule 15Ga-1(c)(3).*

---

[14] Rule 15Ga-1(c)(3) conditions termination of a securitizer's duty to file disclosures required by paragraph (a) on a securitizer having "no asset-backed securities outstanding held by non-affiliates" but does not explicitly require such ABS to have underlying R&W Repurchase Provisions. Market participants have interpreted such a qualification to exist, because paragraph (a) only requires disclosures if such R&W Repurchase Provisions exist in the first place.

ASF Rule 15Ga-1 Market Guide
Page 18

D. Timing of Filings – Form 10-D

(39) <u>If a securitizer is required to make Form 10-D filings for its registered ABS, when must it begin including Rule 15Ga-1 data?</u> Forms 10-D that are filed for an issuing entity after December 31, 2011 are required to contain the Rule 15Ga-1 data regarding the asset pool for such issuing entity, pursuant to Regulation AB Item 1121(c). *Final Release, p. 4505.*

(40) <u>If a securitizer has suspended its obligation to file Form ABS-15G is it excused from providing the Form 10-D disclosure?</u> No, Item 1121(c)(1) requires the information required by Rule 15Ga-1(a) regardless of whether there is currently a separate obligation to provide the same information in quarterly Form ABS-15G filings.

(41) <u>What form should the disclosure take?</u> Item 1121(c)(1) requires that the information required by Rule 15Ga-1(a) be provided in each Form 10-D as it relates to the specified asset pool. If a securitizer has no activity to report, it should indicate that fact in the Form 10-D. Additionally, Item 1121(c)(2) requires the Form 10-D to reference the most recent Form ABS-15G filed by the securitizer together with the securitizer's CIK number. Market participants have interpreted "securitizer" in this provision to mean the securitizer or securitizers, as applicable, in the related offering under Regulation AB that have previously filed a Form ABS-15G. For example, if Sponsor A and Depositor A are involved in an offering of ABS under Regulation AB, the Form 10-D must include a reference to the most recent Form ABS-15G filed by either Sponsor A or Depositor A, or both, if applicable.

III. Disclosure Requirements in Regulation AB Transactions

ABS issuances made in accordance with Regulation AB are required to present in a prospectus for newly-issued ABS data described in Rule 15Ga-1 both (i) regarding the specific asset pool in Form 10-D filings (as described in Part II, above) and (ii) regarding the sponsor's other ABS of the same asset class. *Final Release, p. 4503.*

(42) <u>What new issuances require disclosure of Rule 15Ga-1 information in the prospectus?</u> Regulation AB Item 1104 has been amended to require disclosure of certain Rule 15Ga-1 data (see Item 43, below) for new issuances of certain ABS that have their first *bona fide* offering on or after February 14, 2012. *Final Release, p. 4505.* New issuances of ABS (i) that are ABS for purposes of Regulation AB (i.e., a narrower set of ABS than Exchange Act ABS, which is described in Item 1, above), (ii) that are offered in the registered market and (iii) for which the underlying transaction documents include R&W Repurchase Provisions, will be required to include the Rule 15Ga-1 information in a prospectus. *Final Release, p. 4502.*

(43) <u>What Rule 15Ga-1 information is required to be disclosed in a prospectus?</u> Regulation AB issuers must include all information that is required by Rule 15Ga-1(a) (i.e., all information required to be included by the sponsor, as a securitizer, in a Form ABS-15G) regarding ABS of the same asset class for which the underlying transaction documents contain R&W Repurchase Provisions and that are held by non-affiliates

ASF Rule 15Ga-1 Market Guide
Page 19

during the specified look-back period. The data presented must cover either (i) the prior year (for prospectuses to be filed pursuant to Rule 424 prior to February 14, 2013), (ii) the prior two years (for prospectuses to be filed pursuant to Rule 424 on or after February 14, 2013 but prior to February 14, 2014) or (iii) the prior three years (for prospectuses to be filed pursuant to Rule 424 on or after February 14, 2014). *Regulation AB Item 1104(e)(1)(i) and (ii)*.

The prospectus also must reference the most recent Form ABS-15G that the securitizer filed together with the securitizer's CIK number. *Regulation AB, Item 1104(e)(2)*. Market participants have interpreted "securitizer" in this provision to mean the securitizer or securitizers, as applicable, in the related offering under Regulation AB that have previously filed a Form ABS-15G. For example, if Sponsor A and Depositor A are involved in an offering of ABS under Regulation AB, the prospectus must include a reference to the most recent Form ABS-15G filed by either Sponsor A or Depositor A, or both, if applicable.

(44) How recent must the Rule 15Ga-1 information be that is set forth in a prospectus? The Rule 15Ga-1 information included in a prospectus pursuant to Item 1104 may not be more than 135 days old. *Regulation AB, Item 1104(e)(3)*.

(45) If a sponsor, as securitizer, has suspended its obligation to file Form ABS-15G is it excused from providing this prospectus disclosure? No, Item 1104 requires the disclosure of the information required by Rule 15Ga-1 regardless of whether there is currently a separate obligation to provide the same information in quarterly Form ABS-15G filings.

(46) What form should the disclosure take? The Rule 15Ga-1 disclosure required by Item 1104 should follow the same tabular format required for Form ABS-15G. *Final Release, p. 4502*. If a securitizer has no activity to report, it should indicate that fact in the prospectus.

(47) Reserved.

IV. Other Considerations

(48) What processes should securitizers undertake to request from applicable parties the information required to be disclosed? Aggregating the information required to be disclosed by the Rule will likely require securitizers to request information from certain parties (see Item 24). Market participants have spent considerable time discussing this issue and have determined reasonable procedures by which provision of this information may be effected. A securitizer should choose a procedure that is reasonable for its particular circumstances, taking into account the number of deals outstanding, the uniformity of documentation and transaction parties across issuances, and any relevant provisions within the transaction documents. Below are two examples of ways in which securitizers may attempt to obligate third parties to provide required information. However, the actual provision of such information is largely dependent upon third parties' willingness or ability to accommodate securitizers' new disclosure

ASF Rule 15Ga-1 Market Guide
Page 20

obligations under Rule 15Ga-1 because such parties, including trustees, will most likely not be obligated to do so under existing contracts.

For certain securitizers, an amendment to existing transaction documents may be appropriate to effectuate the required disclosure. For example, auto securitizers may have a smaller number of outstanding transactions both because they have issued ABS less frequently and because the assets underlying such transactions have shorter average lives. An auto securitizer may also have uniform documentation across each transaction that would permit an efficient amendment and may also have had the same transaction parties on all, or nearly all, outstanding transactions. For such a securitizer, an amendment to each outstanding transaction (possibly in the form of an omnibus amendment to the applicable agreements) would be reasonable to obligate a party to provide the required information.

For other securitizers, amending transaction documents for all outstanding deals would be unreasonable simply because it is not feasible. For example, RMBS securitizers may have a larger number of outstanding transactions both because they have issued RMBS more frequently and because the assets underlying the transactions have relatively long average lives. An RMBS securitizer may have varying documentation across transactions and programs that would greatly impede an efficient amendment and may also have considerable diversity among the transaction parties across issuances. For such a securitizer, a memorandum of understanding with a party would be reasonable to obligate them to provide the required information or if such an understanding cannot be reached, some other reasonable means to obtain such information. See Appendix I for a Form Memorandum of Understanding that is intended to provide market participants with a helpful resource and basis for preparation of appropriate memoranda of understanding or other agreements or request letters related to these matters.[15]

---

[15] ASF recognizes that not all of the provisions set forth in the attached Memorandum of Understanding will be relevant or necessary for all transactions or parties and that parties may reach differing understandings or arrangements with regard to these matters, including possible agreements related to reimbursement of transaction parties' related costs and expenses or other compensation arrangements. ASF hopes, however, that industry participants will find the following Memorandum of Understanding to be a fair representation of industry consensus on relative responsibilities and issues related to repurchase activity reporting for outstanding transactions and, therefore, a helpful resource and basis for preparation of appropriate memoranda of understanding or other agreements or letters between transaction parties related to these matters.

APPENDIX I

PRELIMINARY NOTE: *The American Securitization Forum (ASF) provides the following form Memorandum of Understanding as a resource for use by securitizers and related transaction parties to facilitate securitizers' compliance with their obligations to provide reporting of repurchase demand activities under Rule 15Ga-1 of the Securities Exchange Act and on SEC Form 10-D with respect to outstanding transactions. ASF recognizes that not all of the provisions set forth in the attached Memorandum of Understanding will be relevant or necessary for all transactions or parties and that parties may reach differing understandings or arrangements with regard to these matters, including possible agreements related to reimbursement of transaction parties' related costs and expenses or other compensation arrangements. ASF hopes, however, that industry participants will find the following Memorandum of Understanding to be a fair representation of industry consensus on relative responsibilities and issues related to repurchase demand activity reporting for outstanding transactions and, therefore, a helpful resource and basis for preparation of appropriate memoranda of understanding or other agreements or letters between transaction parties related to these matters.*

FORM MEMORANDUM OF UNDERSTANDING

TO: [Transaction Party][16]

FROM: [Securitizer]

DATE: _____, 2011

Repurchase Demand Activity Reporting

THIS MEMORANDUM OF UNDERSTANDING, made as of the date set forth above, specifies the terms of certain understandings between us, [Securitizer], as securitizer of certain asset-backed securities issued in connection with the transactions identified on Schedule A hereto (the "Transactions"), and you, [Transaction Party name], as [Transaction Party] under the terms of the related operative agreements for the Transactions, with regard to the reporting of certain asset repurchase demand activities related to the Transactions.[17]

1. Repurchase Reporting. To assist in our compliance with our obligations as securitizer, we have requested, and you have agreed to provide, certain information regarding certain asset repurchase demand activities related to the Transactions in the manner, timing and format specified below:

> a. Initial Report. [REQUIRED ONLY FOR SECURITIZERS THAT HAVE ISSUED ABS THAT INCLUDE REPURCHASE OBLIGATIONS DURING 2009-2011]. No later than _____, 2012, you have agreed to provide to us information regarding repurchase demand activity during calendar years 2009-2011 related to the underlying

---

[16] It is expected that Securitizers would enter into Memoranda of Understanding with each relevant transaction party.

[17] See Item 23 in the ASF Rule 15Ga-1 Market Implementation Guide for a discussion of "demands."

I-1

assets for each of the Transactions in [substantially the form of Exhibit 1 hereto] [a mutually-agreeable electronic format].

b. Quarterly Reporting. No later than the ___ business day following the end of each calendar quarter (beginning with the first quarter of 2012) in which any asset-backed securities remain outstanding for a Transaction, you have agreed to provide to us information regarding repurchase demand activity during the preceding calendar quarter related to the underlying assets for each such Transaction in [substantially the form of Exhibit 1 hereto] [a mutually-agreeable electronic format].

c. Monthly Reporting. [REQUIRED ONLY FOR TRANSACTIONS SUBJECT TO CONTINUING OBLIGATIONS FOR REPORTING ON FORM 10-D]. No later than the ___ business day of each month (beginning in 2012) in which any asset-backed securities remain outstanding for a Transaction, if any, identified on Schedule A as subject to continuing obligations for filing of reports on Form 10-D, you have agreed to provide to us information regarding repurchase demand activity during the preceding month related to the underlying assets for each such Transaction in [substantially the form of Exhibit 1 hereto] [a mutually-agreeable electronic format].

2. Understandings and Conditions. You have agreed to provide the requested information regarding repurchase demand activities related to the Transactions subject to the following understandings and conditions:

a. Pre-July 22, 2010 Information. We understand and agree that you will provide information related to activity prior to July 22, 2010 only to the extent that you have such information, and we acknowledge that you were under no obligation to gather or retain any such information for this purpose with respect to the Transactions during that period.

b. Post-July 22, 2010 Information. We understand and agree that you will provide information related to activity following July 22, 2010 only to the extent that you have such information or can obtain such information without unreasonable effort or expense; provided that, we agree that your efforts to obtain such information is limited to a review of your internal written records of repurchase demand activity for the Transactions and that you are not required to request information from any unaffiliated parties.

c. Repurchases. We understand and agree that the reporting of repurchase demand activity pursuant to this memorandum is required only in respect of Transactions that include a covenant to repurchase or replace underlying assets upon breach of a representation or warranty.

d. No Implied Duties. We acknowledge and agree that your reporting is limited to information that you have received or acquired solely in your capacity as [Transaction Party] for the Transactions and not in any other capacity. We further acknowledge and agree that, other than any express duties or responsibilities as [Transaction Party] under the Transaction agreements, you have no duty or obligation to undertake any investigation or inquiry related to repurchase demand activity or otherwise to assume any additional duties or responsibilities in respect of any Transaction, and no such additional obligations or duties are implied in this memorandum. In addition, we acknowledge that you are entitled to the full benefit of any and all protections, limitations on duties or liability and rights of indemnity provided by the terms of the Transaction agreements in connection with any actions taken hereunder.

e. <u>Term</u>. Your obligation to provide reporting with regard to each Transaction will continue so long as you serve as [Transaction Party] of the Transaction and any asset-backed securities of such Transaction remain outstanding, or such earlier time as you are notified that such reporting no longer is required.

3. <u>Delivery</u>. Unless and until you are otherwise notified in writing, any information provided hereunder should be provided in electronic format and directed as follows:

Attention: _____

4. <u>Binding Effect; Succession</u>. This memorandum is intended to reflect the understanding and agreement between you and us with regard to the matters described herein. This memorandum is not intended to, and does not, amend or alter, in any manner, the rights or obligations of the parties pursuant to the operative agreements for the Transactions, and does not bind any of the parties' successors or assigns under any agreements for the Transactions. However, in the event of your termination or resignation as [Transaction Party] for any Transaction, you agree to undertake reasonable efforts to assist in the transfer of data regarding repurchase demand activity to any successor.

5. <u>Acknowledgments</u>. By signatures below, you and we acknowledge and agree that this Memorandum of Understanding sets forth our understanding related to the terms of your agreement to provide certain repurchase information to us, as securitizer for the Transactions. We further acknowledge and agree that we, as securitizer, have full responsibility for compliance with all related reporting requirements associated with the Transactions and for all interpretive issues regarding this information.

[_____].
Securitizer

By: _____
Its: _____

[_____],
[Transaction Party]

By: _____
Its: _____

I-3

Schedule A

Transactions

[Listing of Relevant Asset-Backed Securities Transactions]*

---

* Indicates Transactions subject to continuing obligations for filing of reports on Form 10-D after December 31, 2011.

Exhibit 1

ASSET REPURCHASE DEMAND ACTIVITY REPORT[18]

Reporting Period: _____

☐ Check here if nothing to report.

Transaction	Loan No.	Activity During Period[19]		
		Date of Reputed Demand[20]	Party Making Reputed Demand	Date of Withdrawal of Reputed Demand

---

[18] Alternatively, a Securitizer may request that the Transaction Party provide additional or different information than that contained in this Exhibit. For example, such Securitizer may request that the Transaction party provide the information included in the table that appears in the Final Release. See http://www.sec.gov/rules/final/2011/33-9175fr.pdf at 4513.

[19] The Transaction Party should forward any applicable information or documentation relating to any reputed demands to the Securitizer. See Item 11 in the ASF Rule 15Ga-1 Market Implementation Guide for a discussion of what constitutes activity.

[20] See Item 23 in the ASF Rule 15Ga-1 Market Implementation Guide for a discussion of "demands."

I-5

Practice Tool 6: Comparison of Regulatory Regimes under Proposed Regulation AB II

	Offerings Registered on Form SF-1	Offerings Registered on Form SF-3	Exempt Offerings under Rule 144A
SEC Filing and Staff Review:	• Registration statement must be filed with the SEC. • SEC staff may review and comment on registration statement before declaring it effective.	• Registration statement must be filed with the SEC. • SEC staff may review and comment on registration statement before declaring it effective. • After effectiveness, so long as there is remaining shelf capacity and the registrant meets strict ongoing eligibility requirements, offerings may be made at any time.	• Offerings may be made at any time. • Form 144A is required to be filed with the SEC within 15 days after the initial sale. • The issuer must undertake to provide the offering documents to the SEC upon request.
Offering Process:	• All offering-specific communications with investors, whether written or oral, are prohibited before filing. • After filing but before effectiveness, written communications with investors are highly circumscribed. • Sales of securities (including contracts of sale) are prohibited until the registration statement has been declared effective. • Preliminary prospectus must be delivered to purchasers at least 48 hours before confirmation of sale.	• Because registration statement is effective, the restrictions on pre-filing and pre-effective communications do not apply. • After effectiveness, free writing prospectuses may be used (subject to filing requirements). • Preliminary prospectus must be filed with the SEC at least 5 business days before any contract of sale. • Preliminary prospectus must be delivered to purchasers at least 48 hours before confirmation of sale.	• Communications with investors are unrestricted (prohibition on general solicitation has been eliminated). • Contracts of sale may be entered into at any time. • Transaction documents must entitle investors to obtain all required disclosures upon request.

	Offerings Registered on Form SF-1	Offerings Registered on Form SF-3	Exempt Offerings under Rule 144A
Required Disclosures:	• Regulation AB disclosure requirements must be satisfied. • Unclear applicability of some Regulation AB items to esoteric ABS may be resolved through SEC staff review.	• Regulation AB disclosure requirements must be satisfied.	• Must provide same disclosure as S-1 or SF-1 registration. • For ABS, regulation AB disclosure requirements must be satisfied. • Unclear applicability of some Regulation AB items for esoteric ABS. • Unclear scope of disclosure requirements for other structured finance products.
Ongoing Reporting:	• Periodic Exchange Act reports are required. • Reporting is no longer permitted to be suspended after issuer's first fiscal year.	• Periodic Exchange Act reports are required. • Reporting is no longer permitted to be suspended after the issuer's first fiscal year.	• Transaction documents must entitle investors to receive the same information as if the issuer were required to file periodic Exchange Act reports.